an a-z of

social

work

law

Sara Miller McCune founded SAGE Publishing in 1965 to support the dissemination of usable knowledge and educate a global community. SAGE publishes more than 1000 journals and over 800 new books each year, spanning a wide range of subject areas. Our growing selection of library products includes archives, data, case studies and video. SAGE remains majority owned by our founder and after her lifetime will become owned by a charitable trust that secures the company's continued independence.

Los Angeles | London | New Delhi | Singapore | Washington DC | Melbourne

an a–z of
social
work
law

robert johns
jacqueline harry

Los Angeles | London | New Delhi
Singapore | Washington DC | Melbourne

Los Angeles | London | New Delhi
Singapore | Washington DC | Melbourne

SAGE Publications Ltd
1 Oliver's Yard
55 City Road
London EC1Y 1SP

SAGE Publications Inc.
2455 Teller Road
Thousand Oaks, California 91320

SAGE Publications India Pvt Ltd
B 1/I 1 Mohan Cooperative Industrial Area
Mathura Road
New Delhi 110 044

SAGE Publications Asia-Pacific Pte Ltd
3 Church Street
#10-04 Samsung Hub
Singapore 049483

Editor: Kate Keers
Assistant editor: Catriona McMullen
Production editor: Martin Fox
Marketing manager: Camille Richmond
Cover design: Wendy Scott
Typeset by: C&M Digitals (P) Ltd, Chennai, India
Printed in the UK

Library of Congress Control Number:
2021936667

British Library Cataloguing in Publication data

A catalogue record for this book is available
from the British Library

ISBN 978-1-5297-6278-5
ISBN 978-1-5297-6277-8 (pbk)

At SAGE we take sustainability seriously. Most of our products are printed in the UK using responsibly
sourced papers and boards. When we print overseas we ensure sustainable papers are used as
measured by the PREPS grading system. We undertake an annual audit to monitor our sustainability.

Contents

E

F

G

H

I

J

L

About the authors

Robert Johns is a university external examiner, lecturer and author of books on social work law. He was for several years Head of Social Work at University of East London, moving there from De Montfort University. As a social worker and manager, he worked in local authorities in a number of different specialisms, but came to specialise in court work as a children's guardian in Hertfordshire. He has also lectured in Finland, Ukraine, Australia, New Zealand and Sweden. He is the author of a number of articles and books on social work law including *Using the Law in Social Work* (now in its eighth edition, 2020), *Capacity and Autonomy* (2014), and *Ethics and Law for Social Workers* (2016). He contributed chapters to *Critical Issues in Social Work Law* (2017) and *Introducing Social Work* (2020).

Jacqueline Harry is currently a senior lecturer in social work at Kingston University and external examiner at a London university, having previously taught at the University of East London and Birkbeck University. Her extensive practice experience and degrees in law, psychology and social work, have informed her teaching on undergraduate, post-graduate and apprenticeship social work programmes. Since registering as a social worker in 1997, she has worked within mental health, child protection and older adult services, before working with offenders in the probation service. Jacqueline also has many years' experience as a children's guardian undertaking direct work with children and families. This included international private and public law disputes and cases concerning child abduction, honour-related abuse and medical treatment.

About this book

This is the book social work students have been asking for. The authors, both of whom are registered social workers themselves specialising in teaching social work law to students on university qualifying courses, have received many plaintive pleas along the lines of 'if only we had a dictionary to guide us with the legal terms used in social work'. So, here it is: all the terms relevant to contemporary social work practice and probably a few more besides. Doubtless, some may not be where readers expected to find them, but we have endeavoured to make this A–Z as comprehensive, as 'user friendly' and as accessible as possible to students, practitioners and the general reader.

Social work is not essentially about law, but the law is fundamental to social work practice in Britain. Since most social workers in Britain are employed by local authorities, what regulates local authorities matters, and local authorities can only do what Parliament allows them to do. It follows that local authority social workers also can only do what the law says they may or, in some cases, must do. Without the law, such social workers can do nothing. Social workers are accountable to the public who rightly have expectations about the calibre of people employed as social workers and about how they conduct themselves. These expectations are translated into law. Where there is disagreement about what should or should not have happened, or serious issues of safeguarding, the law provides the means of arbitration, of potentially making a definitive decision.

So, in all these ways, the law sets the framework, so it is crucial to understand what it says, but it does not determine exactly what action to take. What social workers do in individual cases is a matter of professional judgement based on a combination of skills and knowledge acquired from a range of sources. Looking up the law may tell you when you must take some kind of action, but law does not tell you how or what you should do in each case. Critically, though, it tells you what you can and cannot do.

Students new to social work are often surprised at the amount of law that it is necessary to cover during qualifying courses, and indeed the UK is somewhat unusual in the extent to which social workers are employed by public bodies who have to operate within clearly defined legal boundaries and lines of accountability. Within the UK itself, those legal requirements vary since social work services are a devolved government responsibility – so social work law varies in each of the four nations. Hence the law in England and Wales, which has a shared heritage, is not identical, although there is enough common ground to enable us to base the dictionary on the law of England and highlight areas where Welsh law deviates, which is what we have done. However, the law and organisation of social work in Scotland and Northern Ireland diverge to an extent that makes this impossible; a dictionary that covered all four countries would result in a weighty tome that would probably confuse rather than elucidate.

Where does this A–Z fit?

Readers should bear in mind that this is not a definitive text where you will find absolutely everything you need to know about every aspect of social work. It is not a manual of practice but rather a quick, concise, accessible guide to social work law. This book offers definitions of selected legal principles that are then related to social work practice. To gain a fuller understanding of some of the issues, readers would be well advised to consult general textbooks on social work law, using this dictionary as a springboard. These generic books generally offer an overview of social work law by adopting a thematic approach, with different chapters exploring law as it applies to particular groups or topics; for example, Brammer, 2020; Carr and Goosey, 2021; Johns, 2020. This dictionary dovetails well with books in this category.

As a dictionary, it is also intended to be complementary to books that focus on specific aspects of social work practice or theory, in particular to those texts that major on one area of practice. There are, for example, books that apply the law to the following areas of practice:

Social work with adults: for example, Braye and Preston-Shoot, 2019; Feldon, 2021; Rogers et al., 2015;

Social work with children and families: for example, Chisnell, 2019; Cocker and Allain, 2019; Davis, 2014; Laing and Jackson, 2018;

Safeguarding and court work: for example, Barnett, 2019; Chisnell, 2019; Cooper, 2014; Cooper and White, 2017; Holt, 2019; Starns, 2019;

Capacity and mental health: for example, Barber et al., 2019; Brown, 2019; Brown et al., 2015; Caxton, 2021; Johns, 2014;

Youth justice: for example, Pickford and Dugmore, 2012; Staines, 2015.

How up to date is this A–Z?

This dictionary is as up to date as it possibly can be. It was checked for accuracy when it went to press. Everyone knows that the law is constantly changing, though, and all social workers know that they have a responsibility to keep abreast of developments in law and practice. This is an intrinsic part of continuous professional development and is firmly embedded in the requirements of Social Work England and the other UK social work regulatory bodies.

The authors are aware of a number of areas where there are likely to be some developments in the near future. At the time of this book going to press, the President of the Family Division's Public Law Working Group released a report entitled *Recommendations to achieve best practice in the child protection and family justice systems (Courts & Tribunals*

Judiciary, 2021). There is also in progress a government-ordered review of the operation of the Human Rights Act 1998. Constantly in the background is the challenge of adapting the law to respond to social change, particularly in relation to social care and the shortcomings uncovered during the 2020 pandemic crisis.

Indeed, the law as it relates to social work is continually adapting to address new or emerging areas of practice. Either existing laws are interpreted to accommodate new challenges, or further legislation and guidance is passed of which social workers need to be aware, since these may inform safeguarding practice in respect of adults or children.

There have been a number of examples that illustrate this. One relevant legal development concerned forced marriage which was criminalised under the Anti-social Behaviour, Crime and Policing Act 2014, following on from the establishment of the Forced Marriage Unit in 2005, a joint project of the Home Office and the Foreign, Commonwealth and Development Office, providing information and multi-agency practice guidance. Another was about enhancing the Female Genital Mutilation Act 2003 by adding new offences and requirements. The Serious Crime Act 2015 criminalised failure to protect a girl from female genital mutilation, introduced dedicated protection orders, and established a duty for specific professionals to notify the police about female genital mutilation. The government's Prevent strategy introduced duties for professionals, and where concerns about children being radicalised have arisen either in public or private legal proceedings this has on occasion necessitated the use of the inherent jurisdiction of the High Court. The Modern Slavery Act 2015 and associated statutory guidance set out processes for identifying and supporting child and adult victims of slavery and includes matters related to child trafficking. The National Crime Agency has asked social workers to be alert to County Lines, whereby criminals exploit children and vulnerable people to move and store drugs using coercion, intimidation and violence. On a more positive note, the Family Drug and Alcohol Court continues as a specialist court that helps families resolve issues related to their substance misuse during care proceedings. The goal here is to ensure better outcomes for children and families.

So, the message is keep up to date and be aware of developments; this is every social worker's ongoing professional responsibility.

Structure and features of the book

As there are so many terms and laws that relate to social work, a dictionary format seemed eminently suitable. So, this is the kind of reference book you can expect to dip into just to look up a specific item in the expectation of a succinct overview of what you need to know and where you might need to go next for more information. Entries vary in length, but the authors have endeavoured to make them as concise as possible. We have also included quite a number of cross-references, both as headings and within entries, in order to make accessing essential information that much easier. We have kept strictly to a dictionary format as this is what students say they need, and none of the other social work law texts takes this approach, preferring in general to address topics in individual chapters.

Most of the topics speak for themselves in that they relate to terms in frequent use in social work and obvious issues that social workers will encounter. However, we also decided to include a number of short entries relating to the legal system, the role of key personnel within it, common legal terms, and what happens in courts. Running alongside these are entries that fall under the human rights umbrella, underpinning the whole legal system and influencing decision-making. There are some specific entries that relate to social workers themselves and their legal status. There are also some generic entries concerning capacity, that is, people's ability to make specific decisions for themselves, since this is such an important issue in contemporary social work. The majority of entries fit into social work categories: adults, children and families, mental health and youth justice. Within each of these we have included an entry for some specific Acts of Parliament that are the bedrock of practice in that area. These are longer entries where we have included a summary of what the Act covers, highlighting those parts of special relevance to social work, for example, the Children Act 1989, the Care Act 2014, the Mental Capacity Act 2005, the Mental Health Act 1983, the Criminal Justice and Immigration Act 2008.

Within entries there are references to source material and signposts as to where to go for further information. Source material includes case law incorporated into an alphabetical reference list at the end of the book; there is no separate list of cases or legislation. Given the dictionary format, we have not included any exercises or guides to further reading within the entries, but instead have included in this introduction some suggestions for complementary and more specialist texts.

Occasionally, we have included references to websites, or at least to organisations that offer reliable information through their websites. We strongly recommend not using internet search engines to look up what the law says: this is not only unreliable since websites are not always kept up to date but can be highly misleading given that many websites are US based. As we have had to tell more than one student, the law of Florida or Pennsylvania is not the law of England and Wales. Instead, we do recommend consulting the websites of organisations that are known to be reliable and authoritative. For example:

For children and families and safeguarding: websites of the National Society for the Prevention of Cruelty to Children, the Children and Family Court Advisory and Support Service, and Child Law Advice, which is operated by the Coram Children's Legal Centre;

For adults: websites of Mind (for mental health), Law Society (for mental capacity), Social Care Institute for Excellence (for Care Act 2014).

Conclusion

This introduction has explained what this A–Z social work law dictionary is about, and how it will be an invaluable source of assistance to anyone embarking on a career in social work, or just curious about what the law says about social work. Both authors are passionate about social work law, believing a sound knowledge of law is an intrinsic part of social work and respected social work practitioners are those who know what the law says and know how to apply it appropriately, ethically and sensitively.

We hope you find the book a valuable resource. Enjoy learning about social work law. Knowledge is power.

Abduction, child See Child Abduction.

Abnormally aggressive or seriously irresponsible conduct is a term that occurs in mental health legislation to reduce the numbers of people who could potentially be subject to compulsory detention in hospital or guardianship. While section 1 Mental Health Act 2007 offers a wide definition of disorder, section 2 of that Act clarifies that compulsory powers under the Mental Health Act 1983 can only be used where someone has a learning disability associated with 'abnormally aggressive or seriously irresponsible conduct'. Nowhere in the Act or in any other legislation is the phrase defined, so presumably it is left to the medical practitioner who certifies that someone has a learning disability to decide also whether their conduct is abnormally aggressive or seriously irresponsible.

However, the rider only applies in relation to the Mental Health Act 1983, so does not apply if someone is being assessed under the Deprivation of Liberty Safeguards or Liberty Protection Safeguards, since these are Mental Capacity Act 2005 related. So, these provisions could theoretically apply to anyone who has a learning disability since in any other context learning disability could be considered a mental disorder.

Acceptable Behaviour Contracts are simply written agreements between the child or young person, their parents and youth justice agencies, usually the Youth Offending Team. The contract sets out the anti-social behaviour that is of concern and the youngster's undertaking not to engage in such behaviour. In order to achieve this disengagement, it may itemise measures to support the young person and divert them from undesirable behaviour. There are no specific sanctions for breaking the contract, although there is always the threat of moving up the scale to **Criminal Behaviour Orders** or action in relation to any criminal offence.

Accommodation of children by local authorities may be needed for a range of reasons. If a **child in need** and their family seek support with accommodation, it is the housing authority that has the main duty to consider their housing needs. A local authority has a power, but important to note, not a duty, to provide accommodation to a child in need with their family (section 17(6) Children Act 1989). Where a local authority is aware of a child who is homeless or threatened with homelessness, they have a duty under section 213B Housing Act 1996 to refer to the housing authority. There are occasions under immigration law where those seeking asylum might be provided with accommodation in the shorter term. If a local authority exercises their power to provide

accommodation under section 17 Children Act 1989, the child will not be considered **looked after** and therefore the local authority does not have ongoing duties to offer support to them when they reach the age of 18.

Section 20 Children Act 1989 requires a local authority to accommodate a child, where there is no one with parental responsibility to look after a child, or the child is lost or abandoned, or the person caring for them is prevented from doing so for whatever reason. This is usually on a temporary basis by way of support; for example, if a parent is in hospital, in prison, or needs to resolve issues, for example around their own drug or alcohol use and there is no one else to assist with accommodating the child. The local authority may not, however, accommodate the child using section 20, if the parent objects. It is not an order of the court. Parents retain **parental responsibility** and can seek the return of the child at any time. Case law emphasises the need for local authorities to avoid using section 20 Children Act 1989 in a way that might be coercive, and the Supreme Court has given guidance on this (*Williams and another v London Borough of Hackney* [2018]). Children accommodated under section 20 do become **looked-after children** and local authorities do have some responsibility for them post-18 (see **Transition to adulthood**).

In certain cases, it may be appropriate for accommodation provided for children under this legislation to be secure (see **Secure accommodation**).

Accountability, employer See Employer accountability and duty of care.

Accountability, local authority See Local authorities, accountability.

Accountability, social worker See Social worker accountability and registration.

Acid test is a test, or rather guidelines, concerning capacity of adults who may not have the ability to make decisions for themselves. The test was laid down in a key legal judgment (see **Cheshire West and Chester**).

An **Action Plan Order** is a community sentence available to courts for 10- to 17-year olds. Its purpose is to prevent re-offending and help young people take responsibility for their offences and the effects of them. It may include any combination of the following specific requirements for a maximum period of 3 months:

- participation in specified activities;
- attendance at group or individual sessions;
- attending an Attendance Centre;
- staying away from specified places;
- attending school regularly;
- making (non-financial) reparation to a victim of crime or the community at large;

A

- in certain circumstances, attending a place for treatment for drug dependency and co-operating with the treatment (consent required);
- attending review hearing.

Courts can only make such orders where there are local schemes available and rely on a probation officer, local authority social worker or Youth Offending Team member to advise them as to what should be contained in the order.

Lack of co-operation with the order may lead to breach proceedings at which the Youth Court has the right to set aside the Action Plan Order and sentence the offender for the original offence.

The relevant law is in sections 69–72 of the Powers of Criminal Courts (Sentencing) Act 2000.

Acts of Parliament are laws that are created by a process whereby Bills pass through both Houses of Parliament. Most Bills are proposed by the government of the day, but individual MPs and members of the House of Lords are occasionally given the opportunity to propose a Bill. If a Bill passes successfully through both Houses of Parliament, albeit with amendments, it then goes through a symbolic process of receiving royal assent and then becomes an Act of Parliament. Such Acts are what constitutes 'statute law', that is, written-down law that can be looked up and checked – in contrast to common law which are legal principles passed down through the ages, but which are not actually codified or written down as such.

Acts of Parliament sometimes set out the law in a broad way with more detailed Regulations produced separately as Statutory Instruments. Sometimes Acts of Parliament will have Schedules at the end that flesh out some of the detail; for example, making it clear which other laws are repealed or amended as a consequence of the new Act. All of these Regulations and Schedules have the force of law; the advantage of **Regulations and Rules** is that they can be amended more quickly when the need arises, simply by asking Parliament to confirm the changes, whereas Acts of Parliament may only be amended through detailed review by Parliament itself.

Acts of Parliament are named by the subject of the law followed by the word Act and then the year the legislation was passed, which is not necessarily the year it was implemented. For further information on how to cite Acts and case law see **Citation of legislation and legal cases.**

The easiest way to check what an Act of Parliament actually says is to look it up on the official government legislation website (see **Legal databases**). Note, however, that this only deals with the content of law; it does not link this to case law, for which reference needs to be made to one of the legal databases such as **Lawtel, LexisNexis** or **BAILII**.

Adoption, or to be more precise an 'adoption order' made in accordance with the law, changes the identity of a child by ending the legal relationship with natural parents.

Parental responsibility and rights held prior to the adoption order come to an end, and the adoptive parents take on all legal responsibilities relating to the adopted child, as if the child were born into the family.

Adoption is seen to offer the security of a permanent home, enabling a child and their adopted parents to feel like a family for the rest of their lives. Case law shows applications to oppose an adoption order require rare and exceptional circumstances and do not include a change of heart.

There has always been adoption of one form or another. Historically, adopted children tended to be either orphans with no family, or children born to unmarried mothers at a time when this attracted stigma. Very young children, usually babies, were often provided to couples that could not have their own child. Changes in society, such as available contraception and reduced stigma around sole parenting, have reduced the number of babies available for adoption.

While many prospective adopters may prefer to adopt a baby, the children currently waiting to be adopted tend to be a little older and separated from their birth families as a result of care proceedings. Those children may have needs arising from those experiences that the adopters will need to consider, which is why information about a child's life will be shared appropriately with prospective adopters. In recent decades, there has been a shift in policy and law that focuses more on providing a child with the family they need, rather than simply providing a family with a child. There do, however, remain some mothers who, for a variety of reasons, decide to relinquish their babies for adoption either at birth or soon after, in the absence of any care proceedings.

The framework of the **Adoption and Children Act 2002**, together with associated Regulations, encourages wider use of adoption for children who are looked after by local authorities, and are intended to provide a simplified adoption process, seeking to address earlier concerns about children waiting in care a long time. This has been supported by amendments made by the Children and Families Act 2014, which provided a mechanism where prospective adopters may foster children with a view to adopting them. Adoption is no longer as closed as it used to be, and consideration is now given as to whether some infrequent form of indirect or direct contact would be appropriate for the child, though such is not imposed on adopters.

The requirement to match a child with adopted parents from a similar ethnic background has also been removed, though it remains a factor for consideration. Despite all efforts, there remain delays in children being adopted from care. In part, this is likely to be because there are not enough prospective adopters who wish to adopt an older child or a child who has additional needs. Minimum National Standards set out practice standards to ensure that there is a consistent approach that ensures the needs of children, parents and prospective adopters are considered by the professionals working with them (Department for Education, 2014a).

Adoption and Children Act 2002 came into full effect on 30 December 2005, replacing the Adoption Act 1976. It consists of three parts, with a number of chapters and sections in each part and is supported by Schedules and a number of Regulations. Statutory guidance on adoption, published by the Department for Education in 2014 supports the implementation of the legislation (Department for Education, 2014a). Part 1 sets out the main adoption process.

Principles

Whenever a judge considers granting an adoption order, they must consider the welfare of the child throughout his or her life. Under Section 1(2) Adoption and Children Act 2002, the judge must consider a welfare checklist that is similar but not the same as the checklist in the Children Act 1989. Section 1(4) includes a requirement to consider the lifelong consequences of the child ceasing to be a member of his or her original birth family and becoming an adopted person. The cases of Re B (A Child) [2013] and Re B-S (Children) [2013] reminded social workers to follow guidance and to provide a comprehensive analysis before making a recommendation of adoption to the court.

Adoption agencies and services

The local authority itself, or in combination with an independent agency that has been appropriately regulated, is known as an 'adoption agency' that provides 'adoption services'. Adoption agencies are required to provide and maintain adoption services for adopters, the child or child's siblings, and/or the natural parents. These services include offering information, guidance and counselling, supporting contact arrangements (where necessary) and, in specific circumstances, providing financial support.

Adoption agencies undertake specialist tasks of assessing and recruiting prospective adopters as well as finding placements suitable for children waiting to be adopted. The Adoption Support Service Regulations 2005 provide a framework for the implementation of adoption processes and for adoption panels. Prospective adopters must first be assessed, and then a specialist report is prepared to place before an adoption panel. A panel is made up of professionals and independent members who consider the suitability of adopters and the proposed arrangements for the child.

Also, under Chapter 5 of the Act, a registrar must maintain records of all adoption orders and link them to birth certificates as evidence of adoption. This is important for children who may wish to trace their natural parents when they reach the age of 18.

Who can be adopted?

An application for an adoption order may only be undertaken in relation to an individual, who is not currently or previously married or in a civil partnership, prior to their eighteenth birthday.

Who can adopt?

Section 49 Adoption and Children Act 2002 states that an adoption order may only be made in respect of adopters who are over the age of 21. The Act enables single people or couples, (whether married, civil partners, or two people of the same sex or different sexes who are living as partners in an enduring family relationship) to adopt. Section 144(5) sets out a list of relationships that are excluded from adoption.

Living with prospective adopters

Prior to the application for an adoption order, the child must have lived with the prospective adopters (section 42 Adoption and Children Act 2002). The amount of time required varies according to the person who is adopting.

Placed with prospective adopters

In order to meet this requirement, a child will need to be placed with prospective adopters. The framework for placement is set out in sections 18–21. The authority for an adoption agency to place a child with prospective adopters is provided either through the consent of the natural parents or by obtaining a placement order through the court, which may dispense with the need for parental consent in specific circumstances. A local authority may seek a placement order at the same time as seeking a care order when adoption is considered to be best for the child, but the duties and obligations of social workers differ under each order. Once placed and having lived with prospective adopters for the required period, the prospective adopters may apply to the court for an adoption order.

Consent to an adoption order

Section 47 Adoption and Children Act 2002 requires that express, informed consent must be obtained from those who hold parental responsibly; this may be done through **Cafcass**. To be legally binding, consent must be provided by the mother six weeks after birth.

Where parental consent is not available, the court must first consider whether adoption is in the child's best interest. If it is, the court must then look to section 52, which sets out two specific grounds for dispensing with parental consent: a parent cannot give consent as either they cannot be found or lack the capacity to do so; or 'the welfare of the child requires the consent to be dispensed with.'

While consent is not specifically required from fathers who do not have parental responsibility, they should be notified, and their views should be sought. There are some specific circumstances where a mother may not wish the father or other family members to know of the child's existence; case law provides some guidance to social workers regarding this in *A, B And C (Adoption: Notification of Fathers And Relatives)* [2020].

Post-adoption contact (section 51A of the ACA 2002)

Each child's circumstances will be different. A judge does not have to make provision for post-adoption contact but should consider if it is in the child's best interests to do so. Any contact is likely to be minimal and usually involves indirect letters on an annual basis, but it can, more unusually, also involve face-to-face meetings. There are concerns about imposing contact on prospective adopters if it is likely to compromise feelings of permanency for the child or have the effect of destabilising the placement.

Part 1 of this Act also sets out the framework for adoptions that include a foreign element.

Part 2 made specific amendments to the Children Act 1989 including provision for unmarried fathers to obtain parental responsibility. It also introduces a new **special guardianship** order by adding section 14A Children Act 1989. Section 120 Adoption and Children Act 2002 adds domestic abuse to the definition of harm given in section 31 Children Act 1989. The requirements for children's **care plans** are also strengthened and clarified.

Part 3 contains miscellaneous provisions and information about registers. In addition to the register outlined in Part 1 of the Act, Part 3 provides for two further registers: a register of children waiting to be adopted (to enable prospective adopters to access and view some of their details); and a register that enables adopted children and natural parents to express interest in finding each other when the child reaches the age of 18 (in recognition of the need for people to have knowledge of their birth heritage).

Adult at Risk is defined as any person aged 18 years and over who is, or may be, in need of adult support services by reason of mental health issues, learning or physical disability, sensory impairment, age or illness and who is or may be unable to meet their care needs themselves or are unable to protect themselves against significant harm or serious exploitation (HM Government, 2020a, para. 14.2). For example, they may be experiencing abuse or neglect, or be at risk of experiencing abuse or neglect, and are unable to protect themselves against that abuse or neglect. They therefore need additional care or support. For legislation governing safeguarding adults against abuse or neglect see **Adult safeguarding**.

Adult safeguarding in social work for many years was hedged around with uncertainty and lack of clarity, principally because there was no clear legal remit for local authorities to protect adults vulnerable to abuse, even where there was a clear need to do so. Prior to 2014, there was no legislation mandating local authorities to take an active role, with reliance instead on official guidance and encouragement for agencies to co-operate and co-ordinate support services. This all changed with the advent of the Care Act 2014, specifically sections 42–46. The equivalent for Wales is sections 126–128 Social Services and Well-being (Wales) Act 2014.

Section 42 Care Act 2014 lays on the local authority the duty to make enquiries where there is 'reasonable cause to suspect' abuse or neglect and where the person experiencing that abuse or neglect is unable to protect themselves against it, by, for example, instituting legal action under domestic abuse protection legislation such as the Family Law Act 1996 (see **Domestic abuse**). The purpose of the enquiries is to enable the local authority 'to decide whether any action should be taken … and, if so, what and by whom.'

This is more or less equivalent to the childcare duty to investigate abuse to be found in section 47 Children Act 1989. Although the duty is similar, one key difference is that there is no parallel to child-related care proceedings, so the scope for legal action is more constrained. There is no Family Court to which the local authority can turn with a request for some kind of formal supervision or imposed care. Instead, the only ultimate legal sanction, aside from any criminal investigation and charges, is to refer the matter to the Court of Protection.

This Court of Protection has, however, a wide discretion as to what orders it can make, although its primary concern is with people who no longer have the capacity to manage their own affairs or look after their own health and welfare interests. Nevertheless, the Court may occasionally intervene where there is clear evidence of abuse, as it did in *DL v A Local Authority and others* [2012] where the parents of an abusive son would not themselves institute any kind of legal proceedings, despite having the capacity to do so. The parents were clearly frightened of the son's physical threats and were at risk of being intimidated and coerced into converting the ownership of the house into his name. Here the Court of Protection felt justified in using its common law (**inherent jurisdiction**) powers to intervene as it considered that it ought to protect vulnerable people.

More information for practitioners as to how to carry out these section 42 duties is to be found in the relevant sections of the **Care and Support Statutory Guidance** (HM Government, 2020a). Note that there are no Regulations connected to adult safeguarding, but the guidance is mandatory (section 78 Care Act 2014).

Every local authority is required under the Care Act 2014 (section 43) to establish a **Safeguarding Adults Board** through which it establishes local safeguarding arrangements designed to enable social workers to work strategically in conjunction with partners to help and protect adults who fall into one of the categories listed in the **Care and Support Statutory Guidance**. This list of types of abuse or neglect, which the Guidance emphasises is not exhaustive, comprises:

- physical abuse, including restraint and physical sanctions and misuse of medication;
- domestic violence, including 'honour' based violence;
- sexual abuse, including pornography and witnessing sexual acts;
- psychological abuse, including emotional abuse, threats, deprivation of contact, humiliation, intimidation, coercion, harassment, verbal abuse, cyber bullying, unjustified withdrawal of services or supportive networks;

- financial abuse, including internet scamming, coercion in relation to wills, property, inheritance or financial transactions, misappropriation of property, possessions or benefits;
- modern slavery;
- discriminatory abuse on the basis of race, gender and gender identity, age, disability, sexual orientation or religion;
- organisational abuse, including neglect or poor care practice;
- neglect and self-neglect: see **Neglect, adult.**

The **Care and Support Statutory Guidance** also itemises 'six key principles' that should underpin adult safeguarding work (HM Government, 2020a, para. 14.13):

- empowerment, with an emphasis on informed consent, which relates to the Mental Capacity Act 2005;
- prevention, which fits with the principles of the Care Act 2014, especially section 1 and promoting well-being;
- proportionality, relevant in ensuring compliance with European Convention on Human Rights and the Human Rights Act 1998;
- protection, including a participative safeguarding process;
- partnership, involving professional collaboration and involvement in the community;
- accountability, which includes transparency.

For more information on the requirements relating to the actual adult safeguarding enquiry see separate **Adult safeguarding enquiries** entry. There are a number of specialist sources for further information: for example, Brammer and Pritchard-Jones, 2019; Cooper and White, 2017; Feldon, 2021; Mandelstam, 2019; Social Care Institute for Excellence, 2020.

Adult safeguarding enquiries implement the local authority's duties under section 42 Care Act 2014 which sets out the duty to investigate possible cases of adult abuse. Section 42 itself is quite short so practitioners need to consult the official guidance for help with carrying out their duties. This guidance is mandatory: social workers employed by a local authority 'must act under the general guidance of the Secretary of State in the exercise of functions given to it by this Part [sections 1–80] or by regulations under this Part' (section 78 Care Act 2014). All references to paragraphs in this entry are to paragraphs in the **Care and Support Statutory Guidance** (HM Government, 2020a).

Aims of adult safeguarding enquiry

Paragraph 14.11 states that the purpose of adult safeguarding is to:

- prevent harm and reduce the risk of abuse or neglect to adults with care and support needs;

- stop abuse or neglect wherever possible;
- safeguard adults in a way that supports them in making choices and having control about how they want to live;
- promote an approach that concentrates on improving life for the adults concerned;
- raise public awareness so that communities as a whole, alongside professionals, play their part in preventing, identifying and responding to abuse and neglect;
- provide information and support in accessible ways to help people understand the different types of abuse, how to stay safe, and what to do to raise a concern about the safety or well-being of an adult;
- address what has caused the abuse or neglect.

The purpose of the enquiry is to decide whether a person or organisation, not necessarily the local authority, should do something to help and protect the adult (paragraph 14.78). It needs to establish whether abuse has taken place and draw up a safeguarding plan to address any abuse or neglect.

What triggers an investigation

Anyone can raise concerns with the local authority, but it is up to the local authority to decide whether there needs to be a 'section 42' enquiry and, if so, whether to conduct that investigation itself or ask another public body, such as the police, to do so (section 42(2) Care Act 2014). It is not a requirement that actual abuse has taken place, since section 42(1) refers also to someone being 'at risk of abuse or neglect'. The local authority may want to undertake an 'initial enquiry' to ascertain whether a full-scale enquiry is warranted. Furthermore, paragraph 144 of the statutory guidance says a local authority may choose to conduct a safeguarding enquiry in order to promote someone's well-being even if the section 42 criteria are not met.

Principles underpinning the enquiry

Six key principles of practice are highlighted in the statutory guidance, and these underpin all Care Act 2014 related work, deriving from Section 1(3) Care Act 2014. These principles were itemised under **Adult safeguarding**: empowerment, prevention, proportionality, protection, partnership, accountability. In addition, reference should be made to *Making Safeguarding Personal* (Local Government Association, 2020) with its emphasis on the process being 'person-led and outcome-focused'.

What should the enquiry process be?

According to the statutory guidance (paragraph 14.94), the process is:

- establish facts
- ascertain the adult's views and wishes
- assess the needs of the adult for protection, support and redress and how they might be met

- protect from the abuse and neglect, in accordance with their wishes
- make decisions as to what follow-up action should be taken with regard to the person or organisation responsible for the abuse or neglect
- enable the adult to achieve resolution and recovery.

To this end, there should be a safeguarding plan, which is essentially a record of what individuals or organisations are going to do to ensure the adult is safe in future, provide support and possible redress, assess future risk, and take any appropriate action in relation to the person or organisation causing the concern (paragraph 14.111). This plan should be reviewed from time to time.

There are useful diagrams or procedures outlined in the statutory guidance (HM Government, 2020a, paragraph 14.92) and Feldon (2021).

Advance decisions, more popularly known as living wills, is the term used in the **Mental Capacity Act 2005**. These are directions or instructions people can give in advance in order to ensure that their wishes are respected concerning medical treatment or social care, principally refusals to accept certain kinds of medical treatment. In effect, these are advance decisions to refuse treatment in certain specified circumstances. For example, if someone has a terminal illness and does not wish their life to be prolonged by what they regard as intrusive medical treatment, they can anticipate this and effectively order doctors not to deploy life-sustaining treatment if there is no reasonable prospect of them recovering. Note the key word 'anticipation': instructions have to be clear, specific and made at a time when someone has full **capacity** to do so.

There are some decisions that will not be acted upon since these may conflict with statute law or court decisions. So, for example, it is not possible to override decisions to impose **compulsory treatment** on someone under the Mental Health Act 1983, or to frustrate a decision made by the **Court of Protection**. However, it is mandatory for health and social care professionals to ascertain whether someone has made an advance decision when their rights to decide for themselves are being overridden, for example, when someone may be made subject to **Deprivation of Liberty Safeguards** or **Liberty Protection Safeguards** (Mental Capacity Act 2005 Schedules A1 or AA1, Mental Capacity Amendment Act 2019).

The key relevant law here is the Mental Capacity Act 2005 sections 24–26. This law was passed as a result of a number of high-profile cases that revealed a gap in the law as they had to be decided by reference to common law **inherent jurisdiction**. The most well known of these was *Airedale NHS Trust v Bland* [1993] which concerned treatment on a life-support machine of a young man whose injuries were sustained in the Hillsborough football disaster in 1989. Medical opinion declared no real possibility of recovery and relatives wanted his life to be ended, but clinicians had no legal authority to do this without reference to the courts.

Do note that advance decisions have significant limitations. They cannot be used to secure certain kinds of treatment or to require that certain services be provided – so there is no point declaring a wish to go to a particular care home and for the local authority to pay for it. Furthermore, they cannot be used to compel someone to break the law. Hence under no circumstances may treatment be deliberately directly given that will hasten someone's death, for under UK law this would be manslaughter; but treatment to keep someone alive, who would otherwise have died, may be withdrawn. This may sound like a subtle distinction, yet it is critically important for practitioners involved in 'end of life' care. Likewise, no one is allowed to assist someone to commit suicide, no matter what wishes are expressed, since this would be a breach of criminal law.

Advocates help other people express their views and wishes, empowering them to defend and promote their own position, regardless of the advocate's own personal views or beliefs. In terms of representing people in court, **solicitors** and **barristers** are the key players, but there are other forms of advocacy, some of which are quite specific.

In court cases involving children, the **children's guardian** plays an important role in care proceedings and adoption cases, being specifically employed for this purpose by the Children and Family Court Advisory and Support Service (**Cafcass**) established by the Criminal Justice and Court Services Act 2000 (sections 11–15). The Mental Capacity Act 2005 (sections 35–41) sets out the important functions of the **Independent Mental Capacity Advocate**. The Mental Health Act 2007 (section 30) created the role of the **Independent Mental Health Advocate**. The Care Act 2014 (sections 67–68) allocates a specific set of responsibilities to **Independent Care Act Advocates**.

For further information on the tasks carried out by these advocates see separate entries for each of them.

After-care services are a specific legal duty under section 117 of the Mental Health Act 1983. They are to be provided for certain categories of patient who have been detained in hospital. These patients are generally those detained on longer term orders: admitted from the community under section 3, via courts under section 37 or 45A, or transferred from prison under section 48. The legislation does not stipulate what constitutes after-care, but the Mental Health Act 1983 Code of Practice provides a wide-ranging list (Department of Health, 2015). Because this legislation is separate from the Care Act 2014, there is no power to charge for after-care provision, but section 75 Care Act 2014 does give the right to express a preference for a particular kind of accommodation.

The **age of criminal responsibility** in England and Wales is 10. This is the minimum age at which a child can be held accountable for actions that are against the law. Under-10s cannot be prosecuted although it is possible to ask the courts to make a **child safety order** in relation to a child under 10. The age of 10 is significantly lower than most other countries, including Scotland where the Age of Criminal Responsibility (Scotland) Act 2019 stipulates an age of 12; this is also the age in Ireland. The Child Rights International Network has full information on the ages of criminal responsibility in other countries in 2019, indicating that in several European countries the age is either 15 (mainly Scandinavian countries) or 14 (several Southern and Eastern European countries).

A report from the Equality and Human Rights Commission strongly recommended the age should be raised to at least 12, as did the Commission on Justice in Wales.

Anti-discrimination legislation attempts to address discrimination
that finds its way into the design and delivery of services which can result in negative outcomes for individuals and groups. One of the most important examples was the Macpherson Report of 1999, which highlighted institutional racism in the police. This was a key influence in promoting the passage of the Equality Act 2010. The Act and its associated Regulations is fundamental to promoting principles of anti-discrimination for it consolidated and amended earlier discrimination laws, broadening their scope, being applicable to organisations providing services to the public as well as to individuals who provide goods or services.

The key provisions of the Equality Act 2010 are found in Chapters 1 and 2 of the Act and in its explanatory notes. These include making it unlawful to treat someone less favourably because of a protected characteristic, that is: age, disability, gender reassignment, marriage and civil partnership, pregnancy and maternity, race, religion and belief, sex or sexual orientation.

The Act recognises discrimination in the following forms: direct and indirect discrimination, dual discrimination; harassment, victimisation; discrimination by perception or association. This includes discrimination because someone is perceived as having a characteristic even if they do not, or because of a person's association with someone that does have a characteristic that is protected under the Equality Act 2010 (*Traveller Movement and Others v J. D. Wetherspoon plc* [2015]).

Section 20 Equality Act 2010 requires organisations to make reasonable adjustments to support access to services for people living with a disability. What is considered reasonable will depend on the type of organisation and the resources it has available to introduce changes, such as making adaptations to a building to make it more accessible.

Section 149 sets out a public sector duty requiring public authorities, in the exercise of their public functions, to have due regard to eliminating discrimination, advancing equality of opportunity, and fostering good relations between persons who have protected characteristics and those that do not (*Kannan v Newham LBC* [2019]).

Sections 158 and 159 permit organisations to take positive action to address disadvantages experienced by some groups through, for example, recruitment policies. Note this is not the same as positive discrimination, that is, actions that actively favour one group over another, which is not lawful. In very limited circumstances indirect discrimination, direct age discrimination, or discrimination related to a disability may be permitted if justified on the basis that it is a proportionate means of achieving a legitimate aim. A legitimate aim would include protecting the health and safety of individuals or the requirements of a business (*Dhinsa v Serco and Another* [2011]). Further exceptions are set out in Schedules to the Act.

Criminal law addresses discrimination through offences related to hate crime; for example, sections 28–32 Crime and Disorder Act 1998, and sections 145 and 146 Criminal Justice Act 2003. The Crown Prosecution Service and police have an agreed-upon definition for identifying hate crimes.

The **British Association of Social Workers (BASW)** 2014 Code of Ethics and **Social Work England's** professional standards both require social workers to challenge their own and others' prejudice. At a minimum, social workers are required to comply with existing legislation, while recognising that the impact it has on reducing discrimination may be limited. This is because the onus is often on individuals to make and resource a claim against those who discriminate, or because legislation fails to capture subtle forms of discrimination or address cumulative disadvantage brought about by deeper structural discrimination. Anti-discrimination legislation generally focuses on individual acts of discrimination since it is difficult to frame legislation to address wider structural issues of racism and other forms of discrimination because of the nature of how the law operates, a point underscored in the Lammy review of the operation of the justice system (Lammy, 2017).

Anti-social behaviour orders now consist of civil injunctions, Community Protection Notices and Criminal Behaviour Orders, which replaced anti-social behaviour orders as a result of the Anti-Social Behaviour, Crime and Policing Act 2014. Injunctions or Community Protection Notices can be made by courts where there are reports of persistent antisocial behaviour from the police, a local authority or landlord. There is some disquiet about them as they are civil orders, that is, the grounds only need be proved on the 'balance of probabilities' yet breaching the order is a criminal offence which, for over 18s, can be up to two years' imprisonment (three months' detention for under 18s).

For more serious anti-social behaviour concerns, courts can make a Criminal Behaviour Order where an offender is convicted of an offence and the behaviour caused, or was likely to cause, harassment, alarm or distress to any person (section 22 Anti-Social Behaviour, Crime and Policing Act 2014). Criminal Behaviour Orders last for a minimum of one year and a maximum of three (section 25). Again, breaching the order is a criminal offence, the maximum penalty for which for under 18s is two years' detention and for over 18s is five years' imprisonment.

Appeals See Courts and the court system.

Appropriate Adult is a specific term used to denote the person who has to be present when a young person (aged 10–17) or vulnerable adult is being interviewed by the police. Most interviews will follow on from that person being detained or asked to attend a police station as a suspect but could be in connection with witnessing a crime. Their attendance is a legal requirement under section 66 Police and Criminal Evidence Act 1984 as amended by the Serious Organised Crime and Police Act 2005. Interviews with young people or vulnerable adults without an Appropriate Adult risk being discounted as evidence by courts. Appropriate Adults should also be present for all 'out-of-court' disposals, such as a **Youth Caution** (sections 136–8 Legal Aid, Sentencing and Punishment of Offenders Act 2012).

While it is clear who young people are, it is less certain who qualifies as a vulnerable adult, but generally this is intended to refer to people with mental health issues or learning difficulties.

In most cases, the most suitable person to act as Appropriate Adult will be the person who knows them best, and for young people that will be a parent, but where the local authority accommodates a young person, a social worker would be the Appropriate Adult. In some cases, the Youth Offending Team will be asked to perform this function since provision of Appropriate Adults is one of their official functions. It is also possible for any 'responsible' person aged 18 or over to act as Appropriate Adult.

In some cases, parents will not be suitable; for example, if they are suspected of complicity in the offence, are witnesses to it, or victims of it, are employed by the police, or where the young person specifically objects. They would also not be suitable if the young person had already admitted the offence to them.

The role of the Appropriate Adult is to protect the interests of the interviewee by effectively putting them in the same position as an adult being interviewed. More specifically, the Appropriate Adult should:

- offer support and advice, but not legal advice (so the Appropriate Adult might wish to encourage the interviewee to insist on advice from a duty solicitor);
- ensure the interviewee understands their rights and that the police act fairly;
- be present when the interviewee is being fingerprinted, photographed, or searched;
- inspect the relevant custody record;
- facilitate communication between interviewee and the police;
- be present when charges are made;
- take up any follow-up action, for example, referral to an organisation that would offer support or further assistance.

It will be seen that the role does require some knowledge of detainees' rights and familiarity with police procedures, so it is difficult sometimes to see how parents can be fully effective in this role. For professionals, specific training is available and there is also a national network of volunteer Appropriate Adults and set of national standards relating to Appropriate Adult schemes (National Appropriate Adult Network, 2018).

Approved Mental Capacity Professionals play a key

role under the **Liberty Protection Safeguards** introduced by the Mental Capacity (Amendment) Act 2019. The Approved Mental Capacity Professional replaces the **Best Interests Assessor** whose functions end when the Mental Capacity (Amendment) Act 2019, along with its associated Regulations and Code of Practice, is fully implemented. Whereas the Best Interests Assessor themselves personally undertook to carry out assessments under the Deprivation of Liberty Safeguards Mental Capacity Act 2005 scheme, under Liberty Protection Safeguards the Approved Mental Capacity Professional receives and reviews the assessments carried out by others at the pre-authorisation review. They must normally then meet the person being cared for and consult with certain other people as specified in Schedule 1 Mental Capacity (Amendment) Act 2019.

An Approved Mental Capacity Professional will, like Best Interests Assessors, normally be a social worker, nurse, occupation therapist, or psychologist who has received additional training, with annual updates, in accordance with requirements laid down by the Regulations. Local authorities approve someone to act as an Approved Mental Capacity Professional.

Approved Mental Health Professionals have a specific role

under mental health legislation. Their principal role is to assess whether people qualify for **compulsory admission and detention** under the Mental Health Act 1983, although they do have other responsibilities in relation to people under **community treatment orders**.

Approved Mental Health Professionals are qualified and registered social workers, mental health nurses, occupation therapists or psychologists who have undertaken further training that meets the requirements of **Social Work England** (section 19 Mental Health Act 2007, section 48 Children and Social Work Act 2017). Their appointment additionally needs to be approved by the relevant local authority (section 114 Mental Health Act 1983).

Approved Mental Health Professionals have the power to apply for a compulsory admission of someone in accordance with sections 2, 3 or 4 Mental Health Act 1983, and also have the power to apply for guardianship under section 7. They do so on the basis of doctors' medical recommendations (for full explanation of procedures see separate entries on **Compulsory admission and detention** and **Guardianship**). They thereby offer an independent assessment of the need for admission and this fulfils expectations of the **European Convention on Human Rights**, in particular the guidance issued by the European Court of Human Rights in the key *Winterwerp* (*Winterwerp v The Netherlands* [1979]) case, namely that:

A

- the existence of a mental disorder must be verified;
- the mental disorder must be of a kind or degree warranting compulsory confinement; and
- the validity of continued confinement has to be justified.

The duties of Approved Mental Health Professionals are to be found in section 13 Mental Health Act 1983. This states that the Approved Mental Health Professional must make an application where they are satisfied that it ought to be made and it is necessary and proper for them to make the application, having considered the wishes expressed by relatives of the patient or 'any other relevant circumstances'. It is a legal requirement under this section for the Approved Mental Health Professional to interview the patient 'in a suitable manner' and satisfy themselves that detention in hospital is 'in all the circumstances of the case the most appropriate way of providing the care and medical treatment of which the patient stands in need'.

Approved Mental Health Professionals' responsibilities in regard to community treatment orders are more general. They are involved in the assessment of a patient detained under section 3 Mental Health Act 1983 where a community treatment order is being considered for them, helping to set up the conditions of the order and making decisions on when to allow someone to return home and when to revoke the order. For a fuller explanation see separate entry on **Community treatment orders**.

In carrying out their duties, Approved Mental Health Professionals need to heed the advice of the relevant Code of Practice (Department of Health, 2015).

Arrest, youth is covered under entries for **Appropriate Adult, Bail,** and **Remands to care or custody.**

Assessment, adult needs refers to an assessment carried out under the Care Act 2014. If an adult believes they need support services, there is nothing to stop them simply arranging them. However, they would then have to pay for them direct, which may be beyond their means, at which point they would need to call on local authority social services to assist. While local authorities have the power to pay for services, they can also charge for them according to someone's ability to pay by applying a means test (sections 14–17 Care Act 2014). They must first establish that the adult objectively needs support services and to what extent, as is made clear by section 9(1) Care Act 2014 which states:

> Where it appears to a local authority that an adult may have needs for care and support, the authority must assess (a) whether the adult does have needs for care and support, and (b) if the adult does, what those needs are.

This is a 'needs assessment'. Assessment is an unconditional entitlement. Section 9(3) says assessment cannot be denied because the local authority takes a different view of need, or because of the person's financial position. Section 9(5) says the assessment must involve the person being assessed, their carer, and any other person requested by the person being assessed or who appears to be interested in their welfare.

There is a separate duty to assess the needs of a carer (section 10 Care Act 2014) (see **Carers**). Significantly, the Act resolves the dilemma of those situations where a carer is desperate for support but the person they care for lacks the capacity to understand how much of a burden they are. This it does by allowing the local authority to carry out the assessment where this is the case and it believes the assessment is in the person's 'best interests' (section 11(2)(a) Care Act 2014).

There are Regulations and statutory guidance specifically associated with the duty to assess, which is the gateway to accessing local authority support. These are:

- Care and Support (Assessment) Regulations 2014
- **Care and Support Statutory Guidance** 2020 (regularly revised) (HM Government, 2020a).

There are also specialist texts that apply the law to social work practice in this area (Feldon, 2021).

Assessment, child includes the gathering and analysing of information that

provides a holistic understanding of a child's needs, any risks they face, how parents meet their needs, any strengths and protective factors. Risks located in the wider community, which a family may have little influence over, must also be assessed where appropriate. Statutory assessments are carried out by social workers if children are considered to be in need or at risk of suffering significant harm. The Department of Health and Social Care Assessment Framework (Department of Health, 2000) prompts consideration of important factors in a child's life whatever their circumstances. The Statutory guidance to the Children Act 1989, **Working Together to Safeguard Children** (HM Government, 2018), requires agencies to share information to support assessments. All assessments should be child focused and undertaken by working in partnership with a family where possible.

Section 43 Children Act 1989 allows the local authority to apply to a court for a Child Assessment Order, if the parents are preventing social workers access to the child and there is reasonable cause to suspect that a child is suffering significant harm. The order lasts for 7 days but orders are rarely applied for since they do not compel the parent to co-operate, and in such cases, it is likely that another order, such as an Emergency Protection Order, would be more appropriate.

Asylum seekers See Refugees and people seeking asylum.

Attendance Centre Orders are non-custodial orders which can

apply to under-18s, who attend junior attendance centres, and to young adult offenders for whom senior attendance centres are provided. In youth justice, Attendance Centre Orders are one of the range of penalties under **Youth Rehabilitation Orders** (section 1(e) Criminal Justice and Immigration Act 2008). Their purpose is to deprive young people of part of their leisure time and to provide a programme that teaches them about involvement in criminal activity. Some centres also teach life skills. Each local youth justice service decides what is appropriate for their area, and orders can only be made if there is provision in the area where the young person lives.

Sessions can be up to 3 hours long and are normally weekly, quite often on a Saturday as they must not interfere with schooling. The aggregate number of hours which the offender may be required to attend is laid down in paragraph 12 of Schedule 1 of the Criminal Justice and Immigration Act 2008. They are as follows:

- Offenders under 14: the maximum number of hours is 12
- Offenders under 16 but over 14: the maximum number of hours is 24
- Offenders over 16: the maximum number of hours is 36

Failing to attend is a breach of the Youth Rehabilitation Order, and Regulations set out in Schedule 2 Criminal Justice and Immigration Act 2008 set out what courts can do if cases are referred back to them.

B

Baby P (aka Baby Peter, Peter Connolly) See **Munro Review**.

Bail is the temporary release of someone accused of an offence, sometimes with conditions attached to ensure they attend court. The Bail Act 1976 (section 4) says there should always be a presumption in favour of someone being bailed rather than held in detention, and there are additional safeguards for young people. For them, the presumption is that they would normally be bailed without conditions. This applies both to the police and the courts.

The police can refuse bail where they believe the young person would not attend court, might commit further offences, or interfere with witnesses, or has previously breached bail conditions, or 'needs' protection or welfare (section 38 Police and Criminal Evidence Act 1984). In such cases, young people would generally be remanded to local authority accommodation (see **Remands to care or custody**).

Courts have additional bail options. For example, they could refer the young person to the **Youth Offending Team** for support and advice through a bail support scheme run by the Youth Offending Team or local agency.

BAILII stands for British and Irish Legal Information Institute which offers a free online reference source for checking legislation and case law. For further information see **Legal databases**.

Barristers See **Courts and the court system**.

Best interests is a term that refers generally to decision-taking on behalf of someone who is not able to make a specific decision for themselves. An obvious example is where someone is unconscious as a result of an accident. There is no doubt it is in that person's interest to be taken to hospital, so it is deemed unnecessary to have specific legislation that says that where a person is unconscious other people can act on their behalf. More controversially, it is assumed that there is a duty on professionals such as health care workers and social workers to prevent people harming themselves, so actively intervening to stop someone committing suicide is not only lawful but expected. Such acts are covered by **common law**, which in this context some might describe as common sense.

However, there are limits to how far this common law principle can be taken, as was seen in the court decision in the **Bournewood case**. Partly as a consequence of this case, the term 'best interests' was clarified in statute law and associated guidance, namely the Mental Capacity Act 2005 and its Code of Practice (Department for Constitutional Affairs, 2007). The relevant sections of the Mental Capacity Act 2005 are sections 1–5, especially sections 1 and 4. Thus, where someone is considered to have lost their ability (capacity) to make decisions for themselves, professionals are obliged to do so in their best interests but in a way that is least restrictive of the person's rights and freedoms (section 1(5) and 1(6) Mental Capacity Act 2005). Even when acting in someone's best interests, professionals must encourage participation in actions or decisions carried out on their behalf (section 4(4) Mental Capacity Act 2005).

There are certain factors that the law says must not impinge on professional decisions to act in someone's 'best interests': age, appearance, behaviour or, in the case of life-sustaining treatment, the desire to hasten someone's death (section 4(5) Mental Capacity Act 2005). The Mental Capacity Act 2005 Code of Practice offers guidance on factors to take into account when assessing 'best interests':

1   the person's past and present wishes and feelings, beliefs and values;
2   the extent to which they can participate on decision-making;
3   the paramount need to avoid discrimination (age, appearance, behaviour);
4   the need not to make assumptions about quality of life;
5   the possibility of regaining capacity;
6   the need to consult with people who care for them, are related to them, or have a formal role under a **Lasting Power of Attorney** or by order of the **Court of Protection** or someone who has been appointed as an **Independent Mental Capacity Advocate**.

Case law

There is an interesting body of case law on interpretation of 'best interests' from which the following cases are drawn.

When an 82-year-old woman with a diagnosis of dementia and resident in a care home wanted to go on a cruise, the local authority decided it was not in her 'best interests' as there was deemed to be an element of risk she was unable to appreciate. This was despite the promise of her partner to take responsibility for her. The court declared that, although there was an element of risk, this was insufficient to go against the presumption in favour of capacity, and that, in effect, 'best interests' does not mean that safety and security trump autonomy (*Cardiff County Council v Ross and Davies* [2011]).

In *K v A Local Authority and Others* [2012], the court confirmed a local authority plan to place a young adult with learning disabilities in a placement away from home as being in his best interests. This was despite the father's objections and claim that family rights under Article 8 **European Convention on Human Rights** should be the paramount consideration. The court ruled that the correct interpretation of the law was to ascertain 'best interests' first by using section 4 Mental Capacity Act 2005 and then checking whether that 'best interests' decision conflicted with Article 8 rights. If it did, then decision-makers had to consider whether that violation was proportionate. In effect, it is 'best interests' that is the paramount consideration.

Best Interests Assessor is a role that continues until the Mental Capacity (Amendment) Act 2019 is fully implemented. The role was to make recommendations to the Supervisory Body concerning the detention of people under the Deprivation of Liberty Safeguards (for explanation see **Deprivation of Liberty Safeguards**). Specifically, the Best Interests Assessor recommended how long deprivation should be for, who should represent the detained person in decision-making, and whether any conditions should be attached to the deprivation of liberty.

This recommendation was based on six assessments, although at least one of these had to be carried out by someone other than the Best Interests Assessor, usually the doctor who carried out the mental health assessment. The other assessments were age, no refusals, capacity, eligibility and **best interests**, the last of which only the Best Interests Assessor could undertake.

Best Interests Assessors would normally be a social worker, nurse, occupation therapist, or psychologist who has received additional training, with annual updates, in accordance with requirements laid down by the relevant Regulations. Local authorities approved someone to act as a Best Interests Assessor.

The role is abolished by the Mental Capacity (Amendment) Act 2019 which replaces the Best Interests Assessor with the **Approved Mental Capacity Professional**. Until it is implemented, practitioners have some useful guidance available (Brown et al., 2015; Hubbard and Stone, 2018; Ministry of Justice, 2008).

Binding over offenders is a power that Courts have had for centuries under both **common law** and **statute law** going right back to the Justices of the Peace Act 1361. It is a means of addressing minor offences, such as assault or breaches of the peace, and is in effect a postponement of sentence on condition that the offender steers clear of trouble. Technically, while binding over orders are themselves civil orders, they are made after a conviction that has to be based on criminal law **burden of proof**. To try to guarantee that the offender complies, the court sets a 'recognisance', that is a sum of money that is forfeited if the offender breaches the binding over order.

Binding over parents is possible in youth justice cases. Under the Powers of Criminal Courts (Sentencing) Act 2000 (section 150), when someone under 18 is convicted of an offence the Youth Court can bind over their parent (or **guardian**) to 'take proper care and exercise proper control' of them. Such orders can only be made in respect of under-16s if the court believes the order is necessary to prevent further offending. Binding over orders can accompany a sentence on the young person, in which case the orders may include a condition that the parent ensures compliance with the community sentence the court passes. The court specifies what actions the parent is to take: for example, ensuring that their son or daughter attends school. Where the court proposes to make such an order, parental consent is required, but unreasonable refusal to consent is punishable with a fine.

So, the parent themselves is not convicted but they are subject to a civil order which will have a recognisance attached to it. The order lasts up to three years or until the young person is 18, whichever is the sooner.

Bournewood case, more properly referred to as *HL v UK* [2004],
established that UK laws relating to mental capacity did not fully comply with the **European Convention on Human Rights**. In 1997, a decision was taken to admit HL to a psychiatric hospital and detain him there against the wishes of his carers, who looked after him on a full-time basis and were effectively, but not legally, his 'nearest relatives' (for explanation of this term see *Nearest relative*). The medical team caring for him determined that he was unable to make his own decision regarding admission, yet was compliant with the hospital regime, and so they were able to keep him in hospital in his 'best interests'. This meant, they believed, that they could exercise a long-standing general common law right to decide what should be done for certain people when it was clear that they were unable to make decisions for themselves, usually where they had a condition that prevented them from doing so. In this case, the condition was a combination of autism and learning disabilities. On this basis, he was kept in hospital for three months; he was not formally detained under the Mental Health Act 1983, but he and his relatives were told that he would be detained if he attempted to leave the hospital. Visits from the carers were discouraged for fear that this would precipitate HL discharging himself.

Legal proceedings were instituted to establish whether **common law** really did give the hospital the right to act in this way. The UK courts decided that they did on the basis that HL's best interests had been determined by medical professionals, HL did not have the capacity to understand his position, but he did not actively object to being in hospital. This was lawful as it was proper and appropriate exercise of the common law doctrine of 'necessity'.

In 2004, the European Court decided otherwise. The Court decided that, given the inability to consent, the default position was that HL was detained in hospital, and so Article 5, the right to liberty, was engaged. Compliance ought not to be taken as consent; professionals cannot assume consent because someone does not demonstrate objection. Clarity in the law was needed so that it could be identified who was taking the decision on HL's behalf, and what specific explicit reasons they had for making a resolution to keep him in hospital.

Furthermore, detention under the common law doctrine of necessity was incompatible with Article 5 because common law was too arbitrary and lacked sufficient legal safeguards, such as the right to appeal enjoyed by patients detained under the Mental Health Act 1983 (see **Compulsory detention and admission**). The European Court also declared that judicial review, the only possible avenue of appeal for HL, was inadequate as it was insufficiently rigorous. As a consequence, HL was not afforded the full legal rights to a judicial hearing envisioned in Article 6, since UK law did not give proper regard to what the Convention expected in terms of how patients could object to detention nor did processes exist for ensuring that their deprivation could be reviewed. There was a gap in UK law: the 'Bournewood gap'.

This gap was filled by the Mental Capacity Act 2005 and its subsequent amendment by the Mental Health Act 2007 which introduced procedures for authorising care and, if necessary, detention of people who were unable to make decisions for themselves. Instead of relying on common law, a statute (section 4 Mental Capacity Act 2005) now declared what was meant by the term '**best interests**'. For further information, see separate entries on **Mental Capacity Act 2005; Deprivation of Liberty Safeguards;** and **Liberty Protection Safeguards.**

British Association of Social Workers (BASW) is the

professional body representing the interests of social workers in the UK. It is not a trade union, nor is it the regulator, so membership is optional, and it has no legal authority as such in contrast to **Social Work England**. It is the guardian of the **Professional Capabilities Framework**, taking over that responsibility from the now-defunct **College of Social Work**.

Burden of proof is responsibility in law, to prove something happened. The

person or body alleging something happened must produce evidence to prove to the court that it did in fact happen. For example, if a local authority in care proceedings asserts that a father hit a child, it is the local authority's responsibility to produce evidence to prove to the court that he did. The burden of proving is not on the father, although he may produce evidence to defend himself. This is similar in criminal law: if the Crown Prosecution asserts that someone broke the law, they must prove it. Not to be confused with the standard of proof.

Butler-Sloss Inquiry See Cleveland Inquiry.

C

Cafcass is The Children and Family Court Advisory and Support Service, a non-departmental public body, formed in April 2001 by the Criminal Justice and Courts Services Act 2000. Cafcass represents children in **Family Court** cases in England and Wales. It employs experienced social workers called family court advisors, sometimes known as **children's guardians** depending on the nature of the proceedings. Family court advisors offer independent advice to the Family Court about children's wishes and feelings, their **best interests** and what is safe for them. Cafcass is involved in national and international public and private law family proceedings, including adoption and medical cases.

See also **Guardians (children's guardians)**.

Capacity is a really important concept for social work and health care professionals since it refers to people's ability to make decisions for themselves; it is those professionals who are most likely to deal with people who have lost, or partly lost, that ability. Those professionals also need to know what the law says about people who have yet to gain fully legal capacity to decide for themselves. The term 'capacity' refers to the physical and mental ability to make decisions, and the law is useful in clarifying both what this means and what can happen when people lose their capacity.

The law also addresses young people's increasing ability to make their own decisions. In this respect, the law assumes that parents make decisions for and on behalf of their children until they reach a certain age. That age is generally 18, the age of majority (section 1 Family Law Reform Act 1969). However, this does not mean that a child or young person under 18 is disqualified from making decisions, far from it. **Statute law** and **case law** have evolved to incorporate the principle that young people's capacity to make certain kinds of decisions develops as they grow older. In relation to medical procedures, the starting point is section 8 Family Law Reform Act 1969 which gives 'a minor who has attained the age of sixteen years' the right to consent to medical or dental treatment without needing parental endorsement. For under-16s the extent of consent depends, critically, on the extent to which the professional who is treating them or caring for them considers them able to understand – a principle that derives from a case law decision in *Gillick v West Norfolk and Wisbech Area Health Authority* [1986]. This case created a new phrase, 'Gillick competence', used in professional circles to describe an under 16-year-old able to make decisions for themselves (see separate **Gillick competence** entry). This right to consent to treatment does not necessarily imply an absolute right to refuse treatment. In some circumstances, compulsory hospital admission and treatment may be authorised under the Mental Health Act 1983 or courts may invoke their **inherent jurisdiction** authority under **common law**. Examples of the latter would include cases where young people refused treatment for anorexia or refused blood transfusions (Johns, 2014).

When it comes to adults, the law assumes total accountability for actions and absolute rights to make any lawful decision. The only grounds for diminishing accountability for criminal actions relate to mental disorder (the law governing this is to be found in Part III of the Mental Health Act 1983). It is not possible to avoid debts, for example, by arguing ignorance, gullibility or lack of wisdom. Indeed, Part I of the **Mental Capacity Act 2005,** the key Act in this area, makes it clear that adults, in effect, have the right to make unwise decisions (section 1(4) Mental Capacity Act 2005). Generally, it is assumed that an individual has capacity and understands the nature and consequences of their actions.

What if there is clear evidence that someone does not have the capacity to make sound decisions? This brings us firmly into the realm of the Mental Capacity Act 2005. The Act starts with a 'presumption of capacity', or in social work we might say an inherent right of autonomy, which people can only lose where it can be clearly shown that they 'lack capacity' to some extent. The Mental Capacity Act 2005 declares that a person lacks capacity if they are unable to make a decision because of 'an impairment of, or a disturbance in, the functioning of the mind or brain' and 'it does not matter whether the impairment or disturbance is permanent or temporary' (section 2 Mental Capacity Act 2005). In practice, this means that decisions that someone lacks capacity are most likely to be made where someone has a learning disability, where someone has mental health issues, has a 'functioning impairment' such as brain injury or dementia or has a life-threatening condition and has become unable to communicate. However, it is quite wrong to think in terms of groups of people to whom the Mental Capacity Act 2005 might apply, a point emphasised in section 2(3) of the Mental Capacity Act 2005 which states that 'a lack of capacity cannot be established merely by reference to a person's age or appearance'. Consequently, assessments of capacity (or rather lack of it) must be firmly based on someone's ability to make decisions (Brown, Barber and Martin, 2015).

Nor is it a simple either-or ('does' or 'does not' have capacity) decision. Capacity can fluctuate from time to time and can vary according to the different kinds of decisions someone has to make. This is made clear in the Mental Capacity Act 2005 itself and its associated Code of Practice (Department for Constitutional Affairs, 2007). As regards overriding people's decision-making autonomy, the fundamental principles underpinning the legislation are:

- lack of capacity must be to do with impairment in mind or brain affecting that decision at that time, sometimes referred to as the causative nexus;
- an inability to make a decision is demonstrated where there is clear evidence of all of the following: that someone is (a) unable to understand information, (b) retain information, (c) use or weigh up information as part of the decision-making process, and (d) communicate their decision (section 3(1) Mental Capacity Act 2005).

In relation to the last point, the law makes it clear that there is an obligation on professionals to facilitate communication and understanding with 'all practicable steps' taken to help someone make a decision (section 1 Mental Capacity Act 2005). If necessary, assessment and reassessment may be needed. The person does not need to understand every single detail but should be able to understand the key points, a point emphasised in case law: for example, *CC v KK* [2012] in which a judge warned against the 'protection imperative' and the danger of professionals conflating the issues of capacity and best interests.

In certain circumstances, where someone loses capacity to understand the danger they might pose to themselves, they may find themselves compelled to remain in a care home or other care provision. These legal provisions are to be found in amendments to the Mental Capacity Act 2005 introduced by the Mental Health Act 2007 and the Mental Capacity Amendment Act 2019. These are known as the **Deprivation of Liberty Safeguards** which are to be superseded by the **Liberty Protection Safeguards**.

The **Care Act 2014** was intended as a consolidating Act, bringing together and updating the welter of legislation that comprised the piecemeal adult care system prior to 2014. It also introduced, for the first time, clear statutory obligations to safeguard adults. The Act is the bedrock of social work with adults inasmuch as it sets the framework for provision of services to support adults who need care and support, including their carers. To achieve this end, the Act is accompanied by several sets of Regulations and the crucial Care and Support Statutory Guidance which is regularly updated (see **Care and Support Statutory Guidance**).

Much of the Act is of direct relevance to social work practice.

The Act starts with the positive principle of promoting well-being (section 1 Care Act 2014). Part 1 of the Act then asserts the principles of preventing future need (section 2), integrating services (section 3), providing information and advice (section 4), and promoting diversity and quality services (section 5). Sections 9–13 cover assessment and eligibility but note that eligibility is determined by reference to Regulations and guidance (see **Assessment, adult needs** and **Eligibility criteria**). Sections 14–17 cover charging for services, while 18–23 distinguish between duties and powers to meet needs.

Other essential sections for social workers (all explored more fully as separate entries) are:

- 25   care and support plans
- 26   personal budgets
- 31–33   direct payments
- 34–36   deferred payments
- 42–44   adult safeguarding
- 47   protection of property

- 58–66   transition to adulthood
- 67–68   Independent Care Act Advocates.

The Care Act 2014 applies only to England. Similar provisions to those listed above are incorporated into the Social Services and Well-being (Wales) Act 2014.

Care and support plans are a key feature of adult care social work

(Feldon, 2021, Chapter 6). Such documents are mandatory where a local authority is required to meet needs under the Care Act 2014 or decides to do so (section 24 Care Act 2014). Section 25(1) states that the care and support plan, or support plan for a carer, includes:

- a statement concerning the needs identified by the assessment, the extent to which the needs meet the eligibility criteria, the needs the local authority is going to meet, and how they will meet them;
- the personal budget for the adult concerned;
- advice and information about what can be done to meet or reduce the needs and what can be done to prevent or delay the development of needs for care and support or of needs for support in the future.

The Care and Support Statutory Guidance (HM Govern-

ment, 2020a) relates to the day-to-day operation of the Care Act 2014 and it is mandatory for local authorities to observe it as this is a stipulation of section 78 of that Act. It provides detailed and comprehensive guidance on several aspects of the Care Act 2014, especially:

- promoting well-being, commissioning services;
- identifying needs;
- charging and financial assessment;
- person-centred care and support planning;
- safeguarding;
- integration and partnership working.

The guidance is regularly updated and practitioners are expected to access it as a working tool. For that reason, it is easily accessible on the internet, but is long: the June 2020 edition, if printed, would be 375 pages.

Care homes, care homes with nursing and nursing homes are

the three key categories of homes providing care. The distinction between establishments that are exclusively care homes and those that also provide nursing care is important because of the regulatory and financial framework. While all kinds of homes fall under the inspection remit of the Care Quality Commission, funding can become complex if people have both social care and nursing needs. This is because section 22 Care Act 2014 prohibits local authorities providing services that the NHS is required to provide under the National Health Service Act 2006. Likewise, the NHS does not provide purely social care. So, in circumstances where someone has both social care and nursing needs, a decision needs to be made as to the extent of each of those kind of needs. Where someone has a 'primary health need' they may qualify for NHS continuing healthcare which is a package that covers the costs of health care, personal care (washing and dressing) and care home fees. This means that, since NHS care is free, adults in this category are financially much better off compared to those with mostly social care needs, since services to meet those needs are chargeable.

Care orders are made in respect of a child under 17 by the **Family Court** under section 31 Children Act 1989. A care order may only be made by the court upon the application of a local authority or authorised person following care proceedings. Before a court may consider making a care or supervision order, first, the whole of the threshold criteria in section 31 (2) Children Act 1989 must be established, and second, the court must have applied the welfare checklist, and considered a care order to be in the child's **best interests**.

A care order provides the designated local authority with parental responsibility, enabling them to make decisions about the child. While in principle, parents retain their parental responsibility, they are not permitted to exercise it while the care order exists. The child will become a **'looked-after' child**, making the local authority a corporate parent and authorising the local authority to remove the child from their family and place them in alternative care arrangements, if necessary. Once made, a care order continues until one of the following occurs: the child is 18, the child is adopted, or the order is discharged. Any orders that were made previously under the Children Act 1989, for example, a **Child Arrangement Order**, will end once a care order is made. Section 34 requires the local authority to consider contact between the child and the family when making a care order.

Interim care orders

There can be some months between the start of care proceedings and the final hearing, during which time there may be concerns about the welfare of the child. Section 38 Children Act 1989 permits the court to make an interim care or supervision order where, on an application for a care order or supervision order, the proceedings are adjourned; or the court gives a direction under section 37(1) Children Act 1989.

An interim care order enables the local authority to share parental responsibility for the child until a final court decision is made. The duration of any interim order will be set out by the court. The court may well add directions to the order that require that the child and the family undergo specific assessments, but the court cannot direct treatments.

The grounds for making an interim care order differ from those required for the making of a final order. Under section 38(2) Children Act 1989, the court may make an order when there are reasonable grounds for believing the threshold is met, rather than needing to be satisfied that the threshold is met. The court must then go on to consider the welfare checklist and interim care plan before making an interim order. If the local authority wishes to use the interim order to remove the child from the family home and make alternative care arrangements, they will need to persuade the court that removal is a proportionate response to the safety needs of the child. The making of an interim care order does not prejudge the final decision, and it may be that at the final hearing, a care order is not made.

Care plans fall under section 31A Children Act 1989 which requires the court

to consider the permanency provisions in the local authority care plan before making a care order. These provisions take into consideration where the child will live, any plans for adoption or long-term care, and how those plans meet the child's current and future needs. Contact between the child and their family will also be considered. The care plan helps the court to determine if a care order would be in that child's best interests. Where a court takes issue with the care plan, it may question the local authority, but it cannot change the plan (Care Planning, Placement and Case Review (England) Regulations 2010).

Care proceedings must follow a specific legal process. To achieve a balance

between the need to protect a child and unnecessary intervention in family life, when a local authority applies to the **Family Court** for a care or supervision order, the court is required to approach the application in two main stages. First, the threshold in section 31(2) Children Act 1989 must be crossed before the court can move on to the second stage, which considers whether making a care or supervision order would be in the child's **best interests**.

The Public Law Outline (PLO) 2014 and section 14 Children and Families Act 2014 require proceedings to be concluded within 26 weeks of the application being made to the court, with limited flexibility to extend this where there are particular complexities. It also provides precise procedures to be followed starting from when care proceedings are under consideration. The Family Procedure Rules 2010 will also be relevant.

In accordance with the PLO, prior to initiating care proceedings, a local authority will have held a legal planning meeting and decided it is appropriate to apply for a care or supervision order. A pre-proceedings letter notifying parents of the local authority decision and a meeting to discuss the actions will be arranged. The parents may access funding for legal representation at this stage. On occasion, pre-proceedings meetings result in an agreement between parents and the local authority about what needs to happen to protect the child, thereby avoiding the need for care proceedings. If not, the application for a care or supervision order is made to the Family Court.

Key documents must accompany an application to the Family Court. These include a local authority statement, chronology of events in the child's life, a threshold statement, decision-making records and the child's interim care plan. Notice of the application must be sent to the parents and those who hold parental responsibility, as well as **Cafcass** who will allocate a **children's guardian** for the child. Those holding parental responsibility and the child separately through their guardian have rights to participate in the court hearings in line with Article 6 **European Convention of Human Rights**. On receipt of the application for a care or supervision order, the court will allocate the matter to an appropriate Family Court.

There are generally three main court hearings in care proceedings. Before each hearing, there will be a legal advocates' meeting where lawyers discuss the plan for preparing the court case.

Between the application and the final hearing, a local authority may ask the court for an interim care order under section 38 Children Act 1989. An interim care order does not mean a child will be removed from their family; it may be that the child can live with their family under an interim care order until the final hearing unless the child's safety requires that they are removed. If the court makes an interim order, it does not necessarily mean it will make a full care order at the final hearing. Directions for assessments of the child or family, but not treatment, may be attached to the interim order.

One of the first court hearings is a Case Management Hearing, where parties negotiate and agree on the information, assessments, facts, witnesses and evidence that will be required for a final hearing. An initial analysis from the **children's guardian** will be provided and updated as enquiries are made. The second hearing is usually the Initial Resolutions Hearing, which allows parties to narrow the issues that the judge needs to consider at the final hearing. For example, parents may agree on facts that the local authority relies on to establish whether the child suffered significant harm that is attributable to parental care, thereby crossing the threshold, but disagree that the child's welfare would be served by the making of a care order. This would then limit the issues at the final hearing to those concerning welfare because threshold is agreed.

If there is disagreement about particular facts, for example, if the local authority says that a parent inflicted injury on a child, which the local authority is relying on to establish threshold being crossed, but the parents deny inflicting the injury, then a court decision about that fact would need to be made. This is because a local authority cannot rely on an allegation to persuade a court that the threshold is crossed; the court can only consider facts to do that. The burden of proof is on the local authority to provide evidence that satisfies the court that something is a fact (*Re A (A child)* [2015]). The standard of proof is on the balance of probabilities – if the threshold is not crossed, the proceedings end.

Final hearing

When considering whether the threshold in section 31(2) Children Act 1989 is crossed or not, the court is not exercising discretion but is making a judgment or evaluation (*Re B (A child)* [2013]). If the threshold is crossed, the court will move to the welfare stage of the hearing, the central part of the proceedings. Each party will have an opportunity to submit their views, or analysis and recommendations, to the court. Social workers and guardians may need to go into the witness box and give evidence on oath, so that they can be challenged by the lawyers acting for the parents and allow the court to test their professional analysis. This is how the court ensures that it is able to undertake a global, holistic assessment of the options by scrutinising and weighing up all the evidence about the child's best interests (*G (A Child)* [2013]; *Re B-S (Children)* [2013], paragraph 50). The court must carefully consider section 1 Children Act 1989, particularly the welfare checklist, and scrutinise how the local authority's care plan would meet the child's current and future welfare needs.

The court may decide not to make a care order; but make a supervision order, a **Child Arrangement Order**, or no order at all. Any order must be proportionate to risk and meet the child's welfare needs.

The **Care Quality Commission** describes itself as the independent regulator of health and social care in England. It was created by the Health and Social Care Act 2008, taking over registration and inspection of care establishments and services from various inspectorates. It also took over the responsibilities of the former Mental Health Act Commission which oversaw standards of care in mental health and arranged for certain patients to be visited in order to safeguard their rights.

The primary function of the Care Quality Commission is to inspect and regulate services to ensure they meet basic standards of quality and safety. They rate services and publish those ratings online. Services evaluated include care homes, hospitals, GPs, dentists, mental health services and social care agencies, all of which receive prearranged and unplanned visits. Where services are inadequate, the Commission has the power to make requirements to remedy any shortfall and enforce necessary changes. Ultimately it has the power to order closures. These powers derive from the Health and Social Care Act 2008, the Health and Social Care Act 2008 (Regulated Activities) Regulations, the Care Quality Commission (Registration) Regulations 2009, and Part 2 of the Care Act 2014.

In Wales, the functions of the Care Quality Commission are performed by the Care Inspectorate Wales, which has a wider remit than the Care Quality Commission under the Regulation and Inspection of Social Care (Wales) Act 2016.

Carers are distinguished in law between adult carers, who have certain rights under the Care Act 2014, and young carers for whom the relevant legislation is the Children and Families Act 2014 section 96, which inserted new sections 17ZA–17ZF into the Children Act 1989.

Statutory support for adult carers has developed piecemeal from the first formal recognition of carers in the Carers (Recognition and Services) Act 1995, which was followed by the Carers and Disabled Children Act 2000 and the Carers (Equal Opportunities) Act 2004. All these Acts were incorporated into the Care Act 2014.

C

Section 10 Care Act 2014 provides for assessment of a carer's need for support on request. The assessment must cover:

- whether the carer is able to provide care for the adult needing care;
- whether the carer is willing to do so;
- the impact of the carer's needs for support;
- the outcomes that the carer wishes to achieve in day-to-day life; and
- whether, and if so to what extent, the provision of support could contribute to the achievement of those outcomes (section 10(5) Care Act 2014).

Section 20 Care Act 2014 lays down that the local authority must meet the carer's needs if those needs meet the eligibility criteria, providing the carer is ordinarily resident in their area. They do this by drawing up a care and support plan which sets out how the local authority plans to meet the eligible needs identified which is then followed by a personal budget (section 25 Care Act 2014). At this point, the carer needs to decide whether to opt for the local authority arranging support services, for direct payments so that they can purchase support services themselves, or for a mixture. For more information see entries on **Eligibility criteria; Ordinary residence; Care and support plans; Direct payments.**

A young carer is 'a person under 18 who provides or intends to provide care for another person' but not as a paid worker or volunteer. Where a local authority believes that a young person may need support, or where an assessment is requested by a parent or young carer themselves, the local authority has a duty to carry out an assessment (sections 17ZA and 17ZB Children Act 1989). The assessment essentially revolves around what the young carer is expected to do, what impact their caring responsibilities have on their physical and emotional health and well-being, and specifically on their ability to participate in education and training (section 96 Children and Families Act 2014). The other issue is whether their caring responsibilities are appropriate, for example:

- personal care such as bathing and toileting;
- carrying out strenuous physical tasks such as lifting;
- administering medication;
- maintaining the family budget;
- emotional support to the adult (HM Government, 2020a, paragraph 6.72).

The assessment must involve the young carer, the young carer's parents, and anyone else requested by the parents or young carer. It must 'have regard to' the young carer's age, understanding and family circumstances, wishes, feelings and preferences of the young carer, any differences of opinion between the young carer, the young carer's parents and the person cared for, and the outcomes the young carer seeks from the assessment (section 2 Young Carers (Needs Assessments) Regulations 2015).

The assessment must 'determine' the amount, nature and type of care the young carer provides, how much the family relies on this, the impact of caring on the young carer's well-being, education and development, whether any tasks are excessive or inappropriate, whether support services are needed, whether the young carer is a 'child in need', and what actions are to be taken, and subsequently reviewed, as a result of the assessment. The young carer's assessment may be combined with other assessments the local authority is undertaking (section 4 Young Carers (Needs Assessments) Regulations 2015).

Case law is a source of law that is derived from judgments and decisions made by judges about cases that appear in courts. Legally significant judgments tend to be recorded and published in law reports. Within the English court structure, the legal reasoning (*ratio decidendi*) contained in judgments and decisions made by judges in one court is a source of legal authority for making decisions about cases that are materially similar, i.e. cases that are alike should be treated alike. This is known as the doctrine of precedent (*stare decisis*). Judgments may be binding, which means, with some exceptions, that they have to be followed by judges making similar decisions in lower courts or a court of the same level; or they may be persuasive, which means that they are not bound to be followed.

Causative nexus is a Latin legal term that social workers may come across when involved in assessing **capacity** under the **Mental Capacity Act 2005**. Section 2 of the Act identifies 'people who lack capacity' and sub-section 1 states that such a person has to be assessed as being unable to make a decision 'because of an impairment of, or a disturbance in the functioning of, the mind or brain'. For a social worker assessing capacity, this means that they must be satisfied that the person's inability to make a decision is as a result of an impairment or disturbance in the functioning of the mind or brain, and they must provide evidence for this, explaining how there is a causal link between the disturbance or impairment of the person's mind or brain and the person's inability to make the decision in question.

The critical word in section 2(1) is *because*. This was confirmed in *Heart of England NHS Foundation Trust v JB* [2014] where the Court of Protection concluded that a woman diagnosed with paranoid schizophrenia did have consent to refuse amputation to a leg that had become gangrenous. Despite her long-standing mental health issues, she was entitled to refuse the treatment strongly advised by doctors. Her psychiatrist had not demonstrated a causal link between her mental health and her alleged incapacity to make a decision about surgery.

There is a whole chapter (Chapter 4) in the Mental Capacity Act 2005 Code of Practice (Department for Constitutional Affairs, 2007) dedicated to capacity assessment. It is entitled 'How does the Act define a person's capacity to make a decision and how should capacity be assessed?' and offers useful practical advice for practitioners.

Cheshire West and Chester is the key legal case concerning mental capacity. It has had a major impact on social work, social care and health particularly in residential and hospital settings, and has become central to considerations of whether people's human rights are being protected, risked or breached.

The case was decided by the Supreme Court in 2014. Essentially, the case concerned whether people were deprived of their liberty or simply subject to necessary restrictions – necessary because of the combination of disabilities and therefore needs. In the course of the judgment, the court provided guidance on defining capacity, and it is this clarification that underpins all related legislation, particularly the **Mental Capacity Act 2005** and Mental Capacity (Amendment) Act 2019.

The Supreme Court explicitly ruled out defining deprivation of liberty by reference to someone's needs. It was not acceptable to justify confining someone to a room, for example, by saying that this was necessary because of their combination of physical and learning disabilities. Rather, consideration of whether someone was deprived of their liberty should use as its reference point what that confinement would feel like to an 'average' (non-disabled) person. In other words, it was to be an objective, not subjective, test, absolute rather than relative. The judgment includes this statement:

> If it would be a deprivation of my liberty to be obliged to live in a particular place, subject to constant monitoring and control, only allowed out with close supervision, and unable to move away without permission even if such an opportunity became available, then it must also be a deprivation of the liberty of a disabled person (*Cheshire West and Chester v P* [2014], judgment para. 46).

The acid test

The Supreme Court offered guidance to social work and health care professionals in order to assist them to decide whether someone is being deprived of their liberty and therefore whether the **Deprivation of Liberty Safeguards** or **Liberty Protection Safeguards** need to be engaged. This guidance is referred to as the 'acid test' and consists of considering the following questions:

1   Is the person subject to continuous supervision and control? and
2   Is the person free to leave?

An individual's objection or otherwise to arrangements that constitute a deprivation of liberty is not a relevant consideration. So, even if the individual is not objecting, the law has to be applied and so the procedures and processes for an application under **Deprivation of Liberty Safeguards** or **Liberty Protection Safeguards** must be undertaken. Of course, the restriction may be for perfectly reasonable reasons, but deprivation of liberty law still has to be applied.

Child abduction
The relevant legislation will depend on the circumstances of the abduction. The Child Abduction Act 1984 creates criminal offences for abducting a child under 16, providing for a sentence of imprisonment. Child abduction often occurs in the context of parental relationship breakdown. The Hague Convention on the Civil Aspects of International Child Abduction 1980 implemented in the UK through The Child Abduction and Custody Act 1985 and the Hague Convention 1996 provides a process through the High Court, for locating and securing the return of a child, whom the other parent has unlawfully removed from the country where the child usually resides.

Child Arrangement Orders
are made by the **Family Court** and set out specifically with whom a child: should live; spend time with. The provision for the orders is in section 8 Children Act 1989. The court orders used to be called contact and residence orders until the name was amended by section 12 Children and Families Act 2014 in order to be more child focused.

Child Arrangement Orders generally relate to separated parents who are unable to agree on the living arrangements for a child. These are private law orders, and do not apply to the arrangements made for parents whose children are the subject of a care order. Section 10(5) Children Act 1989 sets out who may apply for a Child Arrangement Order.

While a Child Arrangement Order is in force, it enables the person with whom the child is living to exercise parental responsibility through making day-to-day decisions about the child. It may also designate parental responsibility to someone who has not previously had responsibility; for example, the father of a child who is not married to the mother, or whose name is not on the birth register.

Section 10 Children Act 1989 sets out when the courts have the power to make a Child Arrangement Order which may be in any 'relevant proceedings'; this recognises that the question of a child's arrangements may arise in other family proceedings and not only by an application by one of the parents.

When making any decisions about the arrangements for a child, the court will carefully weigh up what is in the child's **best interests**. The court will do so by close consideration of the welfare checklist set out in section 1(3) Children Act 1989. A court may request that a social worker from the local authority or **Cafcass** provide an assessment about how arrangements for the child promote their welfare, or request information about a child's family from a local authority.

Applications made in respect of child arrangements have significant implications for the child and the child's family. Section 10(1) of the Act requires that persons attend a family mediation and assessment meeting prior to making an application for a relevant application, which in this case would be a Child Arrangement Order. This seeks to avoid the need to enter into court proceedings in the first place by reaching an agreement.

Section 11 Children and Family Act 2014 introduced an additional subsection into section 1(2A) of the Children Act 1989 reflecting a presumption of parental involvement. This area of law, including recent changes, reflects the culmination of growing concerns that parental or other family separation may lead to disrupted relationships between parents, caregivers and children. The Children and Adoption Act 2006 inserts section 11 A–P into the Children Act 1989 to help facilitate and, if necessary, enforce Child Arrangement Orders.

Child Assessment Orders See Assessment, child.

Child in need is a child under 18, who without the provision of services would be unlikely to achieve or maintain a reasonable standard of health, or their development is likely to be further impaired, or the child has a disability (section 17 Children Act 1989). The broad definition covers a range of children's situations, for example an unaccompanied child seeking asylum, a child involved in crime, or a child whose parent is struggling to meet a child's needs because of their own need for support, for example because of mental health or substance misuse issues.

Local authorities have general duties and powers to support families in order to prevent: a deterioration in a child's development and/or the need for future compulsory measures such as care proceedings. They do not have a duty to meet the needs of every child in their area but a general duty to safeguard and promote the welfare of children within their area who are in need; and promote the upbringing of such children by their families.

The legal definition of a child in need, alongside the general specific duties and powers that local authorities have in relation to them, are set out in Part III Children Act 1989, specifically section 17 and Schedule 2. Statutory guidance on how social workers and other agencies should carry out the duties and powers in section 17 can be found in **Working Together to Safeguard Children** (HM Government, 2018), which is revised regularly.

Local authorities have duties to take reasonable steps to identify children in need in their area and publicise available services. They also have a duty to keep a register of children who have a disability who are automatically considered a child in need and therefore qualify for services under disability legislation (Schedule 2 Children Act 1989).

Before an individual child can benefit from the general duty in section 17 Children Act 1989, they must be brought to the attention of services and be assessed as a child in need. A social worker will complete a child in need assessment drawing on an Assessment Framework that considers many areas, including the child's specific developmental needs and the parent's ability to meet these, and consideration of the wider environmental context and its impact on the child.

If a child is assessed to be a child in need, the local authority has the power to provide services, and has some discretion as to how. A social worker will work with the family and child to produce a child in need plan, which sets out how those needs will be met. Services may be provided directly to the child, for example if they are homeless or need counselling; or provided to the parents, to meet the child's needs such as parenting guidance. The range of services that may be provided are set out in Schedule 2 of the Children Act 1989 and may be one-off or ongoing. Social workers will be involved in completing a child in need assessment, reviewing the plans, and arranging the support services to be provided to the child and family. Section 17 (4) (A) requires social workers to consider the views of the child about the plans to meet their needs.

Child protection See Child safeguarding system.

Child protection conferences are part of a local authority's
decision-making process. Such a conference is a formal meeting where professionals who have information or knowledge about a child can attend and share information, which allows the conference to understand the primary nature of current and future significant harm, for example concerns about neglect. The conference will be chaired by a professional who does not have direct involvement with the child or family. The parents, and if appropriate, the child, will be invited to ensure their involvement in any decision-making process. The conference will make recommendations and may draft a **Child Protection Plan** to address the concerns about risk. The full requirements are contained in **Working Together to Safeguard Children** (HM Government, 2018).

A Child Protection Plan is a plan to keep a child safe from harm.
When a **child protection conference** agrees that a child is at risk of suffering **significant harm,** they agree on a plan to keep the child safe from harm; the plan will be shared with the family and child as appropriate. The plan, as required by **Working Together to Safeguard Children** (HM Government, 2018), will identify the lead social worker, core professionals and family members who will be responsible for completing certain actions within specific timescales. The plan may include support services that are provided to the child and family and require the family to engage with assessments. Regular conferences will review the plans until the risk of significant harm is reduced or the child enters local authority care.

Child Safeguarding Boards See Safeguarding Children Partnerships.

The **child safeguarding system** is underpinned in England by key legislation provided by Children Acts 1989 and 2004, Children and Families Act 2014 and the Children and Social Work Act 2017. **Working Together to Safeguard Children** (HM Government, 2018) provides guidance about how professionals and organisations should implement the law into their practice and is published by the Department for Education (DfE), who are responsible for policy and guidance relating to child safeguarding in England. The more detailed entry on *Working Together* explains the legal basis for its status.

Broadly, the child safeguarding system is a framework that seeks to improve the outcomes of all children. It does this by ensuring a range of organisations, such as schools, health, police, local authority, and even voluntary agencies, have systems in place that enable them to work together to promote children's welfare, and prevent the impairment of children's health and development. Within that framework sit procedures for specific responses to concerns about individual children needing protection. Key agencies, such as health, police and local authorities co-ordinate their services in order to respond to varying levels of need that children in their area have for support and/or protection.

In each area, *Working Together* mandates *safeguarding partners* to ensure effective multi-agency working arrangements between partner agencies. These requirements reflect learning from case reviews where the failure to share information and the overreliance on information from one agency failed to protect children. The London Multi Agency Safeguarding Hubs (MASH) are examples of different agencies that are sharing information in response to concerns about a child. Child safeguarding systems in local authorities will also have a link with other specialist multi-agency arrangement panels; for example, multi-agency public protection arrangements (MAPPA) that assess and manage the risk posed by violent and sexual offenders. Other examples include multi-agency risk assessment conferences (MARAC) that work together to manage high-risk domestic abuse cases.

In each local area, **safeguarding partners** publish a threshold document that identifies factors indicating different levels of need, ranging from children in need of universal services and early help to those with more complex needs, requiring a **child in need** assessment, or children in more acute need, which may result in a duty to investigate under section 47 of the Children Act 1989 or an application for a **public law order**.

The local authority will have a point of contact to receive referrals. Upon receipt of a referral, the local authority must decide on the type of response required within one day and notify the referrer. The response may involve offering general support services, or a child in need assessment. Sometimes a referral may require more specialist responses; for example, concerns about sexual exploitation, Female Genital Mutilation, radicalisation, gang violence or trafficking.

For further information on the local authority role in child safeguarding see **Investigations, child safeguarding**.

Child Safety Orders are used if a child under 10 has committed what would

for an adult or young person be deemed an offence or broken a Local Child Curfew. The child can then be placed on a Child Safety Order. This means they will be supervised by the local Youth Offending Team, and if they do not respond to that supervision, can be referred to court under civil proceedings, with a view to the court making a care order. The maximum length of the order is 12 months.

The relevant law is section 11 Crime and Disorder Act 1998 as amended.

Child, definition of Article 1 of the United Nations Convention on

the Rights of the Child defines a child as anyone under the age of 18. This is reflected in various English and Welsh legislation that considers a child as anyone who has not yet reached their eighteenth birthday. The Children Act 1989 considers that even those who have reached 16 years of age, and may be living independently, are still legally children and it is expected that they should be given the same protection as any other child (HM Government, 2018). Despite technically being children, 16- and 17-year-olds can legally marry, although in England and Wales they require parental consent. Youth justice legislation distinguishes between children and young people, and defines the point at which they become responsible for their actions — see entries on **Young person, definition of** and **Age of criminal responsibility**.

Children Act 1989 is the bedrock of children's statutory social work

and social workers regularly work within the framework of this Act. The Act lays out the factors that must be considered when decisions are being made about a child in either private or public law proceedings. It emphasises that children are best cared for in their own families whenever possible, and their families should be supported with this.

Prior to the Children Act 1989, legislation relating to families and children was contained in a patchwork of different statutes. This made relevant law difficult to follow. High-profile child death cases, including the cases of Jasmine Beckford and Kimberlie Carlisle, led to concerns that children's voices were not being heard; in addition, the Cleveland child abuse scandal of 1987 revealed the potential for local authorities to misuse their power when removing children from their parents. There was also a growing emphasis on children having their own rights.

There are 13 Parts, 100 sections and 15 Schedules in the Children Act 1989 as well as statutory guidance issued under the Local Authorities and Social Services Act 1970, which local authorities must consider when implementing the provisions of the Act.

Part I

Provides that a child's welfare should be the paramount consideration when the court is making decisions about them (section 1(1) Children Act 1989). This is supported by the

welfare checklist in section 1(3), which reflects the important factors that the courts and professionals must keep in mind when making decisions and plans for children.

The importance of decisions being made within a reasonable timescale is reflected in the no-delay principle mentioned in section 1(2), and the no-order principle discussed in section 1(5) requires the court to make an order only when it is in the best interest of the child, rather than because the order has been requested.

The Act introduced a framework for parental responsibility: that requires parents to uphold their children's rights (sections 2–4) and sets out how a parent can acquire parental responsibility. Section 1(2)(a) was added to the Children Act 1989 by the Children and Families Act 2014 and underlines the importance of parental involvement in a child's life.

Section 7 Children Act 1989 enables a court to request information about a child's welfare before making any decisions about the child; this may arise in private law proceedings, after a child's parents have separated. As a social worker, you might find yourself providing information or preparing a report about the welfare of a child because of this section.

Part II

Provides a legal framework for various private law court orders with respect to a child's upbringing or treatment.

Because most of the relevant orders are to be found in section 8 Children Act 1989, **private law orders** have become popularly known simply as section 8 orders. **Specific Issue Orders** relate to a matter that parents cannot agree on, such as a parent wishing to change a child's name. A **prohibited steps order** prevents one parent taking an action in relation to the child, while **Child Arrangement Orders** relate to a child's living arrangements and who they are permitted to see. Applications for these orders are likely to be made by separated caregivers or family members. Courts may seek information from local authorities to check for any previous safeguarding matters such as police being called out to the child's home, or they might request a welfare assessment to ensure they have the information necessary before they make an order.

The legal framework for **special guardianship** and **Family Assistance Orders** are also found within this part of the Act in sections 14 and 16.

Part III

Includes, particularly in section 17, general and specific guidelines for local authorities to identify a '**child in need**' in their area and offer early support to prevent the child's health, welfare and development being compromised, thereby reducing the likelihood of neglect or abuse and the need for compulsory state intervention. The type of support varies from providing children with financial assistance and accommodation to offering them advice, guidance or support to help parents manage children's behaviour. Local authorities may involve other agencies, such as children's centres, when offering services to children in need.

As a social worker, you will be involved in completing assessments relating to the support children and their families require.

This part of the Act also provides the legal structure for some types of accommodation.

Section 20 relates to what is often known as voluntary accommodation of a child which permits the local authority to provide substitute care if those with parental responsibility are not able to accommodate the child in the shorter term. There is a lot of case law offering guidance to social workers about the circumstances in which this section may be used; see **Accommodation of children**.

Section 25 relates to what is called **secure accommodation**, which deprives a child of their liberty in order to protect them from risks they are taking themselves. It contains strict regulations on how, and when, a child can be placed in such accommodation.

Duties owed to children who have been or are currently accommodated can be found in section 22 (see **Looked-after children**).

Part IV

This Part of the Children Act 1989 explains the processes relating to care or supervision orders in sections 31–38, as well as the requirement for children to be represented by someone independent from the local authority or family during public law proceedings (section 41). It is in this Part of the Children Act 1989 and the next, that you will see the term '**significant harm**' feature prominently; this sets out the threshold that must be crossed before it is lawful for a local authority to use compulsion to intervene in a child's life.

Part V

Provides a framework that specifies the circumstances in which a local authority should investigate concerns raised about a child (section 47); it also provides a range of emergency provisions to access children through applying to court for short-term emergency orders, so that social workers can see them (sections 43–44). This might be if there are concerns about a child whom the family are refusing to let the social worker meet. These provisions state that children should not be removed from their homes without an application for a court order (with the exception of emergency police powers in section 46). The court's involvement ensures that compulsory intervention by local authorities is a legitimate and proportionate response to concerns raised about a child.

The remaining Parts of the Act relate to the community, children's homes, private foster care arrangements, child-minding and various miscellaneous provisions.

Children Act 2004 is a response to the Laming Report (2003) following the

inquiry into the death of Victoria Climbié in 2003 and the green paper *Every Child Matters*.

The focus is on strengthening the way agencies are organised and how they carry out functions in relation to children, with an emphasis on multiagency co-operation and accountability. The Act requires agencies to co-ordinate, share responsibilities to promote children's well-being and to develop effective safeguarding strategies. This includes arrangements for the sharing of funds and information services.

If an agency is working with a child, or has specific knowledge about a child, other partner agencies have a duty to co-operate and share information with the local authority. The Act covers a wide range of agencies including police, probation, health authorities, education and youth services – all of which are required to work together. As a social worker, you might work with, or contact, a Multi-Agency Safeguarding Hub, which is an example of an arrangement for multiagency co-operation and information sharing.

The Act comprises 6 Parts and 5 Schedules.

Part 1

Establishes the role, powers and duties of the **Children's Commissioner**. The Commissioner does not represent individual children but has oversight of, and investigates, the issues that affect children in England, providing reports to the Secretary of State.

Part 2

Provides for inter-agency co-operation and arrangements for the organisation of children's services to ensure children's well-being is promoted. The definition of well-being in Section 10(2) Children Act 2004 sets out five main areas, reflecting the *Every Child Matters* green paper. Section 11 contains a broad duty that requires a wide range of agencies, including some privatised services, to ensure they function in a way that safeguards and promotes children's welfare.

Section 13 first established Local Safeguarding Children Boards to co-ordinate responses to safeguarding matters in their area. Part 2 of the Children and Social Work Act 2017 changed these to Child Safeguarding Practice Review Panels, which now require the Local Authority, Clinical Commissioning Group and Police to hold equal responsibility in co-ordinating responses to local safeguarding needs and to link up with relevant agencies.

Section 18 provides for a Director of Children's Services with sections 19 and 20 providing for integrated inspections of children's services and joint area reviews.

Parts 3 and 4

These relate to children services and proceedings in Wales including provision for **Cafcass**.

Parts 5 and 6

These contain miscellaneous provisions that strengthen and clarify the regulation and monitoring of private fostering arrangements. They also make provision for regulation of child minding and day care. Further emphasis is placed on the importance of educational achievement for **looked-after children**, and the need to obtain wishes and feelings before providing support to children 'in need' (section 17 Children Act 1989) is made explicit.

Section 58 withdraws the common law defence of reasonable chastisement for parents. Section 60 makes certain extensions to the provisions of **Child Safety Orders** under the Crime and Disorder Act 1998. There is a slight relaxation around the publicity of legal cases concerning children, which you may notice if you are in court.

Children and Families Act 2014 contains wide-ranging measures
that seek to improve services for children, especially those with special educational needs or disability, those in the care or adoption system, and children involved in family proceedings. The functions of the **Children's Commissioner** are expanded by the Act. The way social workers carry out their functions are affected by many parts of the Act which comprises 9 Parts and 7 Schedules.

Part 1

Measures designed to streamline the adoption process. These include permitting **looked-after children** to be placed with prospective adopters while awaiting final court outcomes, commonly known as 'fostering for adoption'. Prospective adopters may now, subject to safeguards, directly access a register of children waiting to be adopted. The need for adoption agencies to seek a similar ethnic or cultural match has been removed. Supportive provision for adopters has been set out, as too, has the consideration of post adoption contact with the child's relatives.

Part 2

This Part reflects some of the findings of the Family Justice Review in 2010 and makes changes to both public and private law processes. In order to reduce delay for children, the Act requires care proceedings to conclude in 26 weeks, with reduced use made of expert evidence. Parents who are separated are required to attend family mediation and advice sessions, with a view to resolving disputes before going to court. The Act replaced Residence and Contact orders set out in section 8 Children Act 1989 with **Child Arrangement Orders**. The benefits of both parents being involved in the child's life, if safe, is now added to section 1 Children Act 1989.

Part 3

This substantial Part seeks to improve the support and planning for children and young people with special educational needs or disability, in the community, schools, or detained in youth custody. The functions of local authorities, education and health services have been clarified. A structure for a single assessment and **Education, Health and Care Plans** to be drawn up with children and their families is provided and these plans can extend to age 25. Social workers will be involved in assessing and supporting families with the plans.

A framework for **personal budgets** and **direct payments** enables families to have more flexibility.

Part 4

Provides clarification about registration of child minders and the organisation of early years care.

Part 5

Provides miscellaneous general child welfare provisions. This Part includes provisions enabling young people to choose to remain with their foster families until they are 21, known as 'staying put'. There is clarification about how schools can support **looked-after children** and children with medical conditions. Concerns about children smoking are reflected in provisions about nicotine sales. Smoking in cars in the presence of young people under 18 is banned.

Part 6

Extends and clarifies the functions of the **Children's Commissioner**.

Parts 7, 8 and 9

Details statutory rights to leave and pay for parents' time off work for ante-natal care and flexible working.

Children and Family Court Advisory and Support Service See Cafcass.

Children and Social Work Act 2017 consists of three parts with associated Schedules.

Part 1

Generally enhances measures to safeguard children and promote well-being, particularly focusing on **looked-after children**, providing seven corporate parenting principles. Provisions are made for arrangements between schools and local authorities to support looked-after children's education. An addition to the Children Act 2004 changes the arrangements for safeguarding partners and serious case reviews. Permanency provisions in section 31 Children Act 1989 are extended and courts are required to consider these before making orders under Part IV Children Act 1989 (provision for care proceedings).

Part 2

Provides for a regulatory framework for social workers in England. In December 2019, Social Work England took over the regulatory functions previously held by Health Care Professions Council. Regulatory objectives include protection of the public, promoting public health and well-being, maintaining public confidence in the profession and setting professional standards. **Social Work England** provides approval for qualifying courses, setting out required education and training standards. They also maintain a register of qualified social workers, entitled to practise and call themselves social workers. Registration requires disclosure of matters that may impact practice. On occasions when the practice of social workers may be failing to adhere to the standards, Social Work England carries out investigations into concerns that a social worker may not be fit to practise and they have the power to suspend registration on the basis of findings made.

Part 3

Provides the power to make Regulations under the Act, including transitional arrangements, such as transferring social workers' registrations from the Health Care Professions Council to Social Work England.

Children and young people's plans relate to how a particular

local area intends to deliver and organise services to meet the needs of local children. Section 194 Apprenticeships, Skills, Children and Learning Act 2009 initially required the plans to be published regularly. The plans can be a helpful resource to identify the services available to children and young people in the local area.

Children's Commissioner was initially established by section 2

Children Act 2004 to promote and protect the rights of children and young people in England. The Commissioner's remit was widened by the Children and Families Act 2014: to consider and report on the needs and views of children and young people leaving or receiving social care. The Commissioner investigates and reports on issues affecting children and young people (including the impact of legislation and policy) and raises awareness of their views. It is an executive non-departmental public body sponsored by the Department for Education. The existence of the Commissioner bolsters England's compliance with the United Nations Convention on the Rights of the Child.

Children's guardians, formerly known as guardians ad litem, are now part

of **Cafcass**, established in 2001 by the Criminal Justice and Court Services Act 2000.

In certain Family Court proceedings, a children's guardian will be appointed for the child to ensure that they have someone independent to represent their views and safeguard and protect their interests. The guardian will instruct a solicitor to manage the legal proceedings in the court process. The guardian provides an independent, child-focused analysis and makes recommendations about the child's best interests. On occasion, the children's views about what is in their best interests may differ from those of their guardians. If the child is considered to be **Gillick competent**, they may be able to instruct a solicitor directly rather than having their views represented through a guardian. This is in line with Article 12 **United Nations Convention on the Rights of the Child 1989**.

The appointment of a guardian differs according to whether the proceedings are public or private law.

Public law proceedings

Section 41 Children Act 1989 specifies the proceedings where a court must appoint a guardian for the child, unless it is satisfied that it does not need to do so to safeguard the child's interest. Examples of specified proceedings include applications related to care or supervision orders; applications for secure accommodation orders (section 25 Children Act 1989); and applications for contested adoption or placement orders.

Sections 41 and 42 Children Act 1989, part 16 Family Procedure Rules 2010 and Practice Direction 16A set out the guardian's duties and obligations. These include supporting and meeting the child to obtain their views and consider their welfare, having reviewed the local authority records, statements, plans and assessments. The guardian will then provide a holistic analysis of the child's welfare for the court and make recommendations that the court will consider. The Public Law Outline 2014 sets out specific timings and expected contents of the guardian's analysis and recommendations.

Private law proceedings

Part 16(4) Family Procedure Rules and the Practice Direction 16A set out the circumstances when the court should consider appointing a guardian in private law proceedings.

A guardian would not be appointed in private law as a matter of course. There are many occasions where a welfare report under section 7 Children Act 1989 or other information would be enough to ensure the child's views are heard. Appointing a guardian and solicitor is reserved for more complex applications for section 8 Children Act 1989 orders and other private law matters, where it is believed that the other parties who are likely to be the child's parents cannot fully represent the child's views.

Children's guardians are not to be confused with guardians under section 5 Children Act 1989, where parents arrange for someone to care for their children in the event of their death, or a special guardian appointed under section 14 Children Act 1989.

Choice rights, choice of accommodation refers to rights
under the Care and Support and Aftercare (Choice of Accommodation) Regulations 2014

that give people the right to make a choice regarding residential care homes, supported living arrangements or 'shared care' (care provided in a professional carer's home). This applies, obviously, where the local authority agrees that this kind of accommodation is the best way of meeting the adult's needs. The accommodation must also be available and the cost of it must fall within the limit of the personal budget. However, if necessary, a third person, not the adult themselves, could top-up the personal budget fund to make the choice feasible, in which case the local authority must comply with the choice made, unless it has reservations about the third party's finances. There are certain other conditions that apply to accommodation provided under section 117 Mental Health Act 1983 after-care arrangements (section 4 Care and Support and Aftercare (Choice of Accommodation) Regulations 2014).

Circulars is a term that refers to letters sent to local authorities by central government ministers setting out how the government wants local authorities to exercise their powers. They are not technically mandatory, but as they often connect to provision of funding, they are in effect, so they become treated as a set of instructions.

In some instances, a circular is mandatory because the legislation to which it connects makes this clear. For example, section 7 of the Local Authority Social Services Act 1970 states that local authorities 'shall act' under the guidance of the Secretary of State.

See also **Local authorities, accountability**.

Citation of legislation and legal cases should be as follows. Acts of Parliament are named by the subject of the law followed by the word Act (always capitalised) and then the year in which the Act was passed. So, for example, the Act that deals with legal measures to address safeguarding children and their welfare generally is the Children Act 1989 as it is an Act that addresses the needs of, or is about, children. It should never be referred to as the Children's Act 1989 since it is not an 'Act' that belongs to children. Acts can sometimes focus on two or more issues which may or may not be connected. The Police and Criminal Evidence Act 1984 is an Act that addresses the powers and duties of the police and procedures relating to evidence in criminal cases. Frustratingly, as a result, Acts can inadvertently imply a connection which is quite wrong: the classic social work law example is the Criminal Justice and Immigration Act 2008 which addresses the two completely distinct subjects of youth justice and then, separately, the law relating to rights of entry and settlement in the UK for everyone of all ages.

Acts of Parliament are a source of authority so can be used as such in assignments as if they were references. So, it would be quite legitimate to make a statement such as 'empowerment includes steps to promote well-being (section 1 Care Act 2014)' without having to state where section 1 of the Care Act 2014 might be cited in an academic text. When referring to an Act of Parliament in a sentence in an assignment, the law should be stated exactly as described here: so the sentence 'Laws such as the Care Act 2014 and Children Act 1989 are of direct relevant to social work practice' is correctly written; 'Laws such as the Care Act (2014) and Children Act (1989) are of direct relevant to social work practice' is not.

Criminal law cases are referred to simply as *R v surname of person accused of crime* where R stands for Regina, Latin for the Queen, and therefore the crown who prosecute all cases, v is Latin for versus meaning against; for example, *R v Smith*. When referred to in case law, the year and location of the record is added; for example, *R v Smith* [2014] EWCA 255 or *R v Jones* [2018] UKSC 26. In these examples, EWCA stands for England and Wales Court of Appeal, UKSC stands for UK Supreme Court.

Civil law cases are where someone sues another person, so are simply referred to as *Applicant (Claimant) v Respondent (Defendant);* for example, *Smith v Jones.* As with criminal cases, in case law the year and source of record is added: *Smith v Jones* [2016] EWCA 133 or *Smith v Jones* [2020] UKSC 34.

Further information on legal citations can be found in social work law textbooks (Brammer, 2020; Carr and Goosey, 2021) and online.

Civil law, as opposed to criminal law, is a means of arbitration or decision-making on people's rights. It results in the court making an order rather than passing a 'sentence'. Civil law actions might concern family disputes, child safeguarding and care proceedings, domestic abuse, personal injuries caused by road accidents or medical negligence, breach of contract including debts. Magistrates' Courts hear certain kinds of civil cases, but the specialist first-tier civil court is the County Court. Civil court outcomes are not sentences as such since the purpose is not punishment; instead it is about enforcing rights, so courts make orders. However, persistently ignoring a civil court order can have serious repercussions including, ultimately, imprisonment for 'contempt of court'. For a civil case application to succeed, the 'applicant' needs to demonstrate that the defendant had a 'duty of care' to the person applying for compensation or redress. Civil law cases are decided 'on the balance of probabilities' as opposed to criminal cases, which are determined 'beyond reasonable doubt'. This is a lower **burden of proof**.

For most social workers, civil law is more important than criminal law. This kind of law is sometimes implemented through **tribunals** which specialise in matters such as residential care home registration or applications by detained patients to be discharged from psychiatric hospitals. Adult care cases concerning capacity are dealt with by the Court of Protection which is also a civil law court.

Clerks, court See **Courts and the court system**.

The **Cleveland Inquiry** followed the removal in 1987 of 121 children from their families by social workers on the basis of disputed and unchallenged diagnoses

of sexual abuse made by two paediatricians. Judge Butler-Sloss led an inquiry (Butler-Sloss, 1988) that found, among other things, an overuse of intrusive examinations and emergency interventions that caused great stress to parents and children alike. The inquiry found that the parents had few rights to challenge the professionals, and social workers regarded children as objects of concern rather than persons in their own right, which left their voices unheard. The inquiry led to significant changes, directly contributing to the Children Act 1989 and its subsequent amendments. It is essential background reading for social work students and practitioners.

Climbié case See Laming Inquiry.

Closure of care homes has direct relevance in law is for two reasons.

First, courts have declared that in certain circumstances closures of homes will be declared unlawful unless certain procedures are followed. Second, the local authority has certain legal duties and responsibilities towards adults who are in residential care homes when these become vulnerable to closure.

What if someone is in residential care and there is a plan to close that home? Courts have taken the view that this decision potentially engages Article 8 of the **European Convention on Human Rights** since a care home is, in effect, their family life as that is where they live all the time. Thus, any plan to close the home should be taken in the same way as families take decisions, that is, through a process of consultation and negotiation. In *R v North East Devon Health Authority ex parte Coughlan* [1999], the courts decided that a health authority decision breached this article of the European Convention as there had been insufficient consultation. However, courts cannot make rulings about the Convention if the service provider is not a public body since the Human Rights Act 1998 only applies to 'public authorities' as defined in section 6 of that Act. So, in *R (on the application of Heather and others) v Leonard Cheshire Foundation* [2001], it was decided by the court that a voluntary organisation was not subject to the Human Rights Act 1998 so the court had no jurisdiction to review the decision taken. Likewise, in *YL v Birmingham City Council* [2007], the House of Lords refused to hear a similar case as the local authority had made the care arrangement with a private sector provider.

What happens to residents of private and independent sector care homes when they are facing closure? Here, local authorities have responsibilities for market-related issues. Section 5 Care Act 2014 requires local authorities to facilitate a diverse, sustainable high-quality market for their local population by promoting the efficient and effective operation of the adult care and support market as a whole. If any service provider fails, and specifically if homes close, the local authority has duties to ensure the continuity of care (sections 48–56 Care Act 2014). This clearly may mean that they have to arrange alternative accommodation.

Codes of Practice and Statutory Guidance directly influence

social work practice. Besides professional codes such as the Professional Standards of **Social Work England**, social workers also need to be aware of the Codes of Practice that connect to specific laws, as these offer much more detail on how specific legal duties are to be carried out. In some instances, legislation directs that practitioners must carry out certain actions. For example, the Police and Criminal Evidence Act 1984 section 66 Code of Practice directs that the police should interview young people in the presence of an **Appropriate Adult**.

Codes of Practice cover a wide range and often direct how practitioners from different professions should work together. The legal status of a Code of Practice varies. Some, such as the Mental Capacity Act 2005 Code of Practice, are simply advice and guidance that it would be prudent to follow, on the assumption that complying with the Code means that the professional is complying with the law. Other Codes are created by a statute law that compels professionals to abide by them, the Care Act 2014 (section 78) being an example. Increasingly, the term 'Statutory Guidance' is used to indicate that there should be no deviation from actions promoted as best practice. Among the most important Codes of Practice and Statutory Guidance of direct relevance to social workers (with dates of most recent version) are:

- Achieving Best Evidence in Criminal Proceedings: Guidance on Interviewing Victims and Witnesses, and Guidance on Using Special Measures. Code of Practice, 2011.
- Anti-Social Behaviour, Crime and Policing Act 2014: Anti-Social Behaviour Powers Statutory Guidance for Frontline Professionals, 2021.
- Care Act 2014 **Care and Support Statutory Guidance**. Frequently revised.
- Care of Unaccompanied Migrant Children and Child Victims of Modern Slavery: Statutory Guidance for Local Authorities, 2017.
- Department for Education Exclusion from maintained schools, academies and pupil referral units in England. Statutory Guidance 2017.
- Department for Education Schools Admissions Code. Statutory Guidance, 2014.
- Mental Capacity Act 2005: Code of Practice, 2007.
- Mental Health Act 1983: Code of Practice, 2015.
- Ministry of Justice Code of Practice for Victims of Crime. Statutory Guidance, 2015.
- Police and Criminal Evidence Act 1984: Code C: Revised Code of Practice for the Detention, Treatment and Questioning of Persons by Police Officers, 2019.
- Working Together to Safeguard Children: A Guide to Inter-Agency Working to Safeguard and Promote the Welfare of Children. Statutory Guidance, 2018.
- Youth Justice Board:
  - o Appropriate Adults: Guide for youth justice professionals, 2014.
  - o Code of Practice for Youth Conditional Cautions, 2013.

    o   Referral Order Guidance, 2018.
    o   Standards for Children in the Youth Justice System, 2019.
    o   Youth Cautions Guidance for Police and Youth Offending Teams, 2013.

College of Social Work closed in 2015. See **Social worker account-ability and registration**.

Commission for Local Administration is the official title of the body that runs the Local Government and Social Care Ombudsman service. It is an independent body funded by government established by the Local Government Act 1974. See **Local Government and Social Care Ombudsman**.

Commission for Social Care Inspection was a public body that was the inspectorate for social care in England until the implementation of the Care Standards Act 2000 which created the Care Quality Commission, for which see **Care Quality Commission**.

Commissioning services, as related to the local authority's role, is covered under **Care Act 2014**.

Common law and common law doctrine of necessity derives from a legal system that developed in England following the 1066 Norman Conquest. The monarchy of the time established a unified system of laws, administered through the creation of a hierarchal court system. Drawing from and developing local customs that varied throughout the country, judges developed a body of legal principles. The law was not codified from the outset; instead, over the course of hundreds of years, legal principles developed from decisions made by judges in courts. Judges in lower courts followed decisions made by judges in higher courts (precedent). Legal systems in the Commonwealth are based on English common law.

An example of the use of common law is the development of the common law doctrine of necessity. This is the legal right to take action that could clearly be seen as necessary for someone else's good. A straightforward example would be the right of firefighters to force entry to a burning building; no one would seriously suggest that they are committing an offence by breaking in to save lives. Likewise, ambulance personnel would have clear legal authority to take people to hospital where their lives were at immediate risk, even if that person had attempted to end their own life. Courts have extended this common law principle to act for people who do not have the ability to give consent. The **Bournewood case** was an example of this. Here, UK courts argued that preventing someone leaving hospital would not be an assault or infringement of liberty because it was 'necessary' for him to remain there. The European Court held that relying on this common law doctrine of necessity breached the European Convention on Human Rights as it was too vague, since, not being written down, people could not know for sure what the law was or how it might be applied.

Community Protection Notices see Anti-social behaviour orders.

Community treatment orders were introduced by section 32
Mental Health Act 2007. They authorise patients detained under section 3 Mental Health Act 1983 to be allowed home on conditions, with the proviso that they receive treatment. If the conditions of the order are broken, the patient is liable to be recalled to hospital.

Before making a community treatment order, the Responsible Clinician, the hospital psychiatrist with overall responsibility for the patient who authorises the conditional discharge, must declare that the patient meets certain criteria, and an Approved Mental Health Professional must agree. The criteria set out in section 17A Mental Health Act 1983 are:

* the patient is suffering from mental disorder of a nature or degree which makes medical treatment appropriate;
* it is necessary for the patient's health or safety or for the protection of other persons;
* the treatment can be provided outside hospital;
* it may be necessary to exercise recall powers;
* appropriate medical treatment is available.

The Responsible Clinician and Approved Mental Health Professional may specify conditions which they consider necessary or appropriate so long as they relate to the need to ensure that the patient receives medical treatment and/or prevent risk of harm to the patient's health or safety and/or protecting other people (section 17B Mental Health Act 1983).

While in the community, the patient may be recalled by the Responsible Clinician if the patient fails to comply with any conditions laid down, or needs treatment and there would be a risk of harm to the health or safety of the patient or to other persons if they were not recalled (section 17E Mental Health Act 1983).

The community treatment order lasts until the original section 3 expires or sooner if it is discharged (section 17C Mental Health Act 1983).

Compensation Orders are governed in law by sections 130–133 Powers
of Criminal Courts (Sentencing) Act 2000. This lays down that Compensation Orders may be made in addition to any other penalties or orders made by the court, and ought to be made even if someone can claim compensation another way, for example, through the **criminal injuries compensation** scheme.

Anyone convicted of an offence which results in another person suffering loss, damage or personal injury may be ordered to pay compensation.

In the case of young offenders, additional rules apply. First, there is a limit of £5,000 compensation payable for an offence committed by a young person. Second, Compensation Orders must be made against the parents of a young person under 16 and may be made against the parents of a young person under 18. Furthermore, where a young person is in the care of a local authority, the local authority can be ordered to pay the compensation.

While the general rule is that a **Referral Order** should not be combined with any other court order, there is an exception for Compensation Orders, which can be made at the same time as a Referral Order.

Competencies, professional Responsibility for professional standards

of practice lies with **Social Work England**, the professional regulator, who is required to 'determine and publish' them (section 41 Children and Social Work Act 2017). A different system applies in Wales where Social Care Wales issues National Occupational Standards for Social Work.

Minimum standards of practice enforced by Social Work England are quite distinct from the more aspirational **Professional Capabilities Framework** issued and promoted by the **British Association of Social Workers (BASW)**.

Complaints procedures can be used by people to make complaints if

they are dissatisfied with decisions made about them (see **Social worker accountability and registration** and **Social Work England** for complaints about professional practice). The law provides a number of avenues for people to follow.

First, each local authority will have its own complaints procedures as, normally, would independent sector providers. In the case of local authorities, this would involve senior managers through to elected councillors, but in some areas specific procedures are laid down by legislation. For example, section 72 Care Act 2014 requires local authorities to comply with the requirements of the NHS Complaints (England) Regulations 2009.

Second, if dissatisfied with the local authority response, someone could make a complaint of maladministration and injustice in which case the matter would be dealt with by an Ombudsman. For the National Health Service, probably of most relevance to social workers employed in hospitals and Care Trusts, the appropriate body would be the Parliamentary and Health Service Ombudsman for England. For local authority services, it would be the Commissioner for Local Administration in England (in Wales the Public Services Ombudsman for Wales). These bodies may only investigate injustice caused by maladministration, that is, procedural matters, not policy decisions concerning allocation of resources. If the injustice is proven, compensation can be awarded but the Commissioner's decision is not legally binding.

Third, if a person has suffered damage or loss as a consequence of actions taken or not taken, for example, failing to protect property properly, there could be an action for damages in a civil court. Lack of care or negligence would have to be proved.

Fourth, it is possible to appeal to the courts for **judicial review** of a local authority decision or action. Again, courts will not challenge policy decisions but will focus on the processes by which a local authority made its decision. However, courts can and do review how local authorities interpreted the law, specifically taking into account compliance with the **European Convention on Human Rights** as required by the Human Rights Act 1998.

Ultimately, only after exhausting all these avenues, can someone appeal direct to the **European Court of Human Rights** itself, providing there is a case that there has been a breach of one of the conventions of the European Convention on Human Rights. For example, in a landmark case in 1989, the European Court declared that refusing someone access to the records the local authority held on their background, and specifically their adoption, was unlawful as it breached Article 8 (privacy and family life) of the European Convention on Human Rights (*Gaskin v United Kingdom* [1989]).

Compulsory admission and detention in a mental health
facility is possible under mental health law that makes provision for people who have a **mental disorder** to be admitted to a psychiatric hospital and detained there even when they refuse to accept that they need inpatient care. There are various mechanisms to start the process.

If relatives are concerned about someone's mental health, it would generally be appropriate to start with referral to medical services since any application for admission to hospital has to be founded on medical recommendations.

For admission for assessment, section 2 Mental Health Act 1983, two independent medical recommendations are required: one from a specialist, usually a psychiatrist, and the other, if practicable, from a doctor who knows the 'patient', usually the GP (section 12 Mental Health Act 1983). The two medical recommendations must not be more than 5 days apart, and there must be no conflict of interest (sections 12 and 12A). Doctors need to confirm that the patient appears to have a mental disorder and their needs warrant admission to hospital. The grounds for admission are that the patient has a mental disorder of a nature or degree which warrants detention in hospital for assessment (or for assessment followed by medical treatment), and that they ought to be detained in the interests of their own health or safety or with a view to the protection of other persons (section 2). In an emergency, it is possible to admit the patient to hospital with only one medical recommendation, in which case they can be held there for up to 72 hours while a second medical recommendation is sought (section 4). As soon as that recommendation is provided, the section 2 admission is recorded as starting on the day the patient was admitted under section 4, so section 4 is in effect an emergency section 2.

For admission for treatment, section 3, while the rules regarding medical recommendations are identical, doctors must also declare that appropriate medical treatment is available. This is because the grounds for section 3 admission are slightly different from section 2. The patient must have a mental disorder of a nature or degree which means treatment is appropriate; this treatment is necessary for the health or safety of the patient or for the protection of other persons; such treatment cannot be provided unless the person is detained; and such treatment is available (section 3).

In both cases, the application for admission may be made by an **Approved Mental Health Professional** or by the patient's **nearest relative** (section 13). Before making the application, the Approved Mental Health Professional must interview the potential patient 'in a suitable manner' (section 13) and must inform the nearest relative of the admission either before or 'within a reasonable time' after it. In the case of section 3, the nearest relative has the right to veto the admission but could be effectively overruled by a court (sections 11, 29). There is a 14-day time requirement regarding when the person must have been seen by the Approved Mental Health Professional or nearest relative (section 11) and the patient must be conveyed to hospital within 14 days of the date of the second medical assessment (section 6). It may be worth noting that if force or restraint is used to compel people to go to hospital and remain there, the Mental Health Units (Use of Force) Act 2018 applies which makes additional requirements. This Act is known as Seni's law after an incident in which a 23-year old man died after being restrained on a mental health ward by police officers.

The maximum period of detention under section 2 is 28 days, and this cannot be extended (section 2 Mental Health Act 1983). Any further detention would have to meet the stricter criteria of section 3. Anyone detained under section 2 has the right, within the first 14 days, to appeal against detention to a Mental Health Tribunal (section 66). The maximum period of detention under section 3 is 6 months, and this can be renewed any number of times (section 20). At any time during a 6-month period, the patient has the right to appeal to the Mental Health Tribunal (section 66).

There are two circumstances in which, in an emergency, someone might need to be detained in a place of safety pending a mental health assessment.

The first is where they are in a 'place to which the public have access' and come to the attention of the police who consider that they are 'in immediate need of care or control' and it is necessary 'in the interest of that person or for the protection of other persons' to remove that person to a place of safety (section 136 Mental Health Act 1983).

A place of safety is not just a hospital; it can be local authority accommodation, the police station, an independent hospital or appropriate care home or any other suitable place (section 135). This provision is intended to be strictly for emergency use only, with a strict 24-hour time limit which starts when the person arrives at the place of safety (section 82 Police and Crime Act 2017). Nevertheless, its use continues to be controversial given that police are not mental health professionals, and that evidence in the past has suggested that a disproportionate number of black people have been detained using this power. Its continued use also highlights the lack of provision for people who are suicidal.

The second is where someone appears to have a mental disorder and needs assessment, but it is not possible to gain access to them without forcing entry. Here the law states that if it seems that the person may be suffering from a mental disorder and 'has been or is being ill-treated, neglected or kept otherwise than under proper control' or are not able to care for themselves and are living alone, an Approved Mental Health Professional may apply to a magistrate for a warrant to remove that person and take them to a place of safety. This warrant also authorises the police to assist by forcing entry to premises (section 135). The maximum period for which someone can be held at the place of safety pending a full mental health assessment is 72 hours.

Section 131 Mental Health Act 1983 gives people the right to be agreed to admitted to hospital voluntarily and therefore not subject to compulsory orders. If someone is so admitted, as an 'informal' patient, it is possible nevertheless to compel them to stay if, for example, they attempt to leave. This power can be exercised by the registered medical practitioner or approved clinician providing a report to the hospital managers (section 5 Mental Health Act 1983) and this authorises the detention of the person for up to 72 hours during which, presumably, a full section 2 or section 3 assessment is carried out. If it is so urgent that it is not feasible to wait for the doctor, then a nurse of the prescribed class can issue a holding order for up to 6 hours (section 5).

There are entirely separate procedures addressing the admission and detention in hospital of people who have committed offences or are suspected of having done so. These provisions are found in Part III of the Mental Health Act 1983. Remands to hospital are covered in sections 35 and 36, interim orders in section 38, and longer-term orders in sections 37 and 41. Section 37 can also be for guardianship as well as admission to hospital. Generally speaking, these orders are only of relevance to social workers working in forensic mental health teams.

The law regarding compulsory admission to hospital can appear quite complex, but it is important to remember that this law concerns deprivation of liberty, so must comply with the rights to liberty expectations and requirements of the **European Convention on Human Rights**.

Compulsory protection of adults is used in law in circumstances where an adult may need protection either from themselves, perhaps because of self-neglect, or from other people, such as when they are vulnerable to abuse.

The Care Act 2014 (sections 42–46) has provisions for safeguarding, for which see **Adult safeguarding** and **Adult safeguarding enquiries**. The emphasis in this legislation is acting in accordance with an adult's wishes and intervention cannot normally be imposed on someone. However, if there are serious causes for concern in extreme cases, if no other legislation is applicable, it may be possible to take action through the **Court of Protection** under the **Mental Capacity Act 2005** (sections 45–53) or under **inherent jurisdiction** (see **Adult safeguarding** for case example).

If someone has a medically diagnosed mental disorder and associated serious mental health issues, they may become a danger to themselves or other people and therefore qualify for compulsory admission to a psychiatric hospital under the various provisions of the Mental Health Act 1983. Specifically, if someone is on their own, and refuses to allow professionals to see them, section 135 of that Act may be appropriate (see **Compulsory admission and detention**).

If someone has a medically diagnosed mental disorder and has lost the capacity to make decisions about where they should live, yet is unable to live safely at home, then the provisions for **Deprivation of Liberty Safeguards** or **Liberty Protection Safeguards** may be relevant. Note that generally these do not authorise compulsory removal to a home or hospital, although occasionally the '**best interests**' provisions in the Mental Capacity Act 2005 (section 4) may apply.

In an emergency, such as a person being seen unconscious in their home and clearly in potential need of urgent medical attention or care, the only piece of legislation that allows forcible entry to premises is section 17(1) Police and Criminal Evidence Act 1984. This is a general police power that allows officers to enter and search premises if this is necessary in order to save 'life and limb'.

It may be worth noting that **common law** assumes that action taken without consent to protect someone in immediate danger of death or serious injury is always lawful, although clearly once an adult has recovered enough to be able to articulate their wishes, they are then entitled to refuse any medical treatment or social care, a refusal that can only be countermanded if either the **Mental Health Act 1983** or **Mental Capacity Act 2005** applies.

Compulsory treatment can only rarely be justified, and this justification has to relate either to the Mental Capacity Act 2005 or to the Mental Health Act 1983. UK law starts from the fundamental principle that adults generally have autonomy when it comes to accepting or refusing medical treatment. The only exceptions are where

someone does not have 'capacity' or where they have lost the ability to understand their need for treatment because of serious mental health issues.

The Mental Capacity Act 2005 clarifies capacity by stating that lack of capacity is not demonstrated simply by making unwise decisions, or by acquiring certain characteristics, such as being old – for further explanation of this see separate entry on **Capacity**. It is only possible for someone to be treated under the provisions of this Act where they do not have capacity, which could be temporary, for example in the case of someone who is unconscious or has had a stroke. The assumption would be that someone may be given treatment which is in their **'best interests'** (section 5 Mental Capacity Act 2005).

The Mental Health Act 1983 has a whole section (Part IV) that sets out procedures for overriding someone's refusal to consent treatment for a 'mental disorder'. Such people must already be detained on longer term orders: sections 2, 3, 37, and 41 Mental Health Act 1983. This includes patients under **community treatment orders** who have been recalled to hospital (section 56 Mental Health Act 1983). The treatment that can be imposed must either fall into certain categories which are set out in Regulations (Mental Health (Hospital, Guardianship and Consent to Treatment) Regulations 1983) or else be treatment that the patient has already received for three months (section 58 (1) Mental Health Act 1983). The procedure for overriding consent is set out in section 58 (3) and involves an assessment by an independent doctor who has certified that the patient is 'not capable of understanding the nature, purpose and likely effects of that treatment' or has not consented to it but that 'it is appropriate for the treatment to be given'. Before coming to this conclusion, the independent doctor has to consult with a nurse and someone who is neither a nurse nor a doctor (section 58(4) – a social worker would be an obvious choice). However, none of this applies in an emergency, that is:

- where treatment is immediately necessary to save the patient's life;
- providing it is not irreversible, is immediately necessary to prevent a serious deterioration of their condition;
- providing it is not irreversible or hazardous, is immediately necessary to alleviate serious suffering by the patient or represents the minimum interference necessary to prevent the patient from behaving violently or being a danger to themselves or to others (section 62 Mental Health Act 1983).

Confidentiality and privacy are fundamental principles to which

social work is wedded. Information between social worker and an individual can be shared only by agreement, and generally people can be assured of confidentiality in their dealings with social workers. However, there are some exceptions to that principle.

First, it is a common law principle that people cannot withhold information concerning a crime and in that respect information about abuse to children must also be disclosed. This is reinforced by analysis of child abuse inquiries (Department of Health, 1991).

Second, in cases where someone poses a threat to others, confidentiality may have to be breached, such as where serious mental health issues endanger other family members or the public. For social workers acting as Approved Mental Health Professionals such breaches are inevitable. Case law confirms that psychiatric information must be disclosed where there is a potential threat (W v Edgell [1989]). Here there appears to be a greater ethical obligation relating to genuine risk of harm or need to preserve life.

Privacy falls under the ambit of the **European Convention on Human Rights**. The right to privacy is not absolute, but breaches must be justified on the grounds of 'national security, public safety or the economic well-being of the country, for the prevention of disorder of crime, for the protection of health or morals, or for the protection of the rights and freedoms of others' (article 8(2) European Convention on Human Rights). In 2018, the European Court ruled that comments on a psychiatric patient's health condition and sexual behaviour without her consent amounted to an inference in her private life (Mockute v Lithuania [2018]). In 2019, the European Court ruled that the UK had violated the right to privacy when a lifelong supporter of the peace movement had his personal data included in a police 'extremism database', despite never having being convicted of any offence (Catt v United Kingdom [2019]).

There is, of course, a duty on social workers as employees to maintain confidentiality in relation to the business of their employers, albeit in the public or private sectors. One legal exemption of that obligation arises where it is in the public interest for a disclosure to be made. For example, if abusive practices are observed in a group care setting, this could be considered to qualify as a 'protected disclosure' (section 1 Public Interest Disclosure Act 1998). Protected disclosures may relate to commission of a criminal offence, failing to comply with legal obligations, endangering health or safety, miscarriage of justice, damage to the environment or concealing information in relation to any of these. The Public Interest Disclosure Act 1998 provides protection for people who 'whistle-blow' together with right to a remedy if there are reprisals.

There is a legal obligation on social work agencies to disclose information in accordance with **data protection** and **freedom of information** legislation. However, such information will often be redacted wherever it refers to other people since data protection legislation only permits people information about themselves, it does not entitle them to insist that social work agencies breach confidentiality. Similarly, agencies may refuse requests or partially withhold information under the Freedom of Information Act 2000 on grounds of confidentiality, in which case there is the possibility of an appeal for adjudication to the Information Commissioner's Office.

Consent is a crucial concept in social work. Social work practitioners will obviously be careful to work with people by agreement wherever possible, but will need to look to the law for clarification when there is doubt about people's ability to consent, or what consent actually means.

Undoubtedly, in cases where there are overt safeguarding issues, and particularly in cases where courts have already made orders, social workers may have to override consent, but this may only be done where there is clear legal authority for doing so. Examples of legislation relevant to social work where consent may be overridden are Children Act 1989, Adoption and Children Act 2002, Mental Health Acts 1983 and 2004, Mental Capacity Act 2005, and some youth justice legislation.

With regard to children, the legal presumption is that they are unable to give consent and that parents will do so, or refuse to do so, on their behalf. As children grow older, they will come to acquire the full ability to make their own decisions, which they then automatically acquire at 18 (section 1 Family Law Reform Act 1969). Under that age they acquire the right to agree to medical treatment at 16 (section 8) and case law has evolved which effectively means that professionals decide at what point young people are able to give consent themselves in other circumstances (*Gillick v West Norfolk and Wisbech Area Health Authority* [1986]).

The Mental Capacity Act 2005 section 3 covers people's ability to make decisions (covered in the entry on **Capacity**) and the prerequisites identified there could be adapted to provide a test for judging whether someone can give consent. In brief, does someone understand the information relevant to a decision, can they retain that information in order to process it, can they evaluate it, and can they provide a rationale for that decision? The Mental Capacity Act 2005 in section 1(4) also offers another important principle that could be adopted more broadly, namely that people are entitled to make unwise decisions. Hence someone is entitled to consent to an injudicious course of action.

There is a statutory definition in relation to consent to sexual activity, and this could be used to clarify what is meant by consent more generally. This is simply that someone consents if they agree 'by choice, and has the freedom and capacity to make that choice' (section 74 Sexual Offences Act 2003). This implies that someone must have the capacity to consent, and that the consent must be freely given, not obtained under coercion or constraint. So, in this context, it would not be lawful for an adult in a position of trust to engage in sexual activity with a 16- or 17-year-old, even though the age of consent is 16 (section 16 Sexual Offences Act 2003 applies).

Applying the notion that consent must be freely given without coercion, courts have consistently expressed concern about the misuse of section 20 Children Act 1989, specifically parental requests to accommodate children. For example, asking a mother to agree to have her child accommodated under section 20 Children Act 1989 while she was in hospital under the effects of morphine was not legal (*Coventry City Council v C* [2012]). Likewise, pressurising a parent to make a section 20 application under the threat of care proceedings, which were then delayed for over two years, breached fundamental human rights (*Medway Council v M & T* [2015]).

It may be helpful to distinguish between 'active' and 'passive' consent, since sometimes the law demands an explicit written or oral statement from someone that they agree to a course of action (active consent), whereas at other times consent may be assumed with no confirmatory statement required (passive consent) (Johns, 2014). Here are some examples of passive consent being lawful:

- Section 131 Mental Health Act 1983 in effect gives people the right to become a psychiatric in-patient without being formally (compulsorily) detained. They do not have to make a formal request; they simply have to comply by not objecting to being admitted to hospital.
- Section 5 Mental Capacity Act 2005 allows for care or treatment of someone who does not have the capacity to give active consent to that treatment, providing always that the care or treatment is in that person's **best interests**.
- **Common law** allows someone to be treated if they are unconscious and unable to give consent, for example, in a road accident or after taking an overdose.
- Practitioners also often use the term 'informed consent', meaning that the person must be given all of the information about any proposed plan, including benefits, risks, alternatives, and possible negative outcomes. It is an invaluable principle for professional practice, but is not a phrase used in legislation which simply uses the plain word 'consent'.

Contact orders, care order related connect to care proceedings.

When a child is in the care of the local authority, for example, as a result of an interim care order (see **Care orders**), section 34 Children Act 1989 requires the local authority to consider and arrange reasonable contact. This may include supervised contact. A social worker should ensure that purpose, nature and frequency of contact is considered when writing the child's care plan. If the local authority is satisfied that the contact will not safeguard or promote the child's welfare, they may ask the court to stop or change the contact arrangements. Where this is the case, or there is a dispute about contact, the matter will be determined by the Family Court, who will normally appoint a **children's guardian** to represent the interests of the child.

Contact orders, private family law related See Child Arrangement Orders.

Convention on the Rights of the Child, UN See United Nations Convention on the Rights of the Child.

County Court See Courts and the court system.

The Court of Protection has a general role to safeguard the interests of vulnerable adults. It deals with both property and personal well-being, and in some cases adjudicates on disputes concerning them. It has a long history. Although it is a court with judges, it does not generally sit in public and many of its affairs are conducted without court hearings. Current relevant legislation is sections 15–23 of the Mental Capacity Act 2005.

When someone has lost the capacity to make decisions for themselves, the Court of Protection can appoint a Deputy who has ongoing responsibility for acting on their behalf. The Deputy is always accountable to the Court; and can be removed and replaced if they fail to carry out their duties. Deputies can be a family member, friend, or a professional, although there are caveats about appointing a social worker. First, the social worker would need significant proven competence in administering people's affairs and, second, the social worker's local authority employer may be reluctant to take on what may turn out to be a considerable administrative burden.

The downside of involving the Court of Protection itself in managing people's affairs directly is that there are costs involved. Court fees and payments to professional Deputies make this prohibitively expensive except where there is substantial income involved.

The Court can appoint Visitors to offer the Court or the **Public Guardian** advice, and report on well-being in cases where there is nobody to oversee the welfare of particular individuals.

The Court of Protection has the responsibility of arbitrating in **Lasting Power of Attorney** cases where there is a dispute about its validity or about how it is exercised. It adjudicates in several kinds of cases including, in particular, the operation of the **Liberty Protection Safeguards** (or **Deprivation of Liberty Safeguards**) under the Mental Capacity Act 2005 amendments. Many of its decisions are reported and can be accessed through law reports and therefore through websites. In this dictionary, there are several cases cited that are decisions made by the Court of Protection.

Courts and the court system of England and Wales are, not surprisingly, hierarchical, with the Supreme Court the ultimate court of appeal for all kinds of cases at the top. Below that, courts are generally split between courts that hear civil and criminal cases, although the Magistrates' Court can hear both kinds of case, usually doing so in quite clearly demarcated sessions. Figure C1 sets out the basic structure with the broad arrows representing potential routes for any appeal. Note that some appeals are only allowed on points of law, and this chart does not include tribunals, which have their own hierarchy: see separate entry on **Tribunals**. The courts at the bottom of the hierarchy are known as 'courts of first instance' since nearly all cases start there – even the most serious criminal cases start at the Magistrates' Court, although in these the court can only decide whether there is a 'case to answer' and then refer the matter up.

Court structure

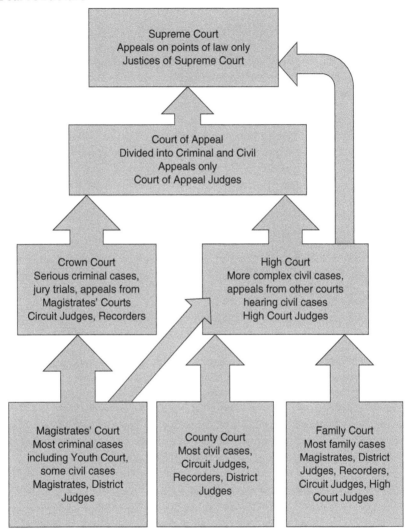

Figure C1   Court structure

The courts that are of most relevance to social workers are the Youth Court, which is a division of the Magistrates' Court, and the Family Court which usually comprises magistrates, but in more complex care proceedings or adoption cases will be determined by a Judge.

Court layout

Most courts are laid out in the traditional way with an elevated bench for Magistrates or the Judge above the well of the court, with lawyers and the defendant or applicant facing them and the witness box to one side. At the back of the court, or in the gallery, sit the press and members of the public. Witnesses wait outside until they are called.

However, in cases that involve social workers, the layout will generally be more informal with everyone on the same level, often around a table. While rules of evidence must be observed in the **Youth Court** and the **Family Court**, proceedings are less formal with wigs and gowns generally absent.

Court personnel: Magistrates or Justices of the Peace

It is surprising to many people that, although Magistrates' Courts hear the majority of cases, magistrates themselves are volunteer lay people who are appointed from the local community. The term 'Justice of the Peace' is synonymous with the term 'magistrate'. Modern Justices of the Peace do undergo training, and those who serve in the Youth Courts or Family Courts have additional specialist training. Magistrates are often referred to as 'the bench' as they used to sit in threes on a bench, although these days they prefer more comfortable chairs. It is customary for only one magistrate, the chair, to speak for the bench.

Court personnel: Judges

Judges are professional lawyers, predominantly experienced barristers, although they can come from the ranks of solicitors. If they sit in the Magistrates' Court, they sit alone. Judges sitting in the Family Court are chosen for their experience in cases involving children and families. Judges are allocated to specific courts according to their experience and rank – there is a hierarchy of judges. In the Appeal Courts and Supreme Court, judges often hear cases together in a panel of three or five, or even more.

Court personnel: Barristers and solicitors

Barristers and solicitors are legal professionals who present cases in court. Barristers, often called 'counsel', are specialist court advocates who usually take instructions through a solicitor. Solicitors deal with a wide range of cases, spending only a minority of their time engaged in advocacy. There are rules regarding who can appear in which court, the general notion being that only barristers have the requisite skills to advocate in the highest courts.

Court personnel: Court clerks and ushers

Clerks of the court are generally legally qualified when serving a Magistrates' Court since magistrates are lay people and therefore need access to a lawyer to advise them. In other courts, they can be purely administrators, but in all spheres their principal job is to organise court rotas and ensure that everything runs efficiently, including recording of evidence and court outcomes. They also oversee implementation of penalties and court decisions such as fines or awards of compensation. An important role in care proceedings for the clerk is to preside at directions hearings where the timetable for the case is set up and orders are made concerning the disclosure of documents and evidence.

Ushers assist the court by calling people into court at the appropriate time, showing people where to go and administering the oath or affirmation. It is their job to ensure that people are where they should be, so in a sense they are court receptionists.

Court personnel: Crown Prosecution Service and police

These two organisations only have a regular role in criminal cases. The Crown Prosecution Service provides lawyers to present the prosecution case in, for example, the Youth Court. The police will only appear in court when required to do so, for example, as witness in criminal cases when requested by prosecution or defence or, very occasionally, care proceedings cases. Outside of court, the Crown Prosecution Service is charged with analysing which cases and what charges should be brought before the Magistrates' or Crown Court. The Crown Prosecution Service has no involvement in care proceedings in which cases are presented in court by local authority lawyers.

Court personnel: Children's guardians

It is the role of the children's guardian in care proceedings to ensure that the local authority's plans and arrangements for children are in their best interests, offering the maximum protection and potential for the future. To this end, they make independent enquiries, having rights of access to local authority records (section 42 Children Act 1989), and then appear in court, instructing a solicitor to represent the child and call witnesses unless the child is of an age to do this themselves (section 41 Children Act 1989). They also have the right to give evidence in court as witnesses and can be required to do so by other parties in the case. In adoption cases, they conduct enquiries about the adoption applicants and the child's circumstances, also interviewing (and witnessing consent of) parents who are giving up a child for adoption. In private law proceedings, the guardian conducts enquiries and makes recommendations to the court, acting as expert witness and independent advisor. Children's guardians are all employed by **Cafcass**, the Child and Family Court Advisory and Support Service.

Court personnel: Social workers

Social workers in court are officers of the court as well as being local authority employees. This means their first duty is to the court, to tell all that they know, to answer all questions openly and honestly, and to offer independent advice when asked. In this context, they have dual accountability. In care proceedings cases, the social worker will often be the key witness for the local authority bringing the case as they will have all the evidence. To this end, they will construct a chronology of events in date order and collate background information, presenting this as a statement to court through the local authority legal representative. At the same time, the social worker is a professional witness, so it is legitimate for them to offer an opinion and advice about the best options for the child in question. In the Youth Court, the social worker's role is to prepare **pre-sentence reports** in accordance with the requirements of the court and the **Youth Justice Board**. Social workers can also on occasion act as independent expert witnesses, for example, if someone wants the social work equivalent of a 'second opinion' or has instituted a legal claim for compensation on the basis of allegations of past professional negligence.

Criminal Behaviour Orders See Anti-social behaviour orders.

Criminal injuries compensation is a scheme administered by the Criminal Injuries Compensation Authority. It assesses compensation claims from people who have been injured – physically, emotionally or psychologically – as the result of a violent crime. Anyone can claim within two years of the commission of the crime; there is no requirement for the culprit to have been caught. The scheme is government funded and the official government website has detailed advice on how to support someone to make a claim. There is also an appeals procedure through the Criminal Injuries Compensation Tribunal.

The Criminal Justice and Immigration Act 2008

is the principal Act of Parliament setting out the powers available to the **Youth Court** when sentencing young offenders for their offences. Part I covers the range of outcomes known as **Youth Rehabilitation Orders**. The rest of the Act covers criminal law generally but some parts of it are specific to youth offenders: for example, sections 35–37 cover **Referral Orders**. Of significance to practitioners are the Schedules at the end of the Act – remember, these have the same force of law as the Act itself. Schedules 1–4 cover Youth Rehabilitation Orders, setting out in much greater detail what is involved in each of the requirements. For further information see **Youth Rehabilitation Orders** entry.

Criminal law is what people generally associate with the word 'law' since criminal law lays down what are offences, how offences are defined, and the range of penalties courts can impose on those who 'break' the law. The common phrase 'it's against the law' refers to this kind of law and the sanctions it attracts on those who transgress it. Such sanctions or penalties are referred to as 'sentences' which are in effect court-ordered punishments.

Criminal law matters most to social workers who work in the field of youth justice for whom the Criminal Justice and Immigration Act 2008 is key, since it stipulates the range of sanctions that apply when young people break the law. These are quite distinct from those that apply when adults commit offences.

Criminal law cases can be heard by Magistrates' Courts or Crown Courts, and then can be appealed to the Court of Appeal and, ultimately, the Supreme Court if there is a specific point of law that is to be clarified.

Criminal law cases have to be proved 'beyond reasonable doubt', which is a higher 'burden of proof' than 'on the balance of probabilities' that applies to criminal law cases. In the more serious cases, whether someone is guilty or not guilty is determined by a jury, after which the judge decides what sentence to pass.

Criminal law cases are referred to in case law as:

R (standing for rex or regina, king or queen, i.e. the crown) v (standing for versus or against) the surname of the alleged offender [year].

For example, in writing:

R v Smith [2017]

But spoken:

The Crown and Smith [2017].

Criminal Records Bureau See Disclosure and barring.

Crown Court See Courts and the court system.

Crown Prosecution Service See Courts and the court system.

Cultural considerations are significant as a child's culture and religion form part of their history and identity. When a local authority makes plans in relation to a child it is accommodating, section 22(5)(c) Children Act 1989 requires that they give due consideration to the child's religious persuasion, racial origin, cultural and linguistic background. In relation to adoption, section 3 Children and Families Act 2014 removed the express provision in the Adoption and Children Act 2002 to give due consideration to finding an ethnic match between children and prospective adopters because of concerns this focus on a match might delay adoption.

Custody has a number of different meanings. It is most often used to refer to detention of convicted offenders in prison for a specified time. For young offenders this form of custody takes the form of a **Detention and Training Order**.

Custody may also be used to detain people accused, but not convicted of, an offence as a means of ensuring that the offender attends court. This form of custody is an alternative to **bail** but only where bail would be inappropriate for specific reasons.

For young offenders this takes the form of remands to local authority accommodation or, in certain circumstances, to '**youth detention accommodation**', which is the term used to denote all forms of custody for young offenders (section 91 Legal Aid, Sentencing and Punishment of Offenders Act 2012). As a short-term measure, a young person accused of an offence could be detained in police custody but must be brought before the court as soon as possible.

In the past, the term 'custody' has also been used in family law to refer to the arrangement after married couples separate or divorce where one of the couple becomes the main carer for a child. The term in this context is now obsolete, although it is still unfortunately widely used by people unfamiliar with the law. The Children Act 1989 substituted the term 'residence order' for custody, but this term itself is now redundant, as the Children and Families Act 2014 (section 12) introduced '**Child Arrangement Orders**' to cover care of children and contact with them when parents split.

Data protection covers data held by social work agencies, as all data held in written format including electronically, is subject to data protection legislation which is principally to be found in the Data Protection Acts 1998 and 2018. The Data Protection Act 2018 confirmed people's right to information about themselves but with some exceptions and exclusions, set out in Schedule 3 of the Act. These centre on withholding information where the 'serious harm test' is met where it could be argued that 'the data would be likely to prejudice carrying out social work, because it would be likely to cause serious harm to the physical or mental health of the data subject or another individual' (section 7(2) Schedule 3 Data Protection Act 2018).

The Data Protection Acts 1998 and 2018 accord rights for people to obtain information about themselves only. They cannot compel social work agencies to breach confidentiality: for information in this aspect, see **Confidentiality and privacy**.

Deferred payment is in effect a long-term loan set up to pay care home fees. So, for example, if someone needs residential care but cannot afford it, they can ask the local authority to pay the fees for them on the understanding that all these fees paid are a loan, secured against the property they currently own. This means that when the home they own is eventually sold, the loan is repaid to the local authority from the proceeds. The adult can delay repaying the local authority until they choose to sell their home, or until death.

In order to qualify for a deferred payment, the adult must be, or about to be, receiving long-term care, have less that the current specified amount in savings, and be the owner of a home which has no spouse, partner, child or relative over 60 living in it.

The actual qualification criteria are slightly different in Wales.

Local authorities are not obliged to offer a deferred payment, but if they do not, they must give reasons in writing (Care and Support (Deferred Payment) Regulations 2014).

Delay, no delay principle See **No delay principle**.

Deprivation of Liberty Safeguards derive from an amendment to the Mental Capacity Act 2005 introduced by the Mental Health Act 2007 to provide a legal framework that would address the shortcomings of the law identified by the European Court of Human Rights in the **Bournewood case**. The Mental Capacity (Amendment) Act 2019 replaced the Deprivation of Liberty Safeguards with Liberty Protection Safeguards, but implementation of these was deferred in 2020 because of the COVID-19 pandemic. Both sets of Safeguards fulfil the same legal purpose and are based on the same principles; the Liberty Protection Safeguards were intended to simplify processes and procedures and permit them to be applied more widely – see separate **Liberty Protection Safeguards** entry for further information. They apply potentially to any adult who falls outside mental health law compulsory detention provisions, but who has some form of mental disorder connected to their lack of capacity (see **Capacity** and **Causative nexus**).

The intention of the Safeguards is to make a Mental Capacity Act 2005 **best interests** decision on behalf of someone who has lost the ability to make a decision concerning where they need to be cared for or treated. The Deprivation of Liberty Safeguards only apply where someone is already in a care home or hospital and needs to be detained there; they do not apply to people living in their own homes, although the Court of Protection itself does have other powers under section 16 Mental Capacity Act 2005 that could apply. This shortcoming is corrected in the Liberty Protection Safeguards which potentially have wider applicability.

The following procedures apply until Liberty Protection Safeguards come into force:

The Deprivation of Liberty Safeguards are to be found in Schedules A1 and 1A added to the Mental Capacity Act 2005, supplemented by a dedicated Code of Practice (Ministry of Justice, 2008). They are a mechanism for authorising a vulnerable person to be kept in a registered care home or hospital against their wishes. The authorisation is issued by a Supervisory Body, usually a local authority, which has to be independent of the Body responsible for the care of the resident or patient (the Managing Authority). This Body organises the assessment by the **Best Interests Assessor**, usually a local authority social worker. All Mental Capacity Act 2005 (sections 1–5) principles apply, including, in particular, the requirement to empower people to make decisions for themselves to the maximum possible extent, and also the requirement that any deprivation of liberty should be proportionate to need. The application process will be started by the organisation that is currently offering care to the patient or resident, that is, the Managing Authority.

Before a Deprivation of Liberty can be authorised, six assessments need to be carried out. At least one has to be carried out by someone other than the Best Interests Assessor. They are:

1   Age: the vulnerable person must be 18 years or above
2   No refusals: the deprivation must not conflict with advance decision or wishes expressed
3   Capacity: the vulnerable person does not have the capacity to make decisions in relation to their need to continue residing in the care home or hospital
4   Mental health: the person has to have a mental disorder as defined by section 1 Mental Health Act 2007

5   Eligibility: compulsory detention under Mental Health Act 1983 is not appropriate
6   Best interests: deprivation of liberty is necessary to prevent harm and is proportionate to need.

On the basis of the six assessments, the Best Interests Assessor then recommends:

- how long deprivation should be for (maximum 12 months);
- who should in future represent the detained person in decision-making;
- whether any conditions should be attached – these must be related to need for deprivation of liberty.

The Best Interests Assessor has 21 days to carry out this task, except in an emergency when the Managing Authority has had to issue to itself temporarily the authority to deprive someone of their liberty. In this case, the assessment process is constrained to a maximum seven days.

In practice, the first important consideration is whether there really is a deprivation of liberty and not just a permissible restriction of liberty, such as locking a front door at night, or not allowing people access to a garden after dark.

What is meant by deprivation of liberty has been decided in an important legal case, *Cheshire West and Chester Council v P* [2014], which declared that whether someone is deprived of their liberty is an objective issue. A comparison should be made between the situation of the vulnerable person and that of an ordinary person. So, for example, being behind locked doors during the night is not a deprivation of liberty since most people would consider that reasonable and normal, whereas not being allowed out of one's room without supervision and being completely under the control of members of staff would be experienced by most people as a definite deprivation of liberty. As the judgment in the case says:

> The fact that my living arrangements are comfortable, and indeed make my life as enjoyable as it could possibly be, should make no difference. A gilded cage is still a cage (*Cheshire West and Chester v P* [2014], judgment para. 46).

Detention and Training Orders are the main custodial sentence
available for 12 to 17-year-olds. The law relating to custodial sentences for young offenders is covered in Chapter 2 of the Powers of Criminal Courts (Sentencing) Act 2000, with provisions for Detention and Training being in sections 100–107.

For certain very serious offences such as murder, young offenders may be 'detained during Her Majesty's pleasure' (section 90). The aim of the Detention and Training Order is to combine re-education with detention, obliging young offenders to address issues such as relationship difficulties, drug and alcohol misuse, anger management, and the effects of their crime. It is stipulated that half the sentence will be spent in custody, with the remainder being in the community under the supervision of a member of the **Youth Offending Team**. Breaching requirements, or committing further offences while under supervision, can result in them being returned to custody.

The length of the Detention and Training Orders is not entirely at the court's discretion as they can only last for a specified period of 4, 6, 8, 10, 12, 18 or 24 months (section 101). Detention and Training Orders can only be made in relation to 12 to 14-year-olds where they are deemed to be persistent young offenders (section 100) and such offenders would normally go to a Secure Training Unit. 15 to 17-year-olds would be sent to a Young Offender Institution.

The **Youth Justice Board** and Ministry of Justice publish an annual overview of youth justice statistics for the previous year. The Report on the year 2019–2020 revealed that the number of young offenders who received a caution or sentence has fallen by 82% over the last ten years. In the year ending March 2020, there was an average of 780 children or young people in custody. This is a fall of 68% compared to 2010. However, Black young people accounted for 28% of the youth custody population – an increase from the 15% of ten years ago (Ministry of Justice, 2021: 38). This point was underlined in an Equality and Human Rights Commission Report (Equality and Human Rights Commission, 2019: 37–40) and in the Lammy Report (Lammy, 2017: 3–4) which pointed out the youth justice system 'is regarded as one of the success stories of the criminal justice system, with published figures showing that, compared with a decade ago, far fewer young people are offending, reoffending and going into custody' yet the proportion of BAME young people being drawn into the youth justice system through offending, reoffending or going into custody is increasing.

Direct payments are sums of money allocated after an assessment of need by a local authority which can then be used to purchase the support and care needed. Direct payments can be paid to families with children under the Children Act 1989 or Children and Families Act 2014, or to adult service users or carers under the Care Act 2014.

Section 17A Children Act 1989 makes provision for direct payments to parents caring for a child or young person with disabilities. They can also be paid to a young person aged 16 or 17. They are paid after a local authority assessment of need, when it is agreed that support is necessary, and a care plan is drawn up. There are three ways of implementing the care plan: by the local authority arranging all the care to meet identified needs; by families buying a mixture of care they need; or a mixture. Direct payments are typically used to provide specialist equipment, respite care, employing a carer, placement at day nursery, after-school support, or short breaks. They cannot be used to employ someone already resident in the same household, unless that person has been specifically employed as a live-in care assistant (Community Care, Services for Carers and Children's Services (Direct Payments) (England) Regulations 2009 as amended).

Direct payments provisions in the Children and Families Act 2014 relate to the Education, Health and Care Plans which were introduced by that Act (see **Education, Health and Care Plans**). An Education, Health and Care assessment is 'an assessment of the educational, health care and social care needs of a child or young person' (section 36(2) Children and Families Act 2014). Provision of services by local authorities following the assessment can last beyond attainment of adulthood, right up until the young person is 25 (section 46 Children and Families Act 2014). A local authority that maintains an Education, Health and Care Plan must prepare a personal budget on request, and this identifies a sum of money available to secure services needed. This sum can then be paid direct to the parent (or over-16s themselves in some cases) to secure the necessary provision. Direct payment arrangements stipulating, among other matters, how they may or may not be spent, are covered by associated Regulations: the Special Educational Needs (Personal Budgets And Direct Payments) Regulations 2014 and Special Educational Needs and Disability Regulations 2014.

Sections 31–33 Care Act 2014 cover direct payments. These lay down that the option for direct payments must be made available on request and can be made to the applicant or a nominated person. The adult must have capacity (section 31 Care Act 2014). There must be a personal budget already in place (see **Personal budgets**) which stipulates the sum of money the local authority agrees is required to meet assessed need. The adult can ask for all, some, or none of that money to be paid direct to them – if none, the local authority then has the responsibility to make the care arrangements. If someone is unable to manage their own finances, they can nominate someone else to manage direct payments on their behalf, but this person must be approved by the local authority. People may opt to switch from direct payments to local authority responsibility for payments, and vice versa, at any time.

The Care and Support (Direct Payments) Regulations 2014 (revised from time to time) specify how the direct payments system is to work. In essence, payments must relate to the care plan, there is a monitoring system, and they can be used to pay for most community services, but not for residential care or to pay anyone else living in the same household, unless that person is specifically employed as a live-in carer.

Direct payments (but not personal budgets) are available in Wales but there are some slight differences about how the scheme works.

The **Director of Public Prosecutions** is the head of the Crown Prosecution Service, which is the organisation responsible for prosecuting most criminal cases in England and Wales.

Disclosure and barring is a system for vetting people who work with any 'vulnerable' group, including children, and is widely known as DBS or Disclosure and Barring Service. This is the name of the organisation set up by section 87 Protection of

Freedoms Act 2012 which updated the Safeguarding Vulnerable Groups Act 2006 by merging the Independent Safeguarding Authority and the Criminal Records Bureau.

There are two barred lists: one for people working with children, and one for those working with adults. The term 'working' includes voluntary work. The basic principle is that anyone who works with either children or vulnerable adults will be subject to scrutiny, but the degree of scrutiny depends on what the person is doing, in particular whether they are engaged in a 'regulated activity' which essentially means direct work with vulnerable people, excluding family members. Regulated activities would include social work, health care, personal care, foster care, childminding, teaching, conveying someone for these purposes, help with shopping, helping someone managing their affairs and moderating internet chatrooms. It is a criminal offence for someone to seek work from which they are barred. It is also an offence for employers or voluntary organisations to appoint barred people to work in regulated activities.

Furthermore, there are legal responsibilities laid on employers and organisations to report any incidents that give rise to the potential need to bar someone (Safeguarding Vulnerable Groups (Miscellaneous Provisions) Regulations 2012). These provisions stand alongside other procedures such as applying to the professional regulatory body to remove someone from the professional register. There are rights to make representations about decisions to bar, and to appeal, given that someone who is barred will not be able to secure any kind of employment in social work and, of course, would be dismissed if they were already in employment.

Disempowerment See Empowerment.

Domestic abuse
On average, two women a week are killed by their current or former partner in the United Kingdom (UK), and many experience domestic abuse in their lifetime (Office for National Statistics, 2020). Domestic abuse is not confined to one gender, ethnicity, socioeconomic status, religion, age, or type of family. Abuse can take many forms.

The Offences Against the Persons Act 1861 makes it a criminal offence to physically assault someone. Section 76 of the Serious Crime Act 2015 makes controlling or coercive behaviour a criminal offence. The Domestic Violence, Crime and Victims Act 2004 provides for further protection including restraining orders. At the time of writing, the long-awaited Domestic Abuse Act 2021 received royal assent. Though many of the measures are yet to come into force, this Act offers support for those who experience domestic abuse and clearer sanctions for those who behave abusively.

Part 1 offers a statutory definition of domestic abuse in relation to those aged over 16 who are 'personally connected to each other'. This includes physical or sexual abuse, violent or threatening behaviour, controlling or coercive behaviour, economic abuse, psychological abuse or emotional abuse. The behaviour may consist of a single incident or a course of conduct. The Act explicitly recognises children who experience the effects of abuse as being victims.

Part 2 establishes the office for the Domestic Abuse Commissioner with specific functions.

Part 3 updates the framework for Domestic Violence Protection Notices (DVPNs) and Domestic Violence Protection Orders (DVPOs), which allow the police, based on reasonable grounds for believing a person has been abusive to someone they are personally connected, to issue a notice or seek an order preventing further abuse, it will be a criminal offence to breach either of these.

Part 4 requires the local authority to consider providing accommodation to those who are at risk of domestic abuse and establish domestic abuse safeguarding boards.

Part 5 sets out special measures for witnesses and victims of domestic abuse in both family and criminal law proceedings to protect them from possible intimidation.

Part 6 creates offences relating to non-fatal strangulation or suffocation, and the sharing of intimate images, for example of one's ex-partner.

Part 7 provides a framework for the prosecution of offenders under the Act. It places what is known as 'Clare's law' on a statutory footing. This permits someone to ask the police and the police to consider sharing information relating to a person's abusive past.

Civil and Family Law

Part IV of the Family Law Act 1996 as amended by the Domestic Violence, Crime and Victims Act 2004 offers protection for victims through a non-molestation order and/or an occupation order.

Section 120 of the Adoption and Children Act 2002 amended section 31 of the Children Act 1989 to include, 'impairment suffered from seeing or hearing the ill-treatment of another': meaning domestic abuse can amount to significant harm. Section 44A of the Children Act 1989 allows an alleged perpetrator to be excluded from the home in specified circumstances.

Where domestic abuse is raised in proceedings related to **Child Arrangement Orders**, a judicial practice direction (PD 12J) sets out what the Family Courts should consider.

Information sharing protocols are in place between a range of agencies including police, children services, housing and probation. For example, Multi-Agency Risk Assessment Conferences (MARAC) share information about high-risk offenders. If police are called out to incidents of domestic abuse, they share that information with children services.

Useful practice guidance is offered by BASW (BASW (England), 2021).

Harassment

A range of behaviours that impose unwanted communications on a person, in a way that could cause them distress, alarm or fear. The Protection from Harassment Act 1997 as amended by the Protection of Freedoms Act 2012 sets out when unwanted behaviour amounts to a criminal offence. Behaviours include spying, calling, texting or using social media to harass or stalk. Social workers may meet with families where harassment or stalking forms part of domestic abuse. Victims may or may not know who is harassing or stalking them. These behaviours present a risk of physical harm to the victim and affect emotional health.

Duty of care, local authority See Local authorities, accountability.

Duty of care, social worker See Social worker accountability and registration.

Duty solicitor is a solicitor who can be consulted as of right, without charge, by someone who is arrested on suspicion of a criminal offence. Social workers are most likely to come across duty solicitors when acting as **Appropriate Adult**. There is also a duty solicitor scheme in relation to court appearances.

Education supervision orders See Education of children and young people.

Education of children and young people means schools

feature significantly in most children's lives but the actual provision of education is not primarily a social work task. However, a number of social workers are employed to work in school settings and schools. Schools naturally play an important role in overseeing the welfare of children, reinforced by law, especially when there is the possibility of a need for safeguarding (section 175 Education Act 2002).

The law requires children to have started school by the time they attain compulsory school age, which is strictly speaking the last day of December, March or August following their fifth birthday. In practice, many start earlier than that. In England, all 3 to 4-year-olds are entitled to 30 free hours of education or childcare for 38 weeks per year (section 1 Childcare Act 2016).

It is education, not school attendance, that is compulsory by law. Unsurprisingly, the vast majority of parents ensure that their child is educated by sending them to school, but section 7 Education Act 1996 says that children may be educated 'otherwise', which in practice means at home, providing parents can convince their local authority that their education arrangements are satisfactory. 'Home schooling' has grown in popularity over several years although not always by choice: it became the only possibility for many during the COVID-19 related lockdowns in 2020–2021.

Parents have the right to express a preference for schooling, but not to insist on their choice. Schools can refuse admission if oversubscribed and if admissions policies, fairly applied, accord priority to other children. There is a right of appeal under the School Standards and Framework Act 1998 enacted through the Schools Admission Code (Department for Education, 2014b).

The local authority has the statutory responsibility of ensuring that children receive full-time education, a duty usually carried out by its education welfare service (or equivalent) who deal with more general welfare issues affecting school performance, as well as attendance concerns. Truancy can result in a parent being prosecuted under section 444 Education Act 1996. Alternatively, a local authority could instigate proceedings under section 36 Children Act 1989 whereby courts can make an education supervision order for a period up to 12 months, although there is provision for this to be extended for up to 3 years by application to the court during the last 3 months of the initial order

(Children Act 1989 Schedule 3 section 15). The order simply requires the child to be supervised and for parents to comply with directions given by the court or the supervisor, with the threat of fines for non-compliance.

Laws governing how schools operate derive from a number of sources. The principal legislation is the Education Act 1996 which was a consolidating Act, but there have been a number of amendments and additions made by successive governments. These may be found in the Education Acts of 2002, 2005 and 2011, the Education and Inspections Act 2006, the Education and Skills Act 2008, the Apprenticeships, Skills, Children and Learning Act 2009; these last two Acts made education or training compulsory up to age 18. The Academies Act 2010, Education Act 2011 and Education and Adoption Act 2016 enable all maintained schools to apply to the Secretary of State for Education to become Academies, state-funded schools independent of local authority control and governance, with ministerial powers to compel certain schools to convert to academy status in certain circumstances.

Of more direct relevance to social workers is the legislative provisions for children with special needs, which falls under the Special Educational Needs and Disability Act 2001 and Children and Families Act 2014 (Part 3) (see **Special educational needs**). The Children and Families Act 2014 introduced birth-to-25 Education, Health and Care Plans to provide better co-ordination and planning across education, health, and social care (see **Education, Health and Care Plans** for full explanation). The same Act declares that all children should be educated in mainstream schooling unless they have special educational needs and their parents wish them to be educated outside the mainstream system (Part 3 Children and Families Act 2014). Section 312 Education Act 1996 entitles children with disabilities to an assessment to determine whether they have learning difficulties arising from their disability. If learning difficulties are confirmed, the local authority has a duty to arrange for those needs to be met (Part 3 Children and Families Act 2014). If parents are dissatisfied with the local authority response, they have the right to appeal to the Special Educational Needs and Disability Tribunal (section 51 Children and Families Act 2014). There is no provision for the child or young person to participate in this process, which contrasts to the position in Wales, where section 6 of the Additional Learning Needs and Education Tribunal (Wales) Act 2018 requires children to be involved in decision-making as fully as possible.

Social workers should also be aware that there are regulations governing schools' disciplinary procedures, for which see **Exclusion from school**.

Education, Health and Care Plans are birth-to-25 documents
drawn up by local authority children's services to provide a co-ordinated approach to addressing needs of young people with special educational needs (section 37 Children and Families Act 2014). The plan should address health care provision 'reasonably required by the learning difficulties and disabilities' and, for under 18s, 'relevant' social care provision.

They can be requested by parents, the young person if they are aged 16–25, or a professional. The Special Educational Needs and Disability Regulations 2014 prescribe time periods within which the local authority must decide whether to carry out an Education, Health and Care Plan. The Regulations stipulate that after the local authority draws up the draft plan, the plan is shared with parents who have 15 days to comment; the local authority then has 20 weeks in which to draw up the final Education, Health and Care Plan (Special Educational Needs and Disability Regulations 2014 Regulation 13). There are procedures for dealing with disagreements including, ultimately, an appeal to the Special Educational Needs and Disability Tribunal.

Once an Education, Health and Care Plan is made, families have the right to opt for a personal budget through which support for their child can be funded. As with social care personal budgets (see **Personal budgets**) there is the option for direct payments for families to buy and manage services, for the local authority to hold the money but families decide how it is to be spent, or for a third party to manage the arrangements.

Education of looked-after children
is important since historically, children 'looked after' by local authorities have underperformed in education – a fact confirmed by government-sponsored research (Department for Education, 2011). To counteract this, specific requirements have been introduced to promote the educational achievement of **looked-after children**. Section 52 Children Act 2004 enhanced the general duties of local authorities towards 'looked-after' children (section 22 Children Act 1989) with a requirement 'to promote the child's educational achievement'. Section 99 Children and Families Act 2014 requires the appointment of a local champion to 'promote the educational achievement of looked after children'. Sections 4–7 Children and Social Work Act 2017 extend these responsibilities to include the appointment of designated school staff members responsible for 'previously looked after pupils'.

Eligibility criteria
in adult care are now governed by legal rules. When a social worker has carried out an assessment of an adult's needs or carer's needs under the Care Act 2014 and has decided they need care and support, the local authority must decide to what extent that need meets the eligibility criteria laid down in the Regulations (section 13(1) Care Act 2014). These are the Care and Support (Eligibility Criteria) Regulations 2015. The Regulations distinguish the needs of an adult, and those of their carer.

In the case of an adult, section 2 Care and Support (Eligibility Criteria) Regulations 2015 says the need must relate to 'a physical or mental impairment or illness' and they are eligible if as a consequence they are unable to achieve certain outcomes and this has a significant impact on their well-being. The outcomes stipulated are:

- managing and maintaining nutrition;
- maintaining personal hygiene;

- managing toilet needs;
- being appropriately clothed;
- being able to make use of the adult's home safely;
- maintaining a habitable home environment;
- developing and maintaining family or other personal relationships;
- accessing and engaging in work, training, education or volunteering;
- making use of necessary facilities or services in the local community including public transport, and recreational facilities or services; and
- carrying out any caring responsibilities the adult has for a child.

In the case of a carer, section 3 Care and Support (Eligibility Criteria) Regulations 2015 states the need must arise as a result of their caring responsibilities and, as a consequence, one of the stipulated circumstances apply, and there is significant impact on the carer's well-being. The circumstances are:

- the carer's physical or mental health is, or is at risk of, deteriorating;
- the carer is unable to carry out any caring responsibilities the carer has for a child;
- the carer is unable to provide care to other people for whom the carer provides care;
- the carer is unable to maintain a habitable home environment;
- the carer is unable to manage and maintain nutrition;
- the carer is unable to develop and maintain family or other personal relationships;
- the carer is unable to engage in work, training, education or volunteering;
- the carer is unable to make use of necessary facilities or services in the local community, including recreational facilities or services;
- the carer is unable to engage in recreational activities.

Having applied the eligibility criteria, the local authority must then give the adult a written record of their decision and 'consider what could be done' to meet needs. It must also decide whether the adult needing care is 'ordinarily resident' in their area (section 13(3) and 13(4) Care Act 2014 – see also **Ordinary residence**).

If the local authority decides that none of the needs meets the eligibility criteria, the local authority must provide written advice and information about what 'can be done to meet or reduce' needs, and what can be done to prevent or delay the development of needs for care and support in the future (section 13(5) Care Act 2014).

The effect of section 13 Care Act 2014 and associated Regulations and guidance is to establish a minimum threshold for adult care and care support. Prior to the Care Act 2014 each local authority had its own eligibility criteria that led to a postcode lottery which the government attempted to address through national guidance called Fair Access to Care Services. The Care Act 2014 system attempts to make the system more consistent and equitable nationally.

Emergency Protection Order section 44 Children Act 1989. See Child safeguarding system.

Employer accountability and duty of care to employees is primarily addressed in the Health and Safety at Work Act 1974. This established the Health and Safety Executive as the key agency responsible for safe working enforcement and providing information. Their website states that it is an employer's duty to protect the health, safety and welfare of their employees and service users and they must do whatever is reasonably practicable to achieve this.

The legal duty of care has developed through common law and is in effect a legal obligation not to act in a way that results in harm. Likewise, there is an obligation not to fail to take action nor to act, or expect others to act, outside their sphere of competence. This duty of care applies to everyone, including all professionals, and therefore there is a particular obligation on social work employers to enable their social workers to be able to act in the best interests of the people they serve.

The key relevant legal case in a social work context established that the employer's duty to provide a safe working environment extended to mental health. In this, the social worker experienced serious mental health issues as a result of a very heavy caseload that was emotionally exhausting. The employer was found to have provided no support when the social worker returned to work, resulting in a recurrence of mental health problems, for which the employer was found liable as they failed to prevent these, but instead dismissed the social worker on health grounds. They were found to have failed in their duty of care (*Walker v Northumberland County Council* [1995]).

Empowerment definitions commonly include themes of autonomy, choice, participation and having control over one's life. It is a state to be achieved through working with someone, not something that is given to someone. **Social Work England's** standards and the **British Association of Social Workers (BASW)** Code of Ethics require social workers to practise in an anti-oppressive manner by recognising their own prejudices and values and not imposing these on others whose values may differ. In addition, social workers should promote social justice through challenging broader policies and practices that conflict with principles of empowerment. Social work often involves tensions between support and control, but even in situations where autonomy and choice may be constrained, participation and engagement are crucial to avoid people experiencing disempowerment.

Legislation that reflects empowerment either through limiting state intervention, respecting people's wishes and decisions, and/or supporting people to build strengths includes:

Human Rights Act 1998

Section 6 **Human Rights Act 1998** obliges public authorities to comply with the **European Convention on Human Rights**. Human rights principles require social work interventions to be proportionate and necessary: for example, ensuring measures are not more intrusive than they need to be, to manage risk.

Mental Health Act 1983

While this Act contains far-reaching power to detain someone, its implementation is subject to human rights principles of proportionality and necessity. In addition, Chapter 1 of the 2015 Mental Health Act Code of Practice places an emphasis on empowerment.

Children Act 1989

The Act promotes family autonomy by recognising that children are better off living with their family where possible and contains measures designed to support this, most especially the duty to safeguard and promote the welfare of children within their area who are in need (section 17 Children Act 1989). In addition, the welfare checklist (section 1 Children Act 1989) ensures that children's views and feelings are considered, and partnership with parents is encouraged. Even where compulsory intervention powers under Part IV of the Act, such as care proceedings, are used to limit parental autonomy, measures must be necessary and proportionate.

Mental Capacity Act 2005

Section 1 Mental Capacity Act 2005 sets out the five core principles that reflect many aspects of empowerment: for example, by supporting participation in the decision-making process, by an assumption of capacity, and by ensuring that any restrictions are proportionate. In the event that someone lacks the capacity to make a decision, section 4 requires that a person's wishes, feelings and views be part of any best-interest decision-making process.

Care Act 2014

Section 1 Care Act 2014 emphasises well-being, choice, participation and control, recognising that the person is best placed to understand their own well-being. Even in the event that an adult requires a safeguarding intervention, the Act promotes the person's participation in that process and, if necessary, the engagement of advocacy services. *Making Safeguarding Personal* from the Association of Adult Directors of Social Services (Local Government Association, 2020) ensures that the person-led approaches set out in the Act are implemented and further integrated into practice.

Enduring Power of Attorney was replaced by Lasting Power of Attorney under the Mental Capacity Act 2005. See **Lasting Power of Attorney**.

Equality and Human Rights Commission is the Body established by the Equality Act 2006 for the purpose of enforcing laws that protect people against discrimination while promoting human rights and equality of opportunity generally.

The key Act which the Commission now enforces is the Equality Act 2010, although it has the right to challenge discrimination in any form; for example, in 2021 it challenged Home Office rules concerning treatment of a 16-year-old asylum seeker as being over 18 on the basis of appearance (*BF (Eritrea) v Secretary of State for the Home Department* [2021]). The Equality Act 2010 lists a number of 'protected characteristics' with which the Equality and Human Rights Commission is mainly concerned. These are: age; disability; gender reassignment; marriage and civil partnership; pregnancy and maternity; race; religion or belief; sex; sexual orientation (section 4 Equality Act 2010).

The **European Convention on Human Rights** was drawn up by the newly formed Council of Europe in the late 1940s and came into force in 1953, drawing its inspiration from the **Universal Declaration of Human Rights**. Its significance is that, unlike the UN Declaration, a formal system of adjudication was instituted through the European Court of Human Rights whereby countries could be declared to be in breach of the Convention and therefore under a moral duty to remedy the shortcoming. The Convention contains rights known as Articles; the Convention Articles and the European Court of Human Rights are completely separate from the European Union (which has 27 members, whereas 47 countries belong to the Council of Europe) and its associated Court of Justice of the European Union.

While the UK has always responded to European Court rulings, in 1998 Parliament agreed to enshrine the Conventions into UK law by passing the **Human Rights Act 1998**. As a result, references to the Convention can now routinely be found in court deliberations and judgments. In social work, this is particularly true in connection with care proceedings cases that inevitably deal with the balance between the rights of the family and the duty of the state to protect and safeguard children, especially when there is a potential threat to life.

The Articles of the Convention that are most relevant to social work are:

* Article 2 right to life. This might apply when there are questions concerning end of life care. However, attempts to argue that closure of a care home is life-threatening because the traumatic stress caused might endanger someone's life proved unsuccessful (*Watts v UK* [2010]).
* Article 3 'No one shall be subjected to torture or to inhuman or degrading treatment or punishment'. This is possibly relevant to extreme lack of quality of care. This Article has also been cited in cases where psychiatric hospital patients have been forcibly fed; this was not considered a violation if 'therapeutically necessary' (*Herczegfalvy v Austria* [1992]).
* Article 5 right to liberty. Very relevant to procedures for detention of people who do not understand their need for care and have lost their decision-making capacity. This was the key issue in the **Bournewood case** (*HL v United Kingdom* [2004]).

- Article 6 right to a fair trial. This had to be considered during the COVID-19 related lockdown when care proceedings cases where held virtually *(Lancashire County Council v M (COVID-19 Adjournment Application)* [2020]). Here, a final hearing had to be adjourned because of the pandemic and was re-arranged with arrangements to hear some evidence virtually, to which a parent objected. These objections were overruled on the grounds that the alternative provision was as fair as possible, with neither parent denied the right to fair trial if required to give their evidence from a remote location.
- Article 8 right to privacy and family life. Clearly relevant to care proceedings and adoption cases. The UK courts have interpreted this to mean that **care orders** should be regarded as temporary measures, and that orders made by courts in care proceedings must be proportionate and necessary *(Re B (A child)* [2013]).
- Article 13 right to effective remedy. Concerning allegations that a local authority had caused harm to children by negligently failing to act in a timely fashion to protect them, the European Court ruled that the UK must allow those who had suffered to sue the local authority concerned, and receive compensation *(Z and others v United Kingdom* [2001]).

These examples are simply illustrative. There is now a substantial body of evidence of application of the Convention to social work cases incorporated into social work law texts (Brammer, 2020; Carr and Goosey, 2021; Johns, 2014, 2020).

European Court of Human Rights is the adjudicating body for interpretation of the European Convention on Human Rights; its jurisdiction applies to all 47 members of the Council of Europe. This court is quite separate from the Court of Justice of the European Union which only has authority over EU members.

Evidence in court is defined as information that courts are permitted to take into account when establishing facts or making decisions. Rules about what constitutes evidence derive from common law and procedural rules, such as Family Procedure Rules or Criminal Procedure Rules. Criminal and civil courts have different rules about evidence.

A court cannot start proceedings of its own accord; proceedings need to be brought before it by a person or body, for example, a local authority in care proceedings, or the Crown Prosecution System in criminal proceedings. The parties to the proceedings will be the applicant, who is the person who brought the case to court, and the respondent, who will respond to the case brought against them.

Courts cannot make decisions on the basis of suspicion; they require proof. There are two relevant concepts here:

The burden of proof

This is the obligation upon a person or body to prove that something happened and is generally a responsibility that lies with the party who brings the allegation. For example, if a local authority in care proceedings assert that the threshold for a care order is met, it is the local authority's responsibility to produce evidence to prove to the court that it is so. If the Crown Prosecution Service asserts that someone broke the law, they must prove it.

The standard of proof

This is the extent to which the evidence must prove the issue, or how far the scales need to be tipped to one side before the courts consider something is proven. In civil law, the standard is the balance of probabilities, which means that the evidence produced needs to show that the event is more likely than not to have happened. In criminal law, the standard of proof is beyond all reasonable doubt, which is self-explanatory and clearly is a higher standard. If evidence produced does not prove that something happened to the required standard, the court case ends.

Admissibility

This is the question of whether evidence will be allowed into court before it can be used to try and prove a case or defend an allegation made. In order to be admitted into court, material or information needs to have been legally obtained and be relevant. What is relevant will depend on the legislation, the allegation and/or the decision that needs to be made. Evidence will generally be disclosed in advance to other parties.

There are broadly three main types of evidence: evidence of a witness to the events; documentary evidence that is contained in various documents, such as case records or a school report; and real evidence often referred to as exhibits, such as fingerprints, DNA or pictures.

Witness evidence is evidence from someone who has seen or heard something directly; for example, 'A' saw 'B' assaulting 'C'. The witness will be asked to submit a witness statement with an attached statement confirming their belief in the truth of the contents. Witnesses may also be asked to attend court and be subject to cross-examination so that their statements can be challenged by other parties. This is in accordance with the rules of a fair hearing.

Social work opinion and analysis

When a social worker writes a witness statement about their involvement with a family, their direct work skills will be combined with their experience and knowledge that they will use to support their analysis and any recommendations. A social worker must not stray beyond the parameters of their knowledge; for example, providing an opinion about a complex aspect of specialist work, of which they have no experience, will not be helpful. There is a distinction between social work and expert witnesses.

The best evidence is that which has the closest relationship to the issue that needs to be proved or decided, so first-hand is best. For example, an eyewitness account would generally be considered as good evidence.

Hearsay

This is like second-hand information: for example, 'A' saw 'B' assault 'C'. 'A' tells 'D' about this and 'D' tells the court. The statement of 'D' is hearsay. The only issue it confirms is that 'A' told 'D' and not that the assault actually happened, although together with other evidence it may help build a picture. The family justice system is more likely than the criminal justice system to admit hearsay evidence into the court, which means that hearsay may be permitted in care proceedings but not normally in criminal cases.

Weight

This relates to how persuasive the court finds a piece of evidence to be. A statement from an independent witness who saw Peter hit Jane is more persuasive than a statement written by Peter's neighbour that says Peter is nice and unlikely to hit anyone. Lawyers for both parties have the task of persuading the court, through their submissions, to attach greater weight to aspects of evidence that support their case.

Once in the witness box, a witness will be required to declare their intention to tell the truth, either by affirming or taking an oath on their preferred holy book. This is followed by:

Examination-in-chief

This is when lawyers obtain evidence from their own witnesses in order to support their case. For instance, a lawyer acting for a local authority will ask a social worker to confirm the contents of their statement and their professional details; they will also be asked to provide an overview of their analysis, including any updates or changes. The lawyer must do this without asking leading questions, and the social worker should have disclosed all their evidence and analysis prior to the court hearing so that the other parties generally know what is being said about them and have a chance to respond.

Cross-examination

This is where the lawyers for each party have an opportunity to challenge the evidence submitted by the other party's witnesses. In care proceedings, for example, a social worker will be cross-examined both by lawyers for the parents and for the guardian and questioned about their statements and analysis. They will often be asked closed and leading questions, that is, questions that imply a particular answer, that are designed to reveal flaws in the analysis and to persuade the court that a certain party's position and evidence should be given more weight. It is the job of lawyers to do the best they can for their clients. Although it is counter-intuitive and unnatural, responses to questions should be directed at the judge and not at the lawyer asking the questions.

Examination-in-chief See Evidence in court.

Exclusion from school is a sanction that has legally set parameters and may only be applied after compliance with specific procedures (Education Act 2002 as amended by Education Act 2011). Exclusion, unless permanent, can total no more than 45 days in any one school year, and is subject to appeal to the school governing body under various Regulations summarised in the relevant statutory guidance (Department for Education, 2017a). Section 52 Education Act 2002 gives the head teacher the right to exclude. However, governors may override this, and parents have the right to appeal against the governors' decision (section 88 Education and Inspections Act 2006; Education and Skills Act 2008).

Expert witness is someone with specialist expertise and knowledge, for example an expert in a specific type of non-accidental injury or with experience of forensic psychiatric conditions. The instruction of experts in court proceedings does not happen as a matter of course, but where necessary to provide the court with information it needs to make decisions. Experts will provide a report for the court and are likely to be cross-examined about the contents of that report. Experts should not offer opinion outside of their area of expertise. Family Procedures Rules 25 and Practice Direction 25B detail the obligations of experts.

F

Fair Access to Care Services is now superseded by national criteria under Care Act 2014. See **Eligibility criteria**.

Family Assistance Orders are made by the Family Court under section 16 Children Act 1989 for up to 12 months. The Family Assistance Order requires a local authority or **Cafcass** to advise, assist and (where appropriate) befriend the family. A Family Assistance Order is not a free-standing order that can be applied for on its own; it may only be requested and made when a court has been asked to make another order, for example, a **Child Arrangement Order**. Family Assistance Orders are occasionally used when a family needs support to make a Child Arrangement Order work. The court can only make the order with the family's and local authority's consent.

Family Court See **Courts and the court system**.

Family Division, High Court has a key role within the High Court as it can hear cases in which children need protection but, for whatever reason, their case cannot be dealt with under the Children Act 1989. It operates under **inherent jurisdiction** in this regard, with the responsibility for making some children 'wards of court' and overseeing their welfare. The court also hears some cases of international child abduction or adoption, cases concerning forced marriage, radicalisation or female genital mutilation. It generally hears complex cases transferred from the Family Court, along with appeals from the Family Court.

Family Justice Council is an advisory body that monitors the family justice system and advises on reforms.

Family law is law that prevents, settles or resolves matters that arise in families, including but not limited to marriage, divorce, arrangements for the care, support or the protection of children, financial arrangements and the division of property when parents separate. A large part of social work relates to, or is regulated by, areas of family law; this includes the Children Act 1989 and the Family Law Act 1996.

Family Proceedings Court was the name given to the Magistrates' Court when hearing care proceedings and similar cases. In 2014, it became part of the Family Court with its own place in the court system. See entry on **Courts and the court system**.

Finance and payment for services relates primarily to adult care services, although do note that parents remain financially responsible for children even when they are **'looked-after' children** and so can be charged for the support which local authority children's services provide.

If someone needs residential care, local authorities may contribute to the cost of this if:

- having carried out an assessment under section 9 Care Act 2014, they agree that the person's care needs are such that residential care is the best option;
- the adult has less than a certain amount in capital – currently £23,250.

Following an assessment of need the local authority draws up a personal budget which includes the amount the adult pays based on a financial assessment, the remaining amount being paid by the local authority. For residential care this covers the cost of care in an actual care home that is available, but if the person prefers a different home, they have the right to choose this. If their home of choice charges higher fees, they could 'top up' the amount. There are detailed Regulations concerning how the financial assessment is carried out and what income and capital is to be disregarded, including the controversial issue of taking into account property the person owns (HM Government, 2020a).

If someone needs support services in their own home, the local authority has the right to charge for the services it agrees someone needs following on from an assessment (sections 14–17 Care Act 2014). If it chooses to do so, it must carry out a financial assessment. This assessment is based on the income and resources of the individual who needs care, not their partner or carer (there are rules and guidance on treatment of income or resources jointly owned). A carer cannot be charged for services provided to support the person they care for but could be charged for services provided directly to them as a carer. The financial contribution should not result in income going below the 'Minimum Income Guarantee'.

Whatever services are provided, local authorities have discretion to decide whether some income or capital has been deliberately placed beyond their reach (section 70 Care Act 2014), and there is no time limit on this (*Yule v South Lanarkshire Council* [1999]).

There are certain services for which the local authority cannot charge:

- the needs assessment itself;
- short-term periods of support, up to 6 weeks normally, to prevent hospital admission or following on from discharge from hospital;
- some minor home adaptations;
- after care following discharge from detention in hospital under section 117 Mental Health Act 1983.

The Regulations and guidance on financing care services are to be found in the Care and Support (Charging and Assessment of Resources) Regulations 2014, and section 8 and various Annexes of the **Care and Support Statutory Guidance.**

Fitness to practise See Social worker accountability and registration.

Former relevant children See Transition to adulthood.

Foster care refers to a wide range of arrangements where individuals or couples provide family environments for children who cannot remain in their parents' care. Foster care is one option local authorities may use to accommodate children who come into their care. Foster care may be short, long term or to provide emergency accommodation.

The approval process for prospective foster carers, which includes suitability, recruitment and the management of training and support, may be carried out by the local authority, or the local authority can choose to work with an independent fostering agency that complies with specific regulations. Fostering services are regulated by the Care Standards Act 2000; Care planning, Placement and Case Reviews Regulations 2010; The Fostering Services (England) Regulations 2011; and the Children Act 1989 guidance and regulations Volume 2.

The suitability of prospective foster carers and their families must be carefully assessed and includes completion of criminal record checks and references. A fostering panel will then approve their suitability and, if approved, may make recommendations on the age and/or number of children a foster carer is permitted to have, or whether they should be approved as a specialist foster carer.

Prior to placing a child with an approved foster carer, an agreed plan must be reached which provides details of the child's placement with that carer and the support that will be available to the foster carer. Foster carers have a right to information about the child to ensure they can meet the child's specific needs. The Fostering Services (England) Regulations 2011 enable the local authority to delegate small day-to-day decisions about children to foster carers. Parental responsibility for a child in foster care remains either with parents or the local authority depending on the route the child entered foster care.

Relative, friend or connected person foster care — also known as kinship care

If a family is struggling to care for a child, it may be in the child's interests to be cared for by a relative, or someone connected to the parents or family in a personal or professional capacity. Where a local authority intends to place a child within its care with a relative or connected person who is not an approved foster carer, they are required by law to arrange a foster care assessment to take place within 16 weeks.

For a child that is not looked after by the local authority, parents themselves can arrange with a close family member or connected persons to care for their child. There may not be social work involvement unless the carers require the local authority to support them with caring for the child.

Private fostering

Informal arrangements made between parents and others who are not connected persons or close family members. The local authority must be notified if the arrangements are, or are intended to be, longer than 28 days. See **Private fostering** entry for more detail.

Freedom of information is governed by the Freedom of Information

Act 2000 which accords the public access to information held by public authorities, but not necessarily independent sector organisations even though they may receive public money. The Act obliges public bodies to publish certain information about what they do, and to give members of the public information they request. This information does not include personal data, since this is covered by subject access requests under data protection legislation. Information includes documents, computer files, emails, photographs, and sound and video recordings.

G

General Social Care Council is the forerunner of the **Health and Care Professions Council**, which in turn is the forerunner of **Social Work England** which is the current regulator appointed in accordance with **Children and Social Work Act 2017**. See **Social worker accountability and registration**.

Gillick competence refers to the ability of young people to make decisions for themselves, for which see general explanation under **Capacity**. It derives from a decision made in a legal case, *Gillick v West Norfolk and Wisbech Area Health Authority* [1986], which concerned a parent prohibiting a GP providing contraceptive advice to anyone in the family under 18. The judgment alluded to the inadvisability of having arbitrary age limits at which young people became competent to make decisions for themselves, preferring an individualist approach instead. This would mean that professionals should decide in each case whether the young person was competent to make a particular decision. If the professional decides that they are competent, then that view holds sway, even if the parent objects. Clearly, this is most likely to occur when medical issues arise, but would be relevant where young people sought social workers' advice without parental consent, or where they disagreed with plans concerning their future.

In determining whether a young person is 'Gillick competent', social workers would obviously want to consider maturity and level of understanding, together with the ability to provide a rationale for the decision made. It would be prudent to deploy the Mental Capacity Act 2005 principles and associated guidance on capacity, especially section 3(1) which suggests that ability to make a decision requires someone to understand and retain information, evaluate it and communicate their decision.

For further information see separate entries on **Capacity** and **Consent**.

Green papers are consultation documents produced by the Government. Their purpose is to invite comment on planned policy or legislative changes. In adult care, prior to the passing of the **Care Act 2014**, there was a whole series of proposals setting out how the government planned to move adult care towards a more person-centred approach. Some of these green papers were:

- A Quality Strategy For Social Care (2000);
- Independence, Well-Being And Choice: Our vision for the future of social care for adults in England (2005);
- Our Health, Our Care, Our Say: A new direction for community services (2006);

- Putting People First (2008);
- A Vision For Adult Social Care: Capable communities and active citizens (2010).

Guardians (children's guardians) See Children's guardians.

Guardianship offers formal supervision of someone who has mental health issues and needs some kind of oversight in the community. Its legal authority derives from sections 7 and 8 Mental Health Act 1983 (plus associated Regulations) and is the only form of community-based compulsory intervention – all other interventions under mental health legislation require the person to be admitted to, and detained in, a psychiatric hospital or unit.

The grounds for making someone subject to guardianship (note: it is not called a guardianship order) are:

- someone has a mental disorder of a degree that warrants 'reception into guardianship';
- it is in the interests of the welfare of the patient or for the protection of other persons.

The procedure for application is similar to Mental Health Act 1983 section 3 admission for treatment, i.e. an **Approved Mental Health Professional** (or nearest relative) applies on the basis of two medical recommendations. Unlike section 3, there is no treatability requirement, but practitioners do have to give reasons in writing as to why guardianship is appropriate.

As guardianship is not a hospital order, a guardian needs to be appointed and this will normally be the local authority. If it is not the local authority, the appointment requires local authority approval. Guardianship is not possible for anyone under 16, who would be more appropriately dealt with through application of childcare or child safeguarding provisions.

All of the above requirements are in section 7 Mental Health Act 1983. Section 8 of the Act sets out the powers of the guardian which are:

- to require the person (referred to as 'patient' in the legislation) to reside in a specified place;
- to require the 'patient' to attend certain places at certain times 'for the purposes of medical treatment, occupation, education or training';
- to require access to the 'patient' to be given to a medical practitioner or Approved Mental Health Professional.

Guardianship is generally regarded as having some intrinsic weaknesses or shortcomings. One textbook succinctly summarises it:

A guardian has limited powers of enforcement, and the provision is only likely to achieve its aims if the person responds well to the imposition of a legislative framework. (Barber et al., 2019: 41)

Harm, significant See **Threshold criteria (care proceedings)**.

The **Health and Care Professions Council (HCPC)** is the predecessor of **Social Work England**, the current regulator appointed in accordance with **Children and Social Work Act 2017**, which abolished the role of the HCPC in relation to social work. See **Social worker accountability and registration**.

Hearsay See **Evidence in court**.

High Court See **Courts and the court system** and **Family Division, High Court**.

Homelessness

Children

Section 17(6) Children Act 1989 explicitly includes the power, not a duty, to provide accommodation under the general local authority duty to safeguard and promote the welfare of children. Section 20 Children Act 1989 lays down a duty to accommodate a child in specific circumstances which would include a homeless child but not their parents with them. For a 'former relevant child' (for explanation see **Transition to adulthood**) there are additional powers to provide assistance which may include providing accommodation (section 23B Children Act 1989). There is guidance on preventing 16 and 17-year olds becoming homeless (Ministry of Housing, Communities & Local Government and Department for Education, 2018).

Adults and families

The key Acts are the Housing Act 1996 (Part VII) as amended by the Homelessness Reduction Act 2017. The 1996 Act set out the local authority's obligations to people claiming to be homeless which includes the definition of homelessness. Generally, local authorities meet these through a housing department or equivalent, not through social services or children's services departments. Hence social workers are not usually involved in homelessness directly, but clearly do need to know what provisions the law makes for people who become homeless.

Sections 175–177 Housing Act 1996 as amended by the Homelessness Reduction Act 2017 state that someone is homeless if:

- they have no accommodation available, or no legal right to occupy accommodation;
- it is unreasonable for them to continue to occupy accommodation;

- they are under threat of violence from any person;
- they are unable to secure entry to accommodation;
- they live in a moveable structure but have no place to put this.

To qualify for local authority assistance, first the person must also be 'eligible', essentially meaning with right of abode in the UK (section 185 Housing Act 1996).

Second, they must be in one of the priority need categories (section 189 Housing Act 1996). The categories are:

- pregnancy;
- having dependent children;
- being 16 or 17 and not being a 'former relevant child';
- being 18–20 if they were accommodated after age 16;
- emergency, such as fire or flood.

There are additional need categories if associated with vulnerability. These are:

- old age, disability, mental health issues;
- formerly **looked-after children**;
- former members of HM Forces;
- served a custodial sentence or been remanded in custody;
- violence or threats of violence.

Third, they must not have made themselves intentionally homeless. Essentially, this centres on someone having done, or failed to do, something which has resulted in them becoming homeless (sections 191–196 Housing Act 1996).

Fourth, they must have a 'local connection' that justifies applying to that particular local authority. In addition to normal place of residence, this includes family ties, employment, or leaving care (section 199 Housing Act 1996).

The Homelessness Reduction Act 2017 broadens and enhances local authorities' responsibilities by adding obligations to prevent and relieve homelessness. There is a Code of Practice associated with this Act to guide local authorities as to how to implement the 2017 Act.

Human Rights Act 1998 integrated the **European Convention on Human Rights** into UK law. While the UK has always responded to European Court rulings on the Convention, in 1998 Parliament agreed to enshrine the Conventions into UK law by declaring that:

- all court decisions should take European Convention on Human Rights conventions into account (section 2 Human Rights Act 1998);

- all legislation was to be compliant with Convention unless specifically 'derogated' (section 14 Human Rights Act 1998);
- all legislation was to be interpreted by reference to Convention and if not compatible to be referred back to Parliament (section 4 Human Rights Act 1998);
- all public bodies to act in a way which was compatible with the Convention (section 6 Human Rights Act 1998).

On this last point, it is worth noting that the Human Rights Act 1998 does not apply to individuals or to independent sector organisations. Thus someone who resides in a care home run by a charity loses the right enjoyed by someone in an NHS nursing home to complain of a breach of Article 8 if the home closes without consultation (*R (on the application of Heather and others) v Leonard Cheshire Foundation* [2001]; *R v North East Devon Health Authority ex parte Coughlan* [1999]).

I

Independent Care Act Advocates are appointed under section 67
Care Act 2014, which requires a local authority to arrange for an advocate to facilitate someone's participation in the care assessment, planning and review process where:

- that person would experience 'substantial difficulty' understanding the process or in communicating their views; and
- there is no appropriate person to help them.

The duty to involve an advocate arises when the local authority is carrying out its duties under:

- section 9: needs assessment;
- section 10: carer's assessment;
- section 25: care and support plan preparation;
- section 27: care and support plan review;
- section 60: child's needs assessment;
- section 62: child's carer's assessment;
- section 65: young carer's assessment.

Section 68 Care Act 2014 requires a local authority to arrange for an advocate where there is a safeguarding investigation under section 42, or safeguarding review under section 44, where someone would experience substantial difficulty:

- understanding information;
- retaining information;
- evaluating information;
- communicating their views, wishes or feelings.

The duty does not arise if there is already an appropriate person who could act as an advocate.

Independent Mental Capacity Advocates (IMCAs)
are empowered to speak for an adult who needs support to represent their own interests, in particular with regards to certain key decisions regarding medical treatment and where they should live. An IMCA would not normally be legally qualified, but would be experienced in dealing with people with capacity issues.

The role was introduced by the **Mental Capacity Act 2005** and the duties are set out in sections 35–41 of that Act. An IMCA must be appointed where there is no one else who can speak for the person and where:

- an NHS body is proposing to provide serious medical treatment for someone who lacks capacity to consent to treatment: serious treatment 'involves providing, withdrawing or withholding treatment in circumstances where … there is a fine balance between its benefits to the patient and the burdens and risks' (section 4 Mental Capacity Act 2005 (Independent Mental Capacity Advocates) (General) Regulations 2006);
- an NHS body proposes to provide accommodation in hospital or a care home, or change that accommodation (section 38 Mental Capacity Act 2005);
- a local authority proposes to provide residential accommodation or change that person's residential accommodation (section 39 Mental Capacity Act 2005);
- there is either an application for authorisation for deprivation of liberty (section 39A Mental Capacity Act 2005) or, when implemented, there is an application for Liberty Protection Safeguards (sections 42–43 Schedule AA1 Mental Capacity Act 2005).

IMCAs are also available for consultation by relatives in connection with **Deprivation of Liberty Safeguards** or **Liberty Protection Safeguards**. They may also be available where an NHS body or local authority wants to review arrangements under a Care Review.

An IMCA may be appointed where there is a safeguarding investigation (section 4 Mental Capacity Act 2005 (Independent Mental Capacity Advocates) (Expansion of Role) Regulations 2006). This applies even if there are friends and family since the circumstances may mean that it would be beneficial to the person concerned.

In order to carry out their work, IMCAs generally have the right to interview the person for whom they are an advocate in private and to examine health and local authority records.

Independent Mental Capacity Advocate services are provided through providers commissioned by local authorities. The Social Care Institute for Excellence (SCIE) website has a list of those providers, along with a lot of useful information about the role.

Independent Mental Health Advocates (IMHAs) play

a specific role under mental health legislation, primarily as advocates to help people understand their rights under the Mental Health Acts 1983 and 2007. They have to be available to certain categories of 'qualifying' patients. These are people who are:

- detained for longer than 72 hours under a provision of the Mental Health Act 1983, including people on leave of absence;

- subject to guardianship under section 7 Mental Health Act 1983;
- subject to supervised community treatment under section 17A Mental Health Act 1983;
- even if not detained, offered certain kinds of treatment.

The legal requirement to appoint Independent Mental Health Advocates is to be found in section 30 Mental Health Act 2007.

Independent Reviewing Officer See Looked-after children.

Independent Safeguarding Authority See Disclosure and barring.

Indictable offences are those that can be tried on indictment, that is, serious enough to be tried at a Crown Court. Some offences are so serious that they must be tried in a Crown Court, for example, rape and murder, while some are of medium seriousness, and are described as triable 'either-way'. These offences, of which theft and burglary are examples, can be tried in the Magistrates' Court unless the defendant chooses to be tried by judge and jury in the Crown Court. Less serious offences, such as most motoring offences, are 'summary' offences and can only be tried in the Magistrates' Court. For young offenders, the Youth Court will deal with all cases except the most serious, which must be sent to the Crown Court.

Inherent jurisdiction is a power held by the Family Division of the High Court that comes from ancient common law obligations to protect children and vulnerable adults called *parens patriae*, and has been developed through case law. Inherent jurisdiction is not generally used where existing legislation provides a legal remedy, but rather for novel or emerging areas of law. For example, if the complete answer to a legal dispute can be found in Children Act 1989, the inherent jurisdiction would not be used. Disputes about adults who come under the framework of the **Mental Capacity Act 2005,** which provides its own court (the Court of Protection) and legal mechanisms, would not generally need recourse to the inherent jurisdiction.

However, inherent jurisdiction remains an important source of law to resolve complex legal issues for some children and adults.

Children

Specific aspects of international child abduction can require the court to use its inherent jurisdiction to locate a child who has been taken abroad and arrange for them to be repatriated – for example, matters concerning individual children and radicalisation. In addition, inherent jurisdiction is drawn on to settle disputes relating to medical treatments and decisions, for example, Charlie Gard in 2017 and Charlotte Wyatt (*Portsmouth NHS Trust v Charlotte Wyatt* [2005]).

A specific way of exercising inherent jurisdiction in relation to children is through wardship. This allows a child under 18 who is a British subject, is physically present in England or Wales, or an ordinary resident there, to be made a ward of the court. Wardship results in the court sharing parental responsibility with the parents and requires the court's consent to any significant steps taken in a child's life, for example, travel abroad, medical or psychiatric assessment. Note that section 100 Children Act 1989 restricts wardship being used instead of care proceedings or the court making decisions about a child subject to a care order.

Inherent jurisdiction has recently been called upon to fill a gap left by existing legislation in order to authorise arrangements that result in a child being deprived of their liberty in circumstances that fall outside of existing legislation because they do not meet the criteria for a Secure Accommodation Order under section 25 Children Act 1989, or other legislation authorising a deprivation of liberty (*D (A Child)* [2019]). This is an evolving and sometimes controversial legal area.

Adults

The Mental Capacity Act 2005 provides measures to protect a vulnerable adult who may not have the capacity to make certain decisions for themselves. The appropriate court in those circumstances would be the Court of Protection. In instances where an adult is considered to have capacity but is vulnerable, there may be gaps in protection. In specific cases and where no other legislation can offer a remedy, the inherent jurisdiction may be drawn upon where the adult is reasonably believed to be; subject to constraint, coercion, undue influence or if the adult is for some reason unable to make a free choice (*Re SA (Vulnerable Adult with capacity: Marriage)* [2005]).

Inhuman or degrading treatment or punishment For relevance to social work of Article 3 of the Convention see **European Convention on Human Rights**.

Injustice, public body See **Rights of redress**.

Inquiries are formal investigations into actions taken in a particular case or in relation to a specific issue, governed by the Inquiries Act 2005. Public inquiries are important in calling public bodies to account and reassuring the public that there is accountability along with a review of what went wrong. The purpose of any inquiry is to establish facts, learn lessons so that mistakes are not repeated, and restore public confidence. A statutory inquiry is one that has the power to compel witnesses to give evidence, provide legal safeguards, and act free of political involvement, although it is the government that sets the terms of reference, budget and selects the members of the inquiry.

In social work, the majority of inquiries have concerned cases where abuse has led to the death of a child, although these can also be addressed by the less public procedure of a serious case review, now known as a Child Safeguarding Practice Review (HM Government, 2018), a procedure established by the **Children Act 2004**. Historically, the most significant public inquiries relevant to social work with children are the Maria Colwell Inquiry 1974, the Jasmine Beckford Inquiry 1984, the Cleveland Inquiry 1988 and the Victoria Climbié Inquiry 2003. While there have also been a number of important inquiries concerning adult abuse, very few were public; although some, like the murder of Steven Hoskin in Cornwall in 2007, concerned abuse of adults with learning disabilities.

Intensive Supervision and Surveillance Programmes comprise one of the Criminal Justice and Immigration Act 2008 Youth Rehabilitation Order requirements (see **Youth Rehabilitation Orders**).

Investigations in child safeguarding cases are governed by both law and guidance. When a local authority receives a referral or information about a child that provides a reasonable cause to suspect that a child in their area is suffering or likely to suffer **significant harm**, or is already the subject of an **Emergency Protection Order** (EPO) or in **police protection**, section 47 of the **Children Act 1989** imposes a duty on that local authority to investigate the concern. Information from the investigation informs decisions about the type of action that is required to safeguard or promote the welfare of the child. Interagency co-operation in the investigation is required by section 47 (9) of the Children Act 1989 and section 11 of the **Children Act 2004** and **Working Together to Safeguard Children 2018**.

Where there are concerns about significant harm, a strategy meeting will be convened by a senior social work manager and involve agencies such as health, local authority and the police. The meeting will share information, consider the grounds for concern and the nature and timescales of the responses. A strategy meeting may decide that other services or assessments can be provided instead of an investigation. If concerns remain, an investigation under section 47 Children Act 1989 will continue. This does not provide legal authority to gain entry to a home or remove a child; if the concerns are immediate, the strategy meeting will need to consider whether an application for an Emergency Protection Order or a **public law order** ought to be made.

If the concerns about a child relate to a criminal offence, such as an assault, a joint investigation between the local authority and the police may take place. There are, of course, circumstances where there might be insufficient evidence for the police to pursue an allegation, but the section 47 Children Act 1989 investigation continues. This is because section 47 Children Act 1989 requires reasonable cause to suspect, whereas criminal matters require a higher **standard of proof** requiring reasonable cause to believe.

The section 47 investigations should be led by a qualified social worker, taking a child-focused approach, and though permission is not required, the worker should collaborate with the child's family where possible. The child should be met with alone and their views, wishes and feelings ascertained where possible. When interviewing the child, the social worker must be mindful that children do not always have the words to explain their experiences or may be hesitant. The worker should be mindful of potential future proceedings and follow the guidance in *Achieving Best Evidence* (Ministry of Justice, 2011). In addition, information from other agencies, such as education, health, criminal justice or other services, should be gathered. If, during the course of the section 47 investigation, the social worker cannot access the child, then subject to the criteria being met, they may need to apply for a **Child Assessment Order** (section 43 Children Act 1989).

During the course of an investigation, as information is gathered and analysed, the concerns may be reduced and end with support services being provided rather than child protection measures being taken. If the concerns remain, a child protection conference will be convened within 15 days of the strategy meeting and a Child Protection Plan put in place.

If at any time it is believed that the child cannot be protected without urgent action, then an application for an Emergency Protection Order (section 44 Children Act 1989) may be considered if the precise criteria within the section are met. The order provides the local authority applicant with temporary parental responsibility and lasts up to 8 days, with the potential to be extended once only for another 7 days, though the child can be returned to the parents sooner if it is deemed safe to do so. The order permits the local authority to enter and remove the child or prevent the child's removal from a safe place, for example, a hospital or foster care. A warrant can be issued to the police to support the local authority (section 48 Children Act 1989).

An EPO sets out specific directions for the health or psychological assessment of the child, although if considered **Gillick competent**, the child may refuse to comply with an assessment. While the application for an EPO is usually made by the local authority, section 44(1)(c) Children Act 1989 does permit applications from others, for example the police, a doctor or NSPCC. An order can be sought by giving notice to the parents of the court hearing, or if particularly urgent, the application for the order can be made *ex parte,* that is, without notice, so the first time the parents will become aware of the order is when the local authority serves it on them and seeks to remove the child. The EPO will set out directions for contact between the child and family while the order is in place. The order is a very serious intrusion into family life, so legal advice should be sought before applying for such an order (*X Council v B (Emergency Protection Orders)* [2004]).

Occasionally, the police become aware of the concerns about significant harm and may use their powers to remove a child or prevent a child being removed from a safe place such as a hospital (section 46 Children Act 1989). It is only the police who can remove a child without an order of the court; though, a family refuses them entry, they may require a warrant to enter premises (section 48). This form of police protection lasts up to 72 hours, and the police must immediately refer the matter to the local authority who must consider whether an Emergency Protection Order is required and will have a duty to investigate under section 47 Children Act 1989.

If a child runs away from, or a parent removes the child from the care provided by the police protection, or the EPO, section 50 Children Act 1989 allows an application to be made to court for a recovery order. This allows police to search for and return the child to the accommodation provided under the EPO or police protection.

Removing a child from their home is very disruptive so, subject to specific criteria in sections 38A and 44A Children Act 1989 being met, there is a power to exclude an alleged abuser from the home rather than removing the child. This power can be attached to an Emergency Protection Order or an **interim care order**.

If, during or at the end of the section 47 investigative process, concerns that the child is suffering or at risk of suffering significant harm are confirmed, an initial child protection conference must be held within 15 days of the start of the investigation to decide on how the child should be protected, either through a Child Protection Plan and/or a consideration of an application for a **care order**. If the local authority considers that the support and measures in place are not sufficient to protect the child from suffering significant harm and a care order is being considered, then a legal planning meeting must be held, and the **Public Law Outline** complied with.

Fur further elaboration of the children safeguarding system see **Child protection conference** and **Child Protection Plan**.

J

Judges See **Courts and the court system.**

Judicial review is an aspect of administrative law based on common law principles and developed through case law. It permits a court to review the lawfulness of the decisions made by public bodies carrying out public functions. This includes, for example, a local authority making decisions that affect adults and children. The relevant court is the Administrative Court in Queens Bench division of the High Court. Judicial review is not an appeal process; the Administrative Court is not empowered simply to change a decision. Rather, it is a review of the decision-making process and the decision's legality. The main grounds for judicial review include the following:

- Illegality: circumstances where the public body has abused its power by acting 'ultra vires', which means beyond the power vested in them, or not applying the law as it should have. An example of this can be found in a case where a local authority removed a child from a mother immediately after birth without a court order (R (G) v Nottingham County Council [2008]). It may also include failing to take into account factors that legislation requires it to consider, for example, views of relevant persons when accommodating a child under sections 20(6) and 22(4) Children Act 1989.
- Irrationality or unreasonableness: this includes taking into account irrelevant factors or not taking into account factors that were relevant and available. Alternatively, arriving at a decision which no reasonable body could have arrived at, known as the Wednesbury principle (Associated Picture Houses Ltd v Wednesbury Corporation [1948]). This can be difficult to establish.
- Impropriety: this is related to principles of natural justice, being biased or failing to follow a specified procedure. This includes not sharing details of a case against a person, leaving them unable to respond accordingly – a principle further reinforced by Article 6(1) **European Convention of Human Rights**; for example, a parent unaware of information shared about them at a case conference.

A claim under the Human Rights Act 1998 and proceedings for judicial review may, on occasion, be combined.

To make a claim for judicial review, the person must first obtain the court's permission to apply. Before providing permission, the court will consider whether the person has sufficient interest in the outcome of the decision subject to review, whether the application is made within three months – unless there is a very good reason that it was not – and whether the alternative remedies, such as complaints procedures, have all been tried. If a judicial review hearing is held and is successful, possible remedies include:

- a mandatory order (formally 'mandamus') requiring the decision-maker to do something;
- an order prohibiting ('prohibition') the decision-maker from doing something that exceeds its power;
- an order that quashes the decision ('certiorari') which is the subject of the complaint, which means the decision may need to be remade;
- damages, which may also be made available (section 31(1) Senior Courts Act 1981).

Justices of the Peace See Courts and the court system.

L

The **Laming Inquiry** is a report of the inquiry into the death in 2000 of Victoria **Climbié**, led by Lord Laming. Victoria died while in the care of her great aunt and her boyfriend, who were later convicted of her murder. The report made extensive findings, including the failures of health, social work and police, to identify or respond to the injuries and neglect, despite the opportunities to do so. Laming found systemic inadequacies and failures in communication at every level, including failure to communicate with Victoria herself and insufficient critical analysis and supervision. The **Children Act 2004** and its subsequent amendments directly incorporate Laming's recommendations.

Lasting Power of Attorney

is essentially an arrangement a person can make in advance in order to ensure that someone they trust is nominated to look after their affairs when they lose the ability (capacity) to do so. The word 'lasting' is important: practitioners must understand the difference between a Lasting Power of Attorney and an ordinary power of attorney, the latter being an arrangement extensively used in everyday business affairs. Nominating someone to look after one's own affairs through a power of attorney is very straightforward and can be done verbally. So, for example, if someone decided to work abroad for a short time, they could delegate managing many of their affairs to someone else – this person legally is then known as a donee (literally person given the power).

The legal rules underpinning power of attorney are strict. It must be possible at all times to check that the person giving the power to the donee (that is the *donor* of the power) has – note has not had, i.e. present tense – full understanding of what they want the donee to do and, critically, that they currently have the legal capacity to delegate this power. The word currently is significant: as soon as someone loses the capacity to delegate powers, irrespective of the reason, an ordinary power becomes void.

This is of limited value if someone knows or anticipates that they will, as they grow older or as their medical condition deteriorates, lose the capacity to delegate. Hence, it is possible to take an additional step to confirm that they want the power of attorney to continue beyond the point at some future date when they lose capacity to delegate the powers. There are, unsurprisingly, some additional safeguards connected to this and specific laws, which are to be found in sections 9–14 of the Mental Capacity Act 2005. These are:

- a Lasting Power of Attorney must be written down and registered with the Office of the **Public Guardian**;

- it needs to be clear whether the Lasting Power of Attorney is intended to deal with financial matters, or health and care, or both, since these are the two distinct kinds of Lasting Power of Attorney;
- there must be proof (usually a medical certificate) when it becomes apparent that the donor who made the Lasting Power of Attorney no longer has capacity to make decisions;
- the donee is under a legal obligation to act in the donor's '**best interests**' (sections 1–5 Mental Capacity Act 2005);
- if it appears that the donee of a Lasting Power of Attorney is not acting in the donor's interests, the matter can be referred to the **Court of Protection**.

As there are two kinds of Lasting Powers of Attorney, it is technically possible to nominate different donees for each one, but it is always advisable to appoint more than one donee for every Lasting Power of Attorney to cover circumstances such as an attorney becoming temporarily or permanently unable to carry out the duties.

The donor may want to stipulate which kinds of decisions the donee may or may not make in the future, which is particularly important with regard to **advance decisions**. The donee of a health and care Lasting Power of Attorney can only make decisions that are not in conflict with an advance decision to refuse treatment.

It is not generally advisable for social workers to take on this role for people they deal with professionally. This is for a number of reasons, but principally to guard against possible disagreements about what should happen to someone who is in receipt of services arranged by a local authority. It would violate the principle of independence if it transpired that the social worker acting as donee was a local authority employee.

Occasionally, social workers may come across references to an Enduring Power of Attorney, which was the predecessor of the Lasting Power of Attorney. Any valid Enduring Power of Attorney automatically became a Lasting Power of Attorney under the **Mental Capacity Act 2005** (Schedule 4).

Law Commission is an independent body created by the Law Commissions Act 1965 whose purpose is to review the law and to recommend changes. In social work, the Commission is chiefly known for its work on the law concerning adult safeguarding. It was influential in drafting the framework for safeguarding provisions in the **Care Act 2014** and was also largely responsible for the Mental Capacity (Amendment) Act 2019 which set up the **Liberty Protection Safeguards**.

Lawtel is connected to Westlaw, which is a reference source for checking what the law currently says. See **Legal databases**.

Leaving care See **Transition to adulthood**.

Legal aid is a system of subsidising the cost of legal assistance to people involved in criminal cases, as defendants, or in civil cases such as divorce, domestic abuse or care proceedings. First established by the Legal Aid and Advice Act 1949, initially the scheme, which was administered by the Law Society, was generous. It provided free legal advice for virtually any kind of case to anyone who could not afford legal fees. The system began to be less generous in the late 1980s and then in 2012 the Legal Aid, Sentencing and Punishment of Offenders Act 2012 (Part 1) abolished the principle that legal aid would available for nearly all cases, substituting a limited range of cases that qualified, although this did include mental health orders and care proceedings. Excluded is much private family law, employment, welfare rights, medical negligence and education law. Furthermore, claimants must not only have a very limited income and few savings, their case must stand more than a 50% chance of success otherwise it will not be supported by the Legal Aid Agency which is the body responsible under the Ministry of Justice for administering the scheme.

Legal databases Checking what statute laws actually say is relatively easy by reference to the government website. However, this does not cover common law or case law (for explanations of these terms see **Statute law**, **Common law**, **Case law**). To do this requires a more comprehensive, completely up-to-date database such as Westlaw/Lawtel, LexisNexis (LexisLibrary) or BAILLI (all website addresses below). These are the most widely used, and which students access does not matter, but will probably depend on which is available on university systems. Of the three, only BAILLI is free, the others being subscription only.

Westlaw (Lawtel)

This database covers all legislation, all cases updated daily, and a range of legal articles. It has a number of powerful tools to search out exactly what is required. It is authoritative, being employed by legal professionals to carry out their everyday work.

LexisNexis or LexisLibrary

This database covers all legislation, legal guidance on procedures, all cases updated with commentaries — it boasts that cases are reported within 90 minutes of the judgments being made. It has a number of powerful tools to search out exactly what is required, together with specific guidance on the status of the law, important where law has not yet been implemented or has been superseded. Like Westlaw, it is authoritative, being employed by legal professionals to carry out their everyday work.

BAILII

The acronym stands for British and Irish Legal Information Institute and offers a free-to-use database of UK and Irish legislation and case law (it is financed by donations). It covers legislation and case law, but does not connect the two. So, for example, it is not possible to locate all the cases that deal with, say, interpretation of section 31 Children Act 1989 (grounds for care proceedings), but it is possible to access cases by their names. It is, however, comprehensive and accurate, although not quite as user-friendly as the subscription services, nor does it have the wide range of research tools.

Websites for legal databases

BAILII: https://beta.bailii.org/

Government website: https://www.legislation.gov.uk/ukpga

Lawtel: https://www.lawtel.com/UK/Home

LexisLibrary: https://www.lexisnexis.com/uk/legal/

Westlaw: http://legalresearch.westlaw.co.uk/

Legal Ombudsman was established by the Legal Services Act 2007. Included here as it is the mechanism by which people can complain if dissatisfied with services received from their solicitors or barristers, for example, in care proceedings cases or in representing them in the Criminal Court or Youth Court.

Legal planning and pre-proceedings See **Care proceedings**.

LexisNexis or LexisLibrary is a reference source for checking what the law currently says. See **Legal databases**.

Liberty Protection Safeguards were introduced by the Mental Capacity (Amendment) Act 2019 and were due for implementation in 2020, but this was delayed due to the COVID-19 crisis. They replace the **Deprivation of Liberty Safeguards**, for which see separate entry.

The rationale for the new Safeguards is that the processes and procedures under Deprivation of Liberty Safeguards needed to be streamlined, principally as a result of the Supreme Court decision in *Cheshire West and Chester v P* (UKSC19) which lowered the threshold for what constituted deprivation of liberty. As a consequence, the number of cases rose significantly with a resultant backlog of cases. There was also an opportunity to remedy some of the shortcomings of the Deprivation of Liberty Safeguards scheme. Specifically:

- Liberty Protection Safeguards can also apply to 16- and 17-year-olds as well as anyone 18 or older;
- Liberty Protection Safeguards can also apply to private and domestic settings as well as hospitals and registered care homes;
- authorisations can last up 12 months, then a further 12 months on renewal, but thereafter can be renewed for 3 years at a time, and renewal will not require a complete new authorisation but will simply require a statement that the grounds continue to be met and no significant change is anticipated;

- 'responsible bodies' replace 'supervisory bodies' to authorise arrangements –
  for NHS hospitals, this will be the 'hospital manager'; for arrangements under
  Continuing Health Care outside hospital, the local Clinical Commissioning Group
  (or Health Board in Wales) will be the responsible body; in all other cases, such
  as care homes or supported living arrangements, the responsible body will be the
  local authority (Sexton, 2020).

The Deprivation of Liberty Safeguards term **Best Interests Assessor** is replaced by
Approved Mental Capacity Professional, with a similar professional background and
additional training as stipulated in the Regulations.

The Liberty Protection Safeguards introduce a new authorisation process which requires
a review prior to authorisation. This must be carried out by someone who is not involved
in day-to-day care or providing treatment to the person being assessed. It can be carried
out by an Approved Mental Capacity Professional or another health care professional, but
in some cases may only be carried out by the Approved Mental Capacity Professional, such
as where a person is objecting to their care and residence. Instead of the six Deprivation
of Liberty Safeguards assessments, there will be three:

- The 'capacity' assessment, since in order to qualify for detention the person must
  lack capacity to consent to the arrangements.
- The 'medical assessment', since to qualify for detention under Liberty Protection
  Safeguards someone must have a mental disorder as defined by mental health
  legislation (see **Mental Health Acts 1983, 2007** entry)
- The 'necessary and proportionate' assessment, required in order to accord with
  the principles of the European Convention on Human Rights, confirming that the
  arrangements are necessary to prevent harm to the person and proportionate in
  relation to the likelihood and seriousness of harm to the person.

There is a rider that Liberty Protection Safeguards cannot be used to authorise detention in a psychiatric hospital, for which mental health legislation is to be preferred (see
Compulsory admission and detention).

When implementing the Liberty Protection Safeguards, practitioners will use the definition
of deprivation of liberty set out in *Cheshire West and Chester v P* (UKSC19), namely that
someone not only lacks capacity to consent to care arrangements but they are also subject
to continuous supervision and control and are not free to leave their care setting. This applies
even if the person is not objecting to the arrangements. The test must be an objective one.

Before arrangements can be authorised, consultation should take place with:

- the person;
- anyone named by the person as someone to be consulted;

- anyone engaged in caring for the person or interested in the person's welfare;
- any donee of a Lasting Power of Attorney or an Enduring Power of Attorney (see **Lasting Power of Attorney**);
- any deputy appointed by the Court of Protection (see **Court of Protection**);
- any appropriate person and any Independent Mental Capacity Advocate (see **Independent Mental Capacity Advocate**).

There is a right of appeal to the Court of Protection against a Liberty Protection Safeguards detention.

A **Litigation friend** is someone whose role is to assist someone through a legal or court process (anyone in theory can be a litigation friend). A litigation friend is not meant as a substitute for a solicitor but rather a litigation friend should empower someone who is at a disadvantage to enforce their legal rights. For example, a parent might take legal action on behalf of their child for compensation for injuries their child received in a car accident. In the **Court of Protection**, an **Independent Mental Capacity Advocate**, a Deputy appointed by the court, or someone who has a **Lasting Power of Attorney** might act for someone who lacks the **capacity** to manage their own court case either with or without a solicitor. Litigation friends only act in **civil law** cases that do not go to tribunals, in **family law** cases, or in the Court of Protection. In some cases where there ought to be a litigation friend but there is nobody suitable, the **Official Solicitor** may agree to act as litigation friend.

Living wills See **Advance decisions**.

Local authorities, accountability concerns the extent to which local authorities are accountable for their actions in the sense of owing a **duty of care** to the people they serve. This is a question that has now been definitively decided by the **Supreme Court** in a case where there was a claim that a local authority breached its duty of care under the **Children Act 1989** by placing a mother and her children on an estate next to a family who, the local authority knew, were anti-social. As a result of harassment from this family, and despite the children being 'children in need' and having social workers, the children suffered physical and psychological harm (*Poole Borough Council v GN and another* [2019]).

As a result of the court judgment, it is now clear that local authorities do not owe a duty of care at common law simply because they have statutory duties, even if these relate to prevention of harm. However, they can come under a common law duty to protect someone from harm in circumstances where the principles applicable to private individuals might be valid. For example, if the local authority took action that they knew posed a danger, such as digging up a road, then they have a clear duty to alert people to the danger and to mitigate it. In this case, though, the local authority itself was not accused of harming the children but was alleged to have failed to protect them.

They knew the children's predicament and, it was claimed, could have used Children Act 1989 powers to remove them.

However, the Supreme Court refuted this. It declared that it could not be said that the family had entrusted their safety to the council, or that the council had accepted that responsibility. The children were not in care, and there were no safeguarding issues relating to the mother. The local authority would have no grounds for care proceedings since, to demonstrate those, it would have to establish that the children were suffering, or were likely to suffer, significant harm attributable to a lack, or likely lack, of reasonable parental care. The harm suffered by the claimants was attributable to the conduct of the neighbouring family, rather than a lack of reasonable parental care. There were simply no grounds for removing the children from their mother.

It could therefore not be said that the local authority was vicariously liable for negligence by the social workers it employed, although clearly social workers were under a contractual duty to the local authority to exercise proper professional skill and care. What this means is that, given that there were no grounds for using powers under Children Act 1989, the local authority did not assume a wider, more general responsibility for the family. In other words, local authorities are responsible for exactly what the relevant legislation says, so do not somehow take on a wider accountability if this falls outside their strictly defined legal responsibilities.

Note the contrast between this case and the Bedfordshire case in which a local authority was held liable for failing to protect children by exercising its Children Act 1989 powers, since in that case the source of the harm was directly attributable to parental neglect and the local authority knew about this (*Z and others v United Kingdom* [2001]).

For information on local authorities' responsibilities as employers, see **Employer accountability and duty of care.**

Local authorities' legal status in essence is that they are **public bodies** and, as such, are created by legislation with their functions clearly defined by law. Unlike individuals, who are free to engage in any action they wish unless the law says that they must not, local authorities may only take an action that is specifically authorised by law. So, for example, there is nothing to stop an individual providing accommodation for someone who is homeless, since they are free to do so even if the action may be unwise, whereas a local authority may only assist homeless people where there is a specific authorisation to do so in statute law, as there is in various Acts of Parliament dealing with homelessness. These Acts may, indeed do, constrain what local authorities can do, making it clear that they may only provide help for homeless people who fall into specific categories.

Every action a local authority takes therefore must be something which the law directs them to do, such as assess adult needs in safeguarding cases (section 42 Care Act 2014), or which the law says they may do, such as promote the educational achievement of children who were formerly in care (section 4 Children and Social Work Act 2017). A local authority that acts without a specific legal authorisation to do so, is said to be acting *ultra vires,* meaning beyond its powers, and would therefore incur sanctions, usually penalties imposed on the councillors who permitted the illegal actions.

Legal authority for local authorities to act comes in many forms in a whole host of legislation but is fundamentally of two sorts: permissive and mandatory powers. Permissive means *may,* mandatory simply means *must.* Permissive means the law states that a local authority has the *power* to do something but has a choice as to whether to do so or not, whereas mandatory means there is more than a power, there is a duty, an obligation that the local authority must fulfil.

As to how local authorities carry out their duties, this may be further clarified through a number of legal mechanisms:

- The **Act of Parliament** that sets out local authority powers and duties may have attached to it Schedules or **Regulations or Rules** (Statutory Instruments) that stipulate how the local authority is required to act, for example, the Schedules attached to the **Mental Capacity Act 2005** or the **Children Act 1989**, or the Children Act 1989 Regulations.
- An Act may authorise the appropriate government minister to issue **Codes of Practice** from time to time which set out how the local authority is expected to act, although it is not illegal to go against what the Code of Practice says. Particularly important for social workers are the **Mental Health Act 1983** Code of Practice, the **Mental Capacity Act 2005** Code of Practice and the **Police and Criminal Evidence Act 1984** section 66 Code of Practice.
- Circulars or Letters issued by government ministers are generally not mandatory as such but can come across as such since they often set out what local authority expenditure central government will cover. Some circulars, however, are mandatory because the parent Act says so. The best example in social work law is the duty in section 7 Local Authority Social Services Act 1970 which states that local authorities 'shall act' under the guidance of the Secretary of State. Thus, any circular issues under this section must be followed.

Internally, local authorities consist of officers, who are appointed paid employees, and members who are elected to decide policy and oversee the effective operation of the local authority, including staff appointments. Social workers are accountable to their managers who, in turn, are accountable to the Directors of Social Services or Directors of Children's Services. Those Directors then report to elected representatives through a cabinet system. The top internal level of accountability is the full council, i.e. all elected representatives.

While organisation of local authorities is largely a matter for them, certain requirements are made such as the appointment of a Director of Children's Services (section 18 Children Act 2004).

If local authorities are failing in their duties to individuals, those individuals can refer the matter to the **Local Government and Social Care Ombudsman** service. If there is a more general failure of the local authority to meet its statutory obligations, it is possible for the appropriate government minister to intervene directly, for example, by appointing a new person to direct the way a particular service is run.

The current overall system was established by the Local Government Act 1972, but there are a number of changes of governance introduced by subsequent legislation, the most recent being the Cities and Local Government Devolution Act 2016.

Local Child Safeguarding Boards See Safeguarding Children Partnerships.

Local Government and Social Care Ombudsman is
a service run by the Commission for Local Administration which deals with complaints from people about maladministration and injustice. The Ombudsman can only adjudicate on procedural matters, not policy. So, for example, a decision to withdraw a service might lead to a complaint on the grounds that the implications had not been properly considered, and that, had the local authority spent less money on roads, it would have been able to fund the service. The first ground is one which the Ombudsman could investigate, the second is not.

The outcomes of cases are regularly reported on the internet and illustrate the kinds of ways complaints are resolved. Some examples from the Local Government and Social Care Ombudsman website:

Case 19 020 245: Ms X complained about the Council's handling of a disabled facilities grant and related works to provide a bathroom adapted for the needs of her son, Y. She said the work was not completed and the work that was done did not meet Y's needs. The Council was at fault. It will apologise, pay Ms X £1,000 for the inconvenience caused, and take steps to put matters right.

Case 19 020 372: Mr X complains about the Council's decision to treat his late mother as having deliberately deprived herself of capital to avoid care charges, resulting in the family having to pay for her care. The Council was at fault for: failing to apply the proper tests for deprivation of capital; for seeking to restrict Mrs Y's personal spending to £30.65 a week when she was funding her own care; and for failing to take proper account of the Office of the Public Guardian's guidance on the scope for gifting. The Council needs to reconsider its decision on the extent to which Mrs Y deprived herself of capital.

Case 19 014 276: Mr B complained about the way the Council responded to his complaint about a care agency. He believed the Council's response simply accepted the agency's comments. The Council's response appeared to be inadequate. Mr B cannot be satisfied the Council has properly considered his concerns. The Council has agreed to remedy the injustice.

Note that decisions are not binding on local authorities or care providers, but it would be highly exceptional for them to be ignored, since this might lead to further legal action.

Looked-after children are children that the local authority is accommodating for longer than 24 hours in accordance with section 22(2) of the Children Act 1989 in either a foster placement or residential accommodation. A local authority may accommodate a child through a range of circumstances, including, but not limited to, section 20 Children Act 1989, wherein the child is considered to be accommodated but the parents retain parental responsibility, or through a **care order** the local authority obtained in respect of that child, in which case the child is considered to be looked after. Children remanded in youth detention or made subject to a supervision order with a condition of residence may also considered to be looked-after children.

The local authority is expected to act like a good parent when providing care for a child. Section 1 **Children and Social Work Act 2017** sets out general corporate parenting principles that the local authority should consider when managing a child's care.

Section 22(3) **Children Act 1989** specifically requires the local authority to safeguard and promote the welfare of the child they are looking after. To achieve this aim, sections 22 A–F Children Act 1989 set out the local authority's responsibilities to the child. For example, the local authority must try to place the child in accommodation that is suitable to their needs, and, if possible, the child should be placed in their local area to maintain continuity of school. The child's background should also be considered when selecting a foster placement.

When a child enters into the local authority's care, a social worker must complete a **care plan** with the child that shows how the child's needs will be met. Care plans must be in language that the child or young person can easily understand and should consider their **wishes and feelings**. The plans should cover a range of matters, including contact between the child and their family and how the child's education and health needs will be met. Care plans must be regularly reviewed. The Care Planning, Placement and Case Review Regulations 2010 set out details for care planning. An **Independent Reviewing Officer** will be assigned to a child when they become looked after and oversee how the local authority implements the child's care plan.

A child will cease to be a looked-after child if they return to the care of their parents, leave care at 18, or are adopted. When a young person has been in care, the local authority has a continuing duty to support them, until they are at least 21 and often until 25, depending on the circumstances (see **Transition to adulthood**).

M

Magistrates See **Courts and the court system**.

Maladministration, public body, in a social work law context, refers to errors or lack of care in making a decision, for example, an incomplete care assessment or failure to consider every aspect of a person's circumstances. Someone would need to be able to demonstrate this in order to have their case considered by the **Local Government and Social Care Ombudsman** service or, indeed, by a judge conducting a **judicial review**. Otherwise, complaints might be more appropriately directed elsewhere. So, for example, a complaint about professional competence might be better directed to the social worker's professional registration body, while complaints about poor quality care in a care home should be directed to the **Care Quality Commission**. Local authority decisions that accord with local authority policy, no matter how much someone might object to that policy, do not qualify as maladministration, whereas misapplication of the policy would.

Mental Capacity Act 2005 is an important Act for social work practice as it clarifies how it is decided whether someone does, or does not, have capacity, that is, the ability to make decisions for themselves. This is critical when it comes to overriding the rights of adults to make decisions for themselves in relation to care, treatment or managing their own affairs.

The Act was passed as a result of long-standing dissatisfaction with the previous system, whereby courts were regularly obliged to use **inherent jurisdiction** to intervene in adult safeguarding. Other provisions, for example in relation to **power of attorney**, were piecemeal and the whole system needed consolidating and bringing up to date. The **British Association of Social Workers** played a significant advisory role, and its influence can be seen in some of its principles – for example, section 3 of the Act states that decisions about capacity must not be based solely on appearance or age.

The Act is divided into three parts followed by a number of Schedules. The Schedules must not be overlooked as they provide considerable detail about how decisions are to be made. For example, some Schedules address procedures for depriving people of their liberty in care situations.

For social work practice, the key parts of the Act are:

- the principles, set out in sections 1–5 in particular (see **Capacity**);
- sections 9–14 (see **Lasting Power of Attorney**);

- sections 35–41 (see **Independent Mental Capacity Advocates**);
- section 44 concerning offences of ill-treatment or neglect of people who lack capacity;
- in a few cases Part 2 may be relevant concerning the **Court of Protection**;
- Schedules A1, AA1, 1 and 1A concerned **Deprivation of Liberty Safeguards** and **Liberty Protection Safeguards**.

Mental disorder is the term used in mental health legislation to identify people who could potentially lose their rights to autonomy in some circumstances. Social workers would probably prefer a more inclusive expression, and one that is not so negative in its connotations, but this is the phrase that underpins the law.

In order to qualify potentially for compulsory admission to hospital or guardianship under the **Mental Health Act 1983**, someone has to have a medically confirmed or potential diagnosis that complies with the legal definition of 'mental disorder'. Before there can be any consideration of making someone subject to deprivation of liberty in a care home or elsewhere under the **Mental Capacity Act 2005 Deprivation of Liberty Safeguards** or **Liberty Protection Safeguards**, there has to be confirmation that the person has a 'mental disorder'.

The definition of mental disorder is to be found in in sections 1–3 **Mental Health Act 2007**. This is very broad. Section 1 simply states, 'mental disorder means any disorder or disability of the mind'. In practice, it is delegated to medical practitioners, sometimes falling into a particular category, to determine whether someone has a mental disorder. The 2007 Act goes on to remove the previous (Mental Health Act 1983) distinctions between four forms of mental disorder: mental illness, mental impairment, severe mental impairment, and psychopathy. Furthermore, it clarifies that learning disability should not qualify someone potentially for compulsory detention or guardianship under Mental Health Act 1983 unless that learning disability is 'associated with abnormally aggressive or seriously irresponsible conduct' (section 2 Mental Health Act 2007). These terms are not further defined. Do note that this consequently does therefore permit Deprivation of Liberty Safeguards or Liberty Protection Safeguards to apply potentially to someone with a learning disability as these Safeguards come under the Mental Capacity Act 2005, not the Mental Health Act 1983.

Section 3 Mental Health Act 2007 makes it explicit that 'dependence on alcohol or drugs is not considered to be a disorder or disability of the mind'. Of course, such a dependence can run alongside something that qualifies as a mental disorder, or indeed could be the cause of it, for example Korsakoff's syndrome. For practitioners, it might be better to understand section 3 as meaning that dependence on alcohol or drugs is not of itself considered to be a freestanding disorder or disability of the mind.

The **Mental Health Act Commission** no longer exists, but you may find references to it in various books and articles. It was established by the Mental Health Act 1983 in order to oversee the operation of compulsory admission, detention and treatment orders, and to visit certain patients who were subject to these legislative provisions. It was formally abolished by the Health and Social Care Act 2008 and its functions incorporated into the remit of the **Care Quality Commission**.

Mental Health Acts 1983, 2007 are the two principal Acts of

Parliament that focus on mental health. Curiously, and perhaps significantly, neither actually defines mental health, nor do they set out a code of rights or entitlements for users of mental health services. Instead, they start from the premise that there exists a group of people (those who have a 'mental disorder') for whom certain protective arrangements need to exist. These arrangements include being detained in specified places against their wishes where there is a danger to 'self or others', and to that end detailed provision is made concerning who can apply for that detention and on what grounds.

The two Acts complement each other. The definition of 'mental disorder' is now to be found in section 1 Mental Health Act 2007. This is very broad: mental disorder 'means any disorder or disability of the mind'. For more information see **Mental disorder**.

Compulsory detention, usually meaning compulsory admission to a psychiatric hospital, features in much of the legislation. Part II of the 1983 Act sets out the grounds for detention, the effects of the various orders, who can apply, and how the period of detention can be ended. The most commonly used detention order is section 2, which covers admission for the purposes of assessment for a period of up to 28 days, during which time the 'patient' may:

- be discharged home;
- agree to remain in hospital on a voluntary basis (section 131, see discussion below);
- be detained for a longer period under section 3 which can last for up to 6 months (section 20).

Elsewhere in the 1983 Act will be found provisions for starting this section 2 assessment procedure in an emergency. There is also provision for detention for people who have committed criminal offences. See **Compulsory admission and detention**.

Sections 7–10 Mental Health Act 1983 cover **guardianship**, a form of formal supervision in the community. This is the only legal provision for imposing restrictions on people in their own homes, since it does not involve admission to hospital, but guardianship powers are limited in respect of requiring people to accept treatment: people can be required to attend at places 'for the purpose of medical treatment'. People under guardianship can be required to live in certain places and mental health professionals have the rights of access to them (section 8 Mental Health Act 1983). Generally, supervising people under guardianship is the responsibility of Community Mental Health Teams which will normally include social workers.

Social workers and medical personnel play important roles in the operation of detention and discharge procedures. Social workers with appropriate additional training (as laid down by section 19 Mental Health Act 2007) can become **Approved Mental Health Professionals** charged with determining whether someone qualifies for detention under the 1983 Act, and with supervising people under guardianship or **community treatment orders**. Doctors with appropriate qualifications and experience can become Approved Clinicians (sections 9–17 Mental Health Act 2007). Approved Clinicians oversee the treatment of the patient in hospital and are empowered to discharge them, either unconditionally or subject to section 17 Mental Health Act 1983.

Section 17 Mental Health Act 1983 covers 'leave of absence' whereby a detained patient can be allowed home but subject to recall if necessary. If the patient is subject to possible recall this is known as a '**community treatment order**' which can have conditions attached to it. The community treatment order ends when the original hospital detention order would have ended, but note that section 20 Mental Health Act 1983 allows for the period to be extended, subject to certain provisions.

The '**nearest relative**' of the patient has certain rights under these two Acts. They can apply for the compulsory admission (or guardianship) of the patient, block a potential compulsory admission (although there is in section 29 the power of County Court to displace them), or order their discharge (subject to section 25 Mental Health Act 1983 power of clinician to block this). Section 26 Mental Health Act 1983 defines who is the patient's nearest relative; the patient does not choose, although they could theoretically apply to court to displace them under section 29.

Part III of the Mental Health Act 1983 (sections 35–55) concerns detention in psychiatric hospitals of people convicted or accused of criminal offences. This part of the Act is of significance to specialist social workers in mental health. It includes provision for admission or guardianship for convicted offenders (section 37), restrictions on discharge of such offenders (section 41) and remands to hospital (section 35).

Part IV of the Mental Health Act 1983 sets out procedures for overriding psychiatric patients' rights to refuse treatment (sections 58–64), and also includes important safeguards to ensure there is a second opinion on irreversible treatments even where the patient consents (section 57).

Of the remainder of the 1983 Act, the following sections are of relevance to social workers:

- section 66 sets out the circumstances where patients have the right to appeal to a tribunal;

- section 114 refers to special procedures for endorsing social workers (and others) as authorised Approved Mental Health Professionals;
- section 115 gives Approved Mental Health Professional power of entry in some circumstances, but note not the power to force entry;
- section 117 sets out provision for after-care;
- section 118 provides authority for the associated Code of Practice to guide practitioners;
- section 127 makes it a criminal offence to ill-treat a psychiatric patient;
- section 129 declares it to be a criminal offence to obstruct anyone authorised to carry out functions under the Act;
- most significantly of all, section 131 declares the overriding general principle that people have the right to agree to enter or remain in hospital on an informal (voluntary) basis, in other words not as detained patients;
- section 135 gives the Approved Mental Health Professional the right to apply to a magistrate for a warrant to force entry into premises in certain circumstances in order to detain someone at a 'place of safety' for assessment;
- section 136 is somewhat controversial, giving the police the right to detain in a place of safety someone who 'appears to a constable to be suffering from mental disorder and to be in immediate need of care or control'.

The Mental Health Act 2007 includes some specific areas not covered in the 1983 Act as well as some amendments which are incorporated in the discussion of the 1983 Act above. These areas are:

- additional safeguards for patients including, in particular, the introduction of **Independent Mental Health Advocates** (section 30);
- supervised community treatment (Chapter 4, sections 32–36).

As mental health law can occasionally be complex, practitioners often rely on specialist guides to assist them in their work; for example, Barber et al., 2019; Golightley and Goemans, 2017; Jones, 2020. There is also an important Code of Practice: Department of Health, 2015.

The **Munro Review** was the outcome of the commissioning of Professor Eileen Munro by the then government to review the child protection system in England in 2010. This was largely due to the concerns about the efficacy of the child protection system and the death of Peter Connelly, known as Baby P, in 2007, who died from abuse and neglect despite social work involvement. Munro recommended a number of reforms designed to provide a child-focused system that reduces bureaucracy and promotes a culture of learning rather than compliance. Some of these were implemented in the Children and Families Act 2014. During her review, Munro spoke with 250 children and young people, as well as a range of frontline and senior professionals.

N

National Occupational Standards, for social workers in England, have now been replaced by the professional standards which **Social Work England**, the professional regulator, is required to enforce (section 41 **Children and Social Work Act 2017**).

However, National Occupational Standards still apply in Wales and there is a specific set of standards that relates to social work enforced by Social Care Wales.

Nearest relative is a specific term used in mental health legislation to identify the person who has certain rights in relation to a relative who may be subject to a **Mental Health Act 1983** compulsory order. These rights, which all derive from the Mental Health Act 1983, are:

* to apply for compulsory admission of their relative to a psychiatric hospital (section 11), although to avoid later family recriminations this might not always be a wise course of action;
* as an alternative, to request the local authority social services department to carry out an assessment with a view to an **Approved Mental Health Professional** making an application under the Mental Health Act 1983 – the nearest relative has the right to have reasons given in writing if the Approved Mental Health Professional declines (section 13);
* to veto an application for admission under section 3 Mental Health Act 1983 (admission for treatment) or section 7 (guardianship), although there are some circumstances when the Approved Mental Health Professional may not have been able to inform the nearest relative, and also the nearest relative could be displaced by a court if their veto is deemed unreasonable (section 29);
* to be informed of their right to discharge their relative who is being detained under sections 2 or 3 Mental Health Act 1983, or who is subject to **guardianship** (section 7) or a **community treatment order** (section 23).

There is therefore considerable power attached to the role, but note that the nearest relative is not necessarily the next of kin. Who is the nearest relative is determined by the application of a set of rules, not by choice. These rules are set out in section 26 Mental Health Act 1983, which sets out a list in hierarchical order of status:

* Husband, wife, or civil partner
* Son or daughter
* Father or mother

- Brother or sister
- Grandparent
- Grandchild
- Uncle or aunt
- Nephew or niece.

The legislation declares that where there is more than one person of the same status, the nearest relative is the eldest. There is also a principle that a nearest relative is to be determined by giving preference to someone who lives with the 'patient', and whole-blood relationships should be preferred to half-blood.

Applying these rules in practice is not usually problematic but can lead to results which do not accord with family wishes. For example, a relative who lives close to, but not with, the 'patient' may not be the nearest relative if there is someone else higher up the hierarchy or older, even though that person never sees the patient. Likewise, in some cultures the omission of cousins from the list seems odd. It is for this reason that recommendations have been made to Parliament that the law should be changed and it is fairly certain that any new mental health legislation will take this on board (Wesseley, 2018).

Practitioners should bear in mind that it is possible for nearest relatives to delegate their responsibilities to someone else, indeed in some circumstances it might be prudent to encourage them, but they cannot be forced to delegate and certainly cannot be ignored.

Neglect of adult has no statutory definition although there are several references to neglect in the **Care Act 2014**. However, the **Care and Support Statutory Guidance** (HM Government, 2020a) itemises various forms of abuse and neglect in paragraphs 14.16–14.18. Paragraph 14.17 states that neglect and acts of omission include ignoring medical, emotional or physical care needs, 'failure to provide access to appropriate health, care and support or educational services' or 'the withholding of the necessities of life, such as medication, adequate nutrition and heating'. If this seems quite general, practitioners may find the Social Care Institute for Excellence (SCIE, 2020) list more helpful:

- Failure to provide or allow access to food, shelter, clothing, heating, stimulation and activity, personal or medical care
- Providing care in a way that the person dislikes
- Failure to administer medication as prescribed
- Refusal of access to visitors
- Not taking account of individuals' cultural, religious or ethnic needs
- Not taking account of educational, social and recreational needs
- Ignoring or isolating the person

- Preventing the person from making their own decisions
- Preventing access to glasses, hearing aids, dentures, etc.
- Failure to ensure privacy and dignity.

Likewise, self-neglect is:

- lack of self-care to an extent that it threatens personal health and safety;
- neglecting to care for one's personal hygiene, health or surroundings;
- inability to avoid self-harm;
- failure to seek help or access services to meet health and social care needs;
- inability or unwillingness to manage one's personal affairs.

The legislation addressing protection of adults who are exposed to neglect or self-neglect is to be found in sections 42–46 Care Act 2014. For further discussion on this see entry on **Adult safeguarding**.

Neglect of children is often referred to in legislation but nowhere specifically legally defined. However, it is generally regarded that neglect means not meeting a child's physical and psychological needs in a way that persists over time and can seriously impact the child's health and development. Examples would include:

- not attending to a child's general medical needs;
- not providing children with enough to eat and drink;
- not taking children to school;
- failing to keep children clean;
- not attending to children's emotional needs;
- not providing adequate supervision.

Indicators of neglect vary according to the age of the child; for example, older children may go missing from home. Note that poverty alone is not an indicator of neglect: some children who experience poverty will also experience neglect, while others will not (Bywaters et al., 2016).

Negligence See **Local authorities, accountability**.

NHS Continuing Healthcare is an adult care package which is free of charge, being funded by the NHS. This is provided after an assessment by the Clinical Commissioning Group which has been carried out in accordance with the National Framework for NHS Continuing Healthcare and NHS-funded Nursing Care (Department of Health and Social Care, 2018). To qualify, the Clinical Commissioning Group must agree that the adult has a primary health need, as the following extract from the Framework explains:

To assist in determining which health services it is appropriate for the NHS to provide under the NHS Act, and to distinguish between those and the services that local authorities may provide under the Care Act 2014, the Secretary of State has developed the concept of a 'primary health need'. Where a person has been assessed to have a primary health need, they are eligible for NHS Continuing Healthcare and the NHS will be responsible for providing for all of that individual's assessed health and associated social care needs, including accommodation, if that is part of the overall need. Determining whether an individual has a primary health need involves looking at the totality of the relevant needs. In order to determine whether an individual has a primary health need, an assessment of eligibility process must be undertaken by a multidisciplinary team. (Department of Health and Social Care, 2018: 19)

If someone is not eligible for NHS Continuing Healthcare, they could receive a joint package of health and social care where an individual's care or support package is funded by both the NHS and the local authority. This would apply where someone has specific needs which are the legal responsibility of the NHS and therefore the local authority would be breaching sections 18–20 of the **Care Act 2014** if it made that provision.

No delay principle

No delay principle, in proceedings related to a child's upbringing, section 1(2) **Children Act 1989**, asserts that delay is generally prejudicial to a child's welfare. Delays in court decisions create uncertainty, possible anxiety and impact a child's relationship with their family. The principle is reflected in the Public Law Outline and in private law proceedings. All parties in proceedings should therefore ensure the timely filing of court documents and reports, keeping witnesses and statements to a minimum. Delay may be permissible where it is planned and purposeful; for example, if a complex medical assessment or the opinion of an expert witness is required.

No order principle

No order principle, section 1(5) **Children Act 1989**, reaffirms that orders should not be made simply because they have been applied for, or as a matter of course. When a court is considering whether to make an order under the Children Act 1989, it is required to ask itself whether making the order will be better for the child than not making the order. Regulating a child's life through a court order should have a purpose related to improving the child's welfare. This applies to both private and public law proceedings.

Non-molestation order

Non-molestation order, under section 42 Family Law Act 1996, provides for a civil order that prohibits a person (respondent) from, for example, threatening or pestering the applicant and any relevant child. Breaching the order is a criminal offence. Often referred to as an injunction, the order is commonly used to protect someone from a former or current partner. Section 62 Family Law Act 1996 explains who may apply for the order. The orders may vary in duration and a respondent may apply to the court to change or end the order.

NSPCC (The National Society for the Prevention of Cruelty to Children) was established in 1884, and specialises in child protection. Named in section 31 (9)(a) **Children Act 1989**, it is the only children's charity with statutory powers to safeguard children, though the NSPCC generally refers matters of concern to the relevant local authority rather than taking the matter to court itself. The charity has service centres throughout the country and undertakes direct work with children and families, provides training and information, undertakes research and offers a support line, resources and consultation. Their website offers essential reading.

Occupation order is a court order made under sections 33–38 Family Law Act 1996 that prevents a person from living in a home they have been occupying with another person, usually their partner or, occasionally, a relative. The order is made on a temporary basis and does not change the legal rights individuals have in their property, such as tenancy or ownership. Section 62(3) Family Law Act only permits 'associated persons' to apply for the order, which includes former couples. Before making an order, a court will consider whether the applicant or any relevant child will suffer significant harm if they do not make the order.

Offences, first time, for a young offender receiving their first conviction by a court invariably means a Referral Order. For more information see the entry for **Referral Orders**.

Official Solicitor See **Litigation friend**.

Ofsted, the Office for Standards in Education, Children's Services and Skills, inspects schools or other education providers, and also regulates services caring for children and young people. This includes local authority children's services, but excludes some independent schools and higher education, although Ofsted is responsible for setting standards in initial teacher training. It is an independent body, reporting directly to Parliament. It publishes the outcomes of inspections with the intention of promoting high-quality services. In social work-related services, it has a particular role in the fields of adoption and fostering, where it oversees the quality of work carried out by agencies. It regularly reviews the quality of childcare work carried out by local authorities and, to this end, may conduct interviews with social workers, senior managers and people who use the local authority's services. Adverse reports can lead to central government ministers intervening by appointing independent trusts to take over the running of children's services under the central direction of the Department for Education. In late 2020, Northamptonshire became the eleventh local authority whose services were ordered to be run independently in this way. Oftsed reports are published online and openly accessible.

Ombudsman See **Local Government and Social Care Ombudsman**.

Ordinary residence, the question of where someone ordinarily resides, is critical to local authorities since it can have major implications for their financial responsibilities to meet care home fees, pay foster carers for looking after children, or providing after care under provisions such as section 117 **Mental Health Act 1983**. There is a considerable volume of guidance and case law on this (HM Government, 2020a; Local Government Association, 2018). From a social work practitioner point of view, the two salient points are:

- Local authorities cannot 'export' their responsibilities by placing someone in a different area, as, for example, when an adult exercises their right to choose accommodation by selecting a care home near their relatives which is outside their 'home' authority area. If this happens, the 'home' area still has responsibility for oversight and financing (section 39 Care Act 2014);
- Where someone no longer lives with their parents because of an arrangement under **Children Act 1989** and the parents subsequently move, the financial responsibility for that person does not move with the parents – this is a very brief resume of the 'Cornwall case' Supreme Court judgment (*R (Cornwall) v Secretary of State for Health* [2015]).

Parent, definition of Not legally as straightforward as people assume. Being a legal parent is a lifelong connection that can only be ended by adoption. It means that there are obligations to maintain a child, the child may have inheritance rights and can claim their parents' nationality. Legal parents may make applications to a court in respect of their child. At the time of writing, there can be only two legal parents. This differs from parental responsibility, which can be shared by more than two people.

Subject to the Human Fertilisation and Embryology Act 2008, the child's father will be the man who is biologically related to the child, and the mother will be the woman who gave birth to the child. There is a legal presumption that a man married to a woman is the father of any child born to the wife during the marriage. There are provisions in section 26 Family Law Reform Act 1969 to rebut this presumption, and section 55A (1) Family Law Act 1986 provides for a declaration of parentage if the child's paternity is disputed.

Currently if a woman has a child and then becomes a man, he will remain the child's mother and not become the father. The law relating to the rights of transgender parents is evolving.

Part 2 of Human Fertilisation and Embryology Act 2008 provides for the assignment of legal parenthood in cases of assisted conception. If a man and woman receive assistance through a licensed clinic to have a child, and the man consents to his female partner using artificial insemination from an anonymous sperm donor, the man who is the woman's partner will be the legal parent. Through section 41 Human Fertilisation and Embryology Act 2008, this provision also applies to lesbian couples: the woman who gave birth will be the mother and her partner will be the other legal parent. While anonymous sperm donors are biologically related to the child, they are not the legal parent. The Human Fertilisation and Embryology (Disclosure of Information) Regulations 2004 provide for a child over 16 and an adult over 18 to obtain information about the sperm donor.

Surrogacy

Sometimes a woman will have a child for a couple or single person who cannot have a child themselves. Legal parenthood in these circumstances is mainly provided for by Human Fertilisation and Embryology Act 2008.

Surrogates may use their own eggs to assist the intended parents. However, gestational surrogacy, where an embryo is transplanted into the surrogate and there is no biological relationship between the surrogate and the child, is very common. The child carried by the surrogate must be biologically linked to at least one of the intended parents by using the woman's eggs and/or the man's sperm. When the child is born, the surrogate is the legal mother, and the intended parents will either need to seek an adoption order or, more usually, a parental order to acquire legal parenthood. Before granting such an order, the court must be satisfied of a number of strict conditions outlined in section 54 Human Fertilisation and Embryology Act 2008. This includes, but is not limited to, the surrogate's consent. The child's welfare is the paramount consideration. Surrogacy arrangements in England and Wales are lawful so long as the arrangement is not a commercial one and expenses received by the surrogate are considered reasonable.

Parental responsibility (PR) is set out in sections 2–4 **Children Act 1989** and refers to a range of legal duties, powers and responsibilities that a parent has in relation to a child. It must be exercised for the benefit of that child, rather than the benefit of the parent. PR provides the power to make decisions about the child's upbringing, such as which school they attend. PR is automatically provided to mothers and married couples. It may also be acquired, for example, by an unmarried father by being registered on the child's birth certificate, agreement with the mother, or through a court order. PR may be conferred to adults through a court order, including **Child Arrangement** or **special guardianship orders**.

Parenting Orders are specific orders and are to be distinguished from a parental binding over order, for which see **Binding over**. The purpose of a Parenting Order is to underline parental accountability for the actions of children. Their declared aim is to help parents stop their children committing further offences, or to ensure that they attend school, or that they cease engaging in anti-social behaviour. While the rhetoric around them emphasises the benign supportive aspect, including providing 'appropriate' packages of help and guidance, it needs to be acknowledged that Parenting Orders reflect a particular ideological view of parental responsibility and accountability (Evans, 2012; Peters, 2012a, 2012b).

Parenting Orders were first introduced in the Crime and Disorder Act 1998 (section 8). They can apply when a young person is convicted of an offence, made subject to an injunction under the Anti-Social Behaviour, Crime and Policing Act 2014, a **Child Safety Order** or a Sex Offender Order. They can also apply when the parent is convicted of an offence under the Education Act 1996, specifically section 443 (failure to comply with a School Attendance Order) or section 444 (failure to secure regular attendance at school of registered pupil). The Anti-Social Behaviour Act 2003 (Part 3) allows Parenting Orders to be made where children are excluded from school, and the Education and Inspections Act 2006 (section 98) allows schools to apply directly to the courts for a Parenting Order because of a child's serious misbehaviour in school. Parenting Orders must also be made where a young person under 16 is subject to an injunction under section 1 of the Anti-social Behaviour, Crime and Policing Act 2014.

Parenting Orders last for a maximum of 12 months. They oblige parents to undergo parental education, counselling or guidance, usually in the form of parenting classes provided by a local agency. The parent or guardian can be required to attend sessions no more than once a week for up to six months. The Parenting Order can also include specific requirements, such as ensuring the young person attends school regularly, or is at home by a certain time each evening. This element can last up to 12 months.

Parenting Orders should be distinguished from parenting contracts which are voluntary agreements between parents, the Youth Offending Team, and the young person. While Parenting Orders do not count as convictions against the parents, failing to comply with them is a criminal offence for which the parent could be fined or given a Community Sentence.

Parliamentary and Health Service Ombudsman See **Complaints procedures**.

Pathway plans fit into the pattern of support for young people moving from care through to adulthood (see **Transition to adulthood** especially for terminology used). Should cover support, health needs, further education, employment plans, accommodation and family relationships, but must be kept quite distinct from the regular local authority review (*R (A) v London Borough of Lambeth* [2010]). Section 3 Children and Social Work Act 2017 provides additional rights for young adults who are 'former relevant children' up to the age of 25, who now have the entitlement to a personal adviser and a pathway plan prepared following an assessment. This assessment must include a determination of whether any local authority services may assist in meeting need and what kind of support and advice is required. This must be offered at least once every 12 months.

Penalties, youth offending For a general explanation of how these work in relation to young offenders see **Youth justice**. For more specific information on court penalties, see **Detention and Training Orders**; **Referral Orders**; **Youth Rehabilitation Orders**.

Personal adviser is a person appointed as part of a package of support for young people moving from care through to independence as adults. See entries on **Transition to adulthood** and **Pathway plans**. Personal advisers often work alongside social workers when young people are between 16 and 18, and then continue providing support once the social worker's role ends at age 18. The personal adviser works with the young person up to age 21, and then up to age 25 if:

- the young adult continues in full-time education; or if
- they have exercised their right to additional support and advice under section 3 **Children and Social Work Act 2017**.

Personal budget is the term used primarily in relation to **Care Act 2014** to

refer to the amount of money a local authority allocates to support a specific individual. After devising a care plan for someone who needs social services help and support, the local authority decides how much that support will cost and declares that sum of money – this is the personal budget. The adult can then decide how the money should be spent, thereby exercising greater control over the choice of services. The relevant law is section 26 Care Act 2014. Once the personal budget has been agreed, the person then has the right to receive that sum as a direct payment.

The term is also used in the **Children and Families Act 2014** in which section 49 sets out provisions for personal budgets and direct payments relating to Education, Health and Care Plans. This stipulates that when a local authority maintains an Education, Health and Care Plan, it must prepare a personal budget on request, which then identifies a sum of money available to secure services needed. For further discussion see entry on **Direct payments**.

Police and Criminal Evidence Act 1984 is significant for

social workers for two reasons: it contains police powers to deal with 'life and limb' situations, and it regulates how police deal with young people and vulnerable adults when they question them, either as suspects or witnesses to a crime.

Generally, the Act balances the powers of the police and the rights of the individual. It covers a wide range of police powers: stop and search (Part I of the Act), powers to enter and search (Part II), powers of arrest (Part III), detention powers (Part IV), questioning (Part V), evidence (Parts VII and VIII), and complaints (Part IX). Part VI of the Act makes observance of the associated Codes of Practice mandatory; there are currently eight such Codes but only Code C has particular relevance to social workers as it sets out the special arrangements concerning questioning young people and vulnerable adults. These centre on the need to have an **Appropriate Adult** present when police carry out certain procedures.

In section 17 (1)(e) of the Act there is a broad police power to enter and search premises for the purpose 'of saving life or limb or preventing serious damage to property'. This may be useful in cases where someone is found to be lying on the floor inside a locked house or flat and is potentially in need of medical treatment. Neither social workers nor health care professionals have the right to force entry into premises in these circumstances; indeed, no one does apart from the police. This is the only law in England and Wales that allows forcible entry for the purpose of safeguarding; what follows thereafter depends on the circumstances. Where someone is unconscious, they can be taken to hospital using **common law** or **Mental Capacity Act 2005** powers. If a mental health assessment is required, this can be initiated, if removal of the person is essential, by using **Mental Health Act 1983** powers by which a magistrate can issue a warrant for the removal to a place of safety (such as a hospital) of 'a person believed to be suffering from mental disorder' who is 'ill-treated, neglected or kept otherwise than under proper control' or is unable to care for themselves and living alone (section 135(1) Mental Health Act 1983).

Police protection order Section 46 Children Act 1989. See **Child safeguarding system**.

Power of attorney See **Lasting Power of Attorney**.

Powers, mandatory and permissive, are the two kinds of powers which an Act of Parliament may give to a local authority. So the law granting a power to do something will always make it clear whether the local authority 'must' (mandatory) or 'may' (permissive). Generally, Acts do not make the provision of specific services mandatory, since what services are provided in a given area will vary according to the needs of that area, and local authorities are best placed to determine that. However, it is often the case that provision of information about services is compulsory, as is the duty to assess whether someone has a need for services – for example, the duty to carry out a needs assessment (section 9 **Care Act 2014**).

It is important that local authorities have both kind of powers. If everything were compulsory, they would have virtually no flexibility, while if everything were permissive there might be a danger of crucial services becoming a postcode lottery. Permissive powers are critical since, without them, local authorities would not be able to do anything, this empowerment being essential as local authorities can act only when and where the law says they can. This contrasts with the position of individual people, who are legally free to do whatever they wish unless the law says that a particular action is proscribed, that is, forbidden by law. A local authority does not have this freedom to act independently. It can do absolutely nothing unless specifically authorised to do so by statute law. See also **Local authorities' legal status**.

Practice directions are issued by the President of the Family Division to the **Family Court**. Practice directions supplement the Family Procedure Rules 2010 which contain rules about how court cases should be conducted in the Family Court. Practice directions tell the courts how specific areas of legal procedure and practice should be conducted. One example is Practice Direction 12J Child Arrangements & Contact Orders: Domestic Abuse And Harm, which address the consideration the Family Court will need to make when being asked to make a **Child Arrangement Order** when there are concerns of domestic abuse.

Pre-sentence reports may be submitted to the **Youth Court** prior to a young person being sentenced once they have admitted or been convicted of an offence. The report is prepared by a member of the **Youth Offending Team** and contains information about the offence and the young person's involvement in it, focusing on their attitude to the offence, together with their family background and circumstances at the time the offence was committed. The report will usually include comments from the offender's school. If there are previous offences, these will be included, together with some commentary on them. Official guidance indicates that the report should also specifically include:

- an offence analysis, including aggravating or mitigating factors, premeditation, culpability, vulnerability to exploitation, impact on victim, acceptance of responsibility and wish to make amends;
- assessment of the child or young person;
- assessment of the need for parenting support including appropriateness of **Parenting Order**;
- assessment of risk to the community and others, including likelihood of reoffending;
- a conclusion.

The pre-sentence report is for the purpose of assisting the court with sentencing options, and also for indicating which of these options would be available; for example, there might not be an Attendance Centre scheme in the area where the young person lives. For certain types of sentences, such as **Youth Rehabilitation Orders**, the report needs to guide the court as to what kind of personalised package would be suitable. The report should also indicate what specifically the **Youth Offending Team** will offer in terms of frequency of supervision appointments. Finally, the report will offer a recommendation, although the court is obviously not obliged to go along with this.

The report will be seen by the young person, their parents, solicitor, the **Crown Prosecution Service**, the clerk of the court and the magistrates. It is not read out in court.

There is official guidance for practitioners on completion of the report (Youth Justice Board, 2019b).

Prevent, reduce and delay duty relates to measures to promote

adults' well-being under the **Care Act 2014**. Section 1(3)(c) of the Act says that local authorities must have regard to 'the importance of preventing or delaying the development of needs for care and support or needs for support and the importance of reducing needs of either kind that already exist'. This reflects the important person-centred, holistic approach and is further clarified in section 2 which says local authorities must 'provide or arrange for the provision of services, facilities or resources, or take other steps' that:

- will contribute towards preventing or delaying the development by adults in its area of needs for care and support;
- contribute towards preventing or delaying the development by carers in its area of needs for support;
- reduce the needs for care and support of adults in its area;
- reduce the needs for support of carers in its area.

To achieve this, local authorities must not only identify services and resources currently available but must also identify unmet needs. They should then presumably work towards developing services and resources to meet those needs; for example, by working with services providers in accordance with the general duty to promote integrated services (section 3) and to promote diversity and quality in provision of services (section 5).

Prevention, crime
Crime prevention is relevant to social work law as there is a statutory obligation on local authorities to prevent offending by children and young persons (section 37 Crime and Disorder Act 1998). The law does not stipulate how local authorities are to achieve this, this is left to them to decide, but they are to formulate a clear strategy for doing so insofar as they must produce annually a 'youth justice plan' (section 40 Crime and Disorder Act 1998). This plan must then be sent to the **Youth Justice Board** for wider dissemination and in order to qualify for funding, and to that end there is published guidance (Youth Justice Board, 2019c).

Privacy and confidentiality
See **Confidentiality and privacy**.

Privacy and family life, right to
For relevance to social work of Article 8 of the Convention see **European Convention on Human Rights**.

Private fostering
arrangements are those where a child under 16, or 18 if they have a disability, is accommodated for 28 days or more by someone who is not the child's parent, does not have **parental responsibility** and is not a relative as defined by section 105 **Children Act 1989** – for example, a great uncle. This kind of fostering does not include children looked after by the local authority. The private foster carer or parent is required to notify the local authority about the arrangement if the arrangements are, or are intended to be, longer than 28 days (section 3 Children (Private Arrangements for Fostering) Regulations 2005). Section 66 Children Act 1989 now requires checks to ensure the welfare of the child is being safeguarded. This reflects the learning from the inquiry into the death of Victoria Climbié, after which local authorities' responsibilities to visit and assess the suitability of private foster arrangements were strengthened.

Private law orders
are made in private family law proceedings (i.e. not involving a local authority) that decide on disputes between individual parents or caregivers in respect of decisions about their child's upbringing – for example, a **Child Arrangement Order**. Other than the court making a decision about the parental dispute, or a local authority or **Cafcass** providing a report or information about the child's welfare, the state is not involved in the dispute or a part to the proceedings. These orders are within sections in Part II of the **Children Act 1989**.

Professional Capabilities Framework is a framework of social work education by which social workers can chart their professional development. The framework is hosted and occasionally refined by the **British Association of Social Workers (BASW)**. It has legal significance in that the framework can be used by social workers as a demonstration of their ability to engage in continuous professional development, which is a condition of renewal of their registration, and is a requirement laid down by **Social Work England**, enforced by its authority derived from the **Children and Social Work Act 2017**.

Professionalism See **Social worker accountability and registration**.

Prohibited steps order is a private law order made under section 8 **Children Act 1989**. It prevents someone taking a particular action in respect of a child for whom they hold parental responsibility. This may include, for example, changing the child's name or removing the child from the UK without consent or permission from the court. A prohibited steps order differs from a **Specific Issue Order** as it prevents, rather than permits, an action. A prohibited steps order should not be used if the same result could be achieved via a **Child Arrangement Order**, for example, if it relates to the person with whom a child should spend time.

Proof, burden of See **Burden of proof** and **Evidence in court**.

Proof, standard of See **Evidence in court**.

Proportionality is a key human rights concept. Public authorities have a great deal of power accorded them by law, including a wide range of discretionary powers. As a general principle, this power is to be exercised in the public interest and for the public good. In individual cases, it is important to have a balance between the need of the state to intervene in someone's life, and that individual's right to self-determination and right to act in a way which accords with their wishes and culture. This is most acute in decisions to compel people to be admitted to a psychiatric hospital and to receive treatment against their wishes under the **Mental Health Act 1983** (Parts 2, 3 and 4). Is the action proportionate to the need?

The principle of proportionality is at the heart of many social work-related cases that have gone to court, since it must be demonstrated that the actions taken by local authorities are 'proportionate', such as the legitimate need to safeguard a child or adult. Proportionality underpins many cases involving alleged breaches of the **European Convention on Human Rights** and the European Court itself often invokes the principle in determining whether cases violate the Convention.

Not surprisingly, there have been several cases where courts have debated whether local authority actions in removing children from parents were proportionate. In one case, members of the Supreme Court disagreed with each other and had to come to a majority verdict that removing a child from a mother from birth on the grounds of likelihood of significant harm (section 31 **Children Act 1989**) was proportionate (Re B (a child) [2013]).

A simple way of understanding proportionality is to remember the adage 'don't use a sledgehammer to crack a nut'.

Protection of property relates to local authority duties in situations

where someone moves into residential accommodation or hospital and there is a 'danger of loss or damage to movable property' and the adult is unable to deal with this or make suitable arrangements (section 47(1) **Care Act 2014**). The local authority 'must take reasonable steps to prevent or mitigate the loss or damage' and to that end may enter the relevant premises in order to deal with the property (section 47(2) and (3) Care Act 2014). Prior to carrying out these duties, the local authority must obtain the consent of the adult concerned or, if they do not have capacity to consent, the permission of the person authorised to act for them. If there is no such person, the local authority may act in the person's '**best interests**' (section 47(4) Care Act 2014). It is an offence to obstruct a local authority carrying out this duty, and the local authority may recover expenses incurred from the adult concerned (section 47(6) and (7) Care Act 2014).

In practice, this is not usually a social work task, but social workers do need to be aware of the local authority's responsibilities, often carried out by administrative or finance staff, and may have to take action in an emergency to ensure property is safe, for example, ensuring a house or flat is secure. This includes taking responsibility for pets left in the house.

Protection of title is a legal term to delineate a name that is reserved for

people who have a particular qualification or entitlement. In this case, the title 'social worker' is reserved for people who comply to the registration requirements made following the **Children and Social Work Act 2017** and enforced by **Social Work England**. Social work was first made a protected title by section 61 Care Standards Act 2000.

Public bodies are formally established organisations that are mainly financed by

public funds in order to deliver a public service. A local authority is clearly a public body, deriving most of its funds from council tax and direct grants from central government, which in turn raises its revenue from a variety of taxes. Local authorities are also financed by charges levied for their services. Some charges are entirely at the local authority's discretion but some, such as charges for adult support services under the **Care Act 2014**, are subject to limitations and requirements laid down in Regulations such as the Care and Support (Charging and Assessment of Resources) Regulations 2014. See also **Local authorities' legal status.**

Public Guardian is the name of the official whose Office is a government

body under the Ministry of Justice that oversees the work of Deputies appointed by the

Court of Protection, donees appointed under a **Lasting Power of Attorney**, and guardians (people appointed to manage the affairs of people who are missing, in prison abroad, or taken hostage). It is also the body that administers applications for Lasting Powers of Attorney and assists Deputies (people appointed by the Court of Protection to manage the affairs, or look after the welfare, of someone who has lost the capacity to do so). Further information may be readily obtained from the Office of the Public Guardian website.

Public law orders permit the state, acting through a local authority, to compulsorily intervene in a family's life because of concerns the child is, or is likely to, suffer significant harm. Public law orders are set out in part IV of the **Children Act 1989**. They include a care or supervision order.

If, during private law proceedings about a child, a court becomes concerned the child is, or is at risk of, suffering significant harm, they may use section 37 Children Act 1989 to direct a local authority to carry out an assessment and provide a report about whether the local authority believe care proceedings should be started in respect of a child. However, the final decisions on whether care proceedings are implemented rests with the local authority.

Public Law Outline See Care proceedings.

Quality assurance, service standards are overseen by various bodies. The **Care Quality Commission** (in Wales, the Care Inspectorate Wales) is responsible for oversight of the quality of residential and at-home care services for adults. As well as investigating complaints, the Commission carries out regular routine inspection of homes and agencies. A similar function for children's services is provided by **Ofsted**, the Office for Standards in Education, Children's Services and Skills (in Wales, the Social Services Inspectorate Wales), who additionally oversee the quality of local authority children's services and the work of **Cafcass** (Children and Family Courts Advisory Service) or Cafcass Cymru.

The legislation that relates to quality of adult care comprises the Health and Social Care Act 2008, the Health and Social Care (Safety and Quality) Act 2015, and their associated Regulations. These are very wide-ranging and quite detailed. For children and families, the **Children Acts 1989 and 2004**, **Children and Families Act 2014**, and **Children and Social Work Act 2017** are key, supplemented by Regulations and detailed guidance most especially that associated with the **Children Act 1989** (Department for Education, 2014c, 2015a, 2015b, 2015c, 2015d).

The body responsible for the quality of professional practice of social workers is Social Work England (in Wales, Social Care Wales). Their role is covered in the **Social worker accountability and registration** and **Social Work England** entries.

See also **Rights of redress**.

R

Referral Orders are compulsory in nearly all cases of first-time offenders who pleaded guilty at the **Youth Court** (section 16 Powers of Criminal Courts (Sentencing) Act 2000). There is no restriction on making further Referral Orders for subsequent offences, if the court considers this appropriate, but this is unusual. A **Parenting Order** may be made by the court to run alongside the Referral Order where appropriate (schedule 34 Criminal Justice Act 2003 as amended). Also, a **Compensation Order** can be made in addition, as can **restraining orders**, **Sexual Harm Prevention Orders** and **Sexual Offences Prevention Orders** (paragraph 3.28, Ministry of Justice and Youth Justice Board, 2018).

The aim of the Referral Order is to divert the offender from the court to a **Youth Offender Panel** who decides what activities the young person is to undertake in order to repair the damage done by their offence, learn to lead a safe and crime-free life, and make a positive contribution to society. The order lasts not less than 3 months and no more than 12. If the young person fails to co-operate the matter can be referred back to the **Youth Court** who may revoke the order and sentence the young person for the original offence.

Refugees and people seeking asylum

Refugees and people seeking asylum have different status under law. An asylum seeker is someone who has fled their country to seek protection from persecution and is waiting for a decision about their claim for asylum. In contrast, a refugee is someone whose asylum claim has been successful. The UK signed the Geneva Convention in 1951 which allows individuals fleeing from persecution to seek asylum in a safe country. The main principles of the convention are reflected in a large body of intersecting legislation and evolving policy (Henry, 2020). The Immigration and Asylum Act 1999 and the Nationality Immigration and Asylum Act 2002 provide key legal frameworks for both the asylum process and access to support. These should be read alongside updated guidance on the Government's website.

Process

People seeking asylum are required to make an application as soon as they enter the UK or shortly thereafter. Delaying the application may leave the claimant without any support and can also compromise their claim later on. Applicants will undergo an initial screening interview, followed sometime later by a substantive interview. Evidence will be gathered on the applicant's circumstances, which includes the country they came from and countries travelled through. If there are concerns about trafficking they will be referred to the National Referral Scheme which seeks to identify and protect victims of trafficking.

While awaiting a decision a person will be required to report to the Home Office. Sometimes applicants will be held in immigration removal centres pending a decision.

If an applicant's claim is refused, they may appeal and/or make a claim that their human rights would be breached if they were returned to their home country. If the appeal fails, remaining without leave is illegal and individuals and families may be liable to detention and removal.

Support

If the applicant is, or would become destitute without support, section 95 Immigration and Asylum Act 1999 provides for applicants to obtain minimal subsistence and accommodation while waiting for a decision on their claim. This may not be available to applicants who make their claim late. Support is generally organised through UK Visas and Immigration, which is part of the Home Office. There is no choice about accommodation, and people tend to be sent outside London, possibly to accommodation centres set up by the Nationality Immigration and Asylum Act 2002.

If the claim is refused and appeal rights are exhausted, section 55 Nationality Immigration and Asylum Act 2002 and sections 4, 95 or 98 of the Immigration and Asylum Act 1999 may permit support for a short period while the applicant prepares to leave the UK.

Schedule 3 and section 55(5)(a) Nationality Immigration and Asylum Act 2002 enable the Secretary of State to use discretion to provide for people, if a failure to do so would breach a person's rights under the European Convention on Human Rights.

An applicant may present to adult social care for support and if they appear to have care and support needs, the **Care Act 2014** permits an assessment, but support will not necessarily be provided. Section 21 Care Act 2014 may prevent the local authority from meeting the needs of asylum seekers who are subject to immigration control, even if they are considered destitute. Applicants would need to establish they have care and support needs arising over and above destitution, for example because of a disability. However, local authorities may undertake a human rights assessment to consider whether refusal of support or assistance under the Care Act 2014 would breach their human rights. If an applicant has a child with needs, support may be provided under section 17 **Children Act 1989**.

Registration of a children's care provider comes under
the Care Standards Act 2000 that requires certain establishments and agencies to be registered with the regulator, currently the Office for Standards in Education, Children's Services and Skills (**Ofsted**). These organisations are:

- residential children's homes of all kinds, residential family centres and residential holiday schemes for children with special needs;
- adoption support agencies, independent fostering agencies and voluntary adoption agencies.

The purpose of registration is primarily to ensure fitness of managers to provide services to children. The Act allows the regulator to lay down conditions attached to the registration. Exempt from registration are local authority adoption and fostering services, private fostering arrangements, secure training centres, and boarding or residential special schools unless they need to qualify as children's homes.

Registration, professional social worker, means that once someone is qualified as a social worker, and wishes to work as such, they must register with the appropriate body, which in England is **Social Work England**. Social Work England determines who is entitled to be registered, how often registration is to be renewed and under what conditions, such as providing evidence of continuous professional development, and how someone can be suspended from and restored to the register, or ultimately removed from the register (section 39 **Children and Social Work Act 2017**).

For certain other tasks, there are additional registration requirements. For example, if a social worker is to become an **Approved Mental Health Professional**, they must comply with the approval process established by Social Work England and their employer. Likewise, a similar process applies to approval as an **Approved Mental Capacity Professional** in accordance with the Mental Capacity (Amendment) Act 2019.

Registration of social care homes is compulsory. In England they must be registered with the **Care Quality Commission** in accordance with the Care Standards Act 2000 and associated Regulations. The Care Quality Commission is a non-departmental public body, part funded by registration fees, created by the Health and Social Care Act 2008. Its job is to inspect homes in all sectors (public, private and voluntary), to enforce minimum national standards and investigate specific complaints as and when these arise. Reports on routine inspections of individual establishments by the Care Quality Commission are openly accessible online.

In Wales, the functions of the Care Quality Commission are performed by the Care Inspectorate Wales, which has a wider remit than the Care Quality Commission under the Regulation and Inspection of Social Care (Wales) Act 2016.

Regulations and Rules are simply instructions that connect to specific Acts of Parliament. They put flesh on the bone in the sense that they amplify how the legal principles in the parent Act are to be implemented. As their legal authority derives from a specific Act, they must be observed in the same way as the Act is. Regulations are not lesser law; they are just as binding as the **Act of Parliament** itself. Some textbooks will therefore refer to Regulations as secondary legislation. The term Regulations and Rules are interchangeable and, as legal entities, are always capitalised when written.

The reason for having Regulations is so that, if necessary, the rules can be amended without having to go back and amend the principal Act, thus saving Parliamentary time. As some Regulations are regularly revised, it is important to check what the latest rules are.

In social work law, examples of Regulations and Rules are:

- Arrangements for Placement of Children by Voluntary Organisations and Others (England) Regulations 2011;
- Care and Support (Charging and Assessment of Resources) Regulations 2014;
- Care and Support (Choice of Accommodation) Regulations 2014;
- Care and Support (Eligibility Criteria) Regulations 2014;
- Care Planning, Placement and Case Review (England) Regulations 2010;
- Care Quality Commission (Registration) Regulations 2009;
- Children Act 1989 Guidance and Regulations
  - o   Volume 1: Court Orders
  - o   Volume 2: Care Planning, Placement and Case Review
  - o   Volume 3: Transition to Adulthood for Care Leavers
  - o   Volume 4: Fostering Services
  - o   Volume 5: Children's Homes Regulations, Including Quality Standards;
- Children (Secure Accommodation) Regulations 1991;
- Family Procedure Rules 2010;
- First-Tier Tribunal (Health, Education and Social Care Chamber) Rules 2008;
- Health and Social Care Act 2008 (Regulated Activities) Regulations 2014;
- Local Authority Social Services and National Health Service (England) Complaints Regulations 2009;
- Safeguarding Vulnerable Groups Act 2006 (Miscellaneous Provisions) Order 2012;
- Special Guardianship Regulations 2005.

Relinquished babies See Adoption.

Remands to care or custody occur when young people have been

denied **bail**; they would normally be remanded to local authority accommodation. The court decides which local authority is to take responsibility and that local authority must accept the child or young person (section 92 Legal Aid, Sentencing and Punishment of Offenders Act 2012). The court can forbid the child residing with a named individual and can impose various conditions including electronic monitoring (sections 93–95).

In certain circumstances covered by sections 98 and 99 Legal Aid, Sentencing and Punishment of Offenders Act 2012, young people can be remanded to **youth detention accommodation**. See that entry for more detailed information on this.

Regardless of whether the young person is remanded to local authority accommodation or youth detention accommodation, the cost of this accommodation must be met by the designated local authority, and the young person attains 'in care' status. This greater financial responsibility for youth detention accommodation encourages local authorities to promote bail packages or other alternatives, such as remands to foster care.

Being 'in care' means that the local authority must adopt a **care plan** to secure arrangements for the young person's support should they be convicted and receive a custodial sentence. In addition, they acquire responsibilities under the **Children Act 1989** to promote family and kinship support (kinship care) for the young person. It may well be that such young people and their families have had no previous direct links with social workers, but it is important that in such cases social workers do not lose sight of the more general Children Act 1989 obligations and liaise closely with **Youth Offending Team** members.

Reparation orders are youth justice non-custodial sentences which aim to
help the young offender understand the effects of crime and make amends. It comprises a programme which may not exceed 24 hours in total which must be completed within three months of making the order (section 74 Powers of Criminal Courts (Sentencing) Act 2000 as amended). Such programmes might include attending group sessions on the effects of crime, apologising to the victim in person or in writing, and carrying out unpaid practical work for them or the local community. Failure to attend or co-operate may mean the offender is returned to court where a fine or Attendance Centre Order could be imposed, or the order discharged and a different sentence imposed for the original offence.

Residence orders See Child Arrangement Orders.

Restraining orders are intended to prevent further harm occurring where
the defendant in a criminal case knows the person they have injured or whose property they have damaged; for example, where they live in the same house, or where the victim runs a local business, or has been targeted in some way. They may be made in cases where the offender is under 18 and restraining orders can run alongside **Referral Orders**. The relevant legislation is section 12 Domestic Violence, Crime and Victims Act 2004 and section 5 Protection from Harassment Act 1997.

These orders differ from injunctions under the Anti-social Behaviour, Crime and Policing Act 2014 in that they are used in domestic situations whereas anti-social behaviour injunctions relate to people in the community. Also, restraining orders are intended to protect named persons whereas injunctions are more general, and not person specific.

Unusually, restraining orders are not limited to cases where the offender is convicted, but can be made where they are acquitted. The rationale for this is that this may be necessary where there is clear evidence that the victim needs protection, but there is insufficient evidence to convict.

Right to fair trial For relevance to social work of Article 6 of the Convention see **European Convention on Human Rights**.

Right to liberty For relevance to social work of Article 5 of the Convention see **European Convention on Human Rights**.

Right to life For relevance to social work of Article 2 of the Convention see **European Convention on Human Rights**.

Right to religion (freedom of religion and belief) is protected by Article 9 of the **European Convention on Human Rights**. This includes the right to have non-religious beliefs, to change religion or beliefs, and not be compelled to have a particular religion. These are absolute rights, whereas the right to manifest beliefs is a qualified right. This means that the state can authorise restrictions where someone chooses to manifest their beliefs by, for example, wearing specific items of clothing. These restrictions would have to be on the grounds of public safety, for the 'protection of public order, health or morals, or for the protection of the rights and freedoms of others'.

The right to religion is relevant to social workers working with children in several respects:

* Section 1 **Children Act 1989** requires courts to consider the child's welfare to be the 'paramount' consideration and in that regard to consider 'background and any characteristics' which would clearly include religious beliefs and culture;
* The Children Act 1989 Statutory Guidance (Department for Education, 2015a, 2015c) refers in various places to the need to consider religion and culture in care planning, reviews and foster carer placements;
* The law requires the local authority to consider the wishes and feelings of any child in its care in decisions made about that child (section 22(4) Children Act 1989). So, should the wishes and feelings of a child be contrary to those with parental responsibility, then these must be duly considered. In making decisions concerning children, the local authority 'shall give due consideration' to the child's 'religious persuasion, racial origin and cultural and linguistic background' (section 22 (5) Children Act 1989).

Rights of redress under law enable individuals to undo wrongs they believe they have experienced by providing independent bodies to which they can appeal along with mechanisms for awarding compensation. For social work services, the first stage of seeking redress, beyond the organisation they think has acted wrongly, depends on which organisation they believe is at fault. So, for example, for complaints about private sector care providers the first line of approach might be the local authority or the **Care Quality Commission**. There is also potential to appeal to the **Local Government and Social**

Care Ombudsman service. In cases concerning children and families, there are a number of decisions that can be contested in the **Family Court**; for example, a dispute about parental visits to a child subject to a **care order**. If not covered by a specific legal procedure, there is the potential of asking the courts for **judicial review**. Ultimately, where there are significant legal issues that relate to the **European Convention on Human Rights**, it may be possible to appeal to the **European Court of Human Rights**.

Rights, child, or children's rights derive from two main direct sources that legislation and social work practice should reflect. The first is the **European Convention on Human Rights**, which applies to both adults and children. The convention became part of English law through the Human Rights Act 1998, which means a child could complain to an English court that their human rights have been compromised. For example, Article 3 of the European Convention on Human Rights sets out a right not to be subjected to inhumane treatment or torture. Leaving a child to suffer significant harm without intervention may be found to breach a child's rights, as happened in *Z and others v United Kingdom* [2001]. The **Children Act 1989** complies with Article 3 by providing a framework for safeguarding children.

The second source of rights for children is the United Nations Convention on the Rights of the Child (UNCRC), which the UK ratified in 1989. For further information on this see entry on **United Nations Convention on the Rights of the Child**. This has not been incorporated into English law, so a child could not complain to an English court that one of their convention rights has been interfered with. However, in ratifying the convention, the UK made assurances that legislation, policy and practice would comply with the convention. Every five years, the United Nations investigates and reports on a country's compliance with the Convention. The Children Act 1989, as amended, together with subsequent child-related legislation, has been designed to comply with the Convention. For example, Article 19 of the UNCRC, which provides for a child's right to be free from abuse and neglect, is reflected in section 17 and part IV of the Children Act 1989. Article 12, which provides a right to participate in decision-making, is reflected throughout the requirement in the Children Act 1989 to ascertain a child's views, wishes and feelings when making decisions and plans – examples include sections 1 (3), 22 and 17 Children Act 1989. Articles 28 and 29 of the UNCRC relate to the rights to education, which is reflected in the Education Act 2006 and in part 3 of the **Children and Families Act 2014**, in relation to providing Education, Health and Care Plans for disabled children. The **Children's Commissioner** for England provides regular reports on how England complies with the Convention.

Case law also reflects an increasing recognition of the child's rights to make their own decisions where they are mature enough to do so, for example, in the Gillick case discussed in the entry on **Capacity**.

Rights, human See **European Convention on Human Rights** and **Human Rights Act 1998**.

S

A **Safeguarding Adults Board** is required for every local authority (section 43 and Schedule 2 **Care Act 2014**). This may be operated jointly with other local authorities, which would be sensible if the result fitted better with NHS Trust and police boundaries. The Board is an inter-agency co-ordinating and oversight body, charged with ensuring that local bodies work together to provide an effective adult safeguarding service. Section 44 Care Act 2014 states that the Board must also conduct a review in serious cases where there are lessons to be learned as a result of death or serious abuse or neglect (see **Safeguarding Adults Reviews**).

Paragraphs 14.133–14.161 of the **Care and Support Statutory Guidance** (HM Government, 2020a) enumerate the functions and responsibilities of the Board. These can be summarised as:

* reviewing and monitoring policy and procedures for responding to abuse or neglect cases;
* sharing information about providers or individuals where there are concerns;
* conducting serious case reviews;
* reviewing and monitoring agreed standards;
* monitoring outcomes of strategy meetings and case conferences to ensure investigations are concluded and actions carried out;
* promoting training for staff, volunteers and carers;
* data collection on the incidence of abuse and outcomes of investigations;
* developing plans based on data;
* auditing and developing services for adults who have experienced abuse, and for perpetrators of abuse;
* developing strategies for reducing risk of abuse and neglect;
* reviewing strategic plans and producing an annual report.

Board membership comprises all agencies engaged in identifying and investigating abuse, supporting families where abuse has taken place or those who deal with perpetrators of abuse; for example, social services departments, NHS Trusts, police, prison and probation service, emergency services, advocacy services.

Section 45 Care Act 2014 makes it mandatory to supply information to the Board if that information is requested 'for the purpose of enabling or assisting the SAB to exercise its functions'.

Safeguarding Adults Reviews are conducted by the

Safeguarding Adults Board for the area and focus on cases which have given cause for concern. Specifically, section **44 Care Act 2014** states that a review must be held where there is concern about how agencies worked together where either an adult has died, or the adult experienced serious abuse or neglect. There is a requirement for agencies to co-operate with the review with a view to 'identifying the lessons to be learnt from the adult's case', and 'applying those lessons to future cases' (section 44(5) Care Act 2014). The **Care and Support Statutory Guidance** (HM Government, 2020a; paragraph 14.164) suggests reviews should be organised so as to identify what 'will promote effective learning and improvement action to prevent future deaths or serious harm occurring again' and they should also be used to explore examples of good practice.

More detail on the precise role of Safeguarding Adults Reviews will be found in paragraphs 14.162–14.179 of the Care and Support Statutory Guidance. From this, it is clear that the role of the Safeguarding Adults Board when conducting a Review is not to hold any individual or organisation to account, but rather it should explore what happened, areas of problematic practice, what should have been done differently, what can be generalised from this case to others, and what remedial action needs to be taken to prevent similar cases occurring.

Safeguarding Children Partnerships (Safeguarding Partners) replaced Local Safeguarding Children's Boards under the **Children and Social Work Act 2017**. These are senior professional teams from the local authority, the clinical commissioning group and police. They have equal and joint responsibilities for developing effective multi-agency working procedures in their area. They develop a strategy to ensure co-ordinated responses to children's needs and timely and integrated investigation of child protection concerns. The partners also review and report on the effectiveness of the local arrangements and report serious injuries or child deaths to a child safeguarding practice review.

Safeguarding, adult See Adult safeguarding.

Safeguarding, child See Child safeguarding system.

Secure accommodation is accommodation that restricts a child's

liberty. The provision is intended for children who have a history of absconding that includes a likelihood of suffering significant harm, or they are likely to injure themselves or others if they remain in other accommodation (section 25 **Children Act 1989**). A local authority may not keep a child they are accommodating or who is looked after by them in secure accommodation for more than 72 hours, without seeking a court order. The court will consider the criteria above and the child's welfare needs. A children's guardian must be appointed. The accommodation must conform to Regulation 10 of the Children (Secure Accommodation) Regulations 1991.

Note that this kind of secure accommodation is provided as a means of addressing children's needs, to protect them from themselves. It is not intended as punitive, nor as part of the judicial system, for which see **Youth detention accommodation**.

Seebohm Report 1968 is a seminal document for social work which

had major ramifications for social work and social work law, its recommendations being implemented by the Local Authority Social Services Act 1970.

The Committee on Local Authority and Allied Personal Social Services, as it was officially called, was appointed in 1965 in order 'to review the organisation and responsibilities of local authority personal social services in England and Wales, and to consider what changes are desirable to secure an effective family service'. At that time, social workers were employed in different local authority departments, split between children, adults and mental health, each of which was responsible to a different government department. When the Seebohm Report was published it recommended the amalgamation of a number of local authority functions to form a single social services department. This department included services provided by the former children's departments, welfare departments, home help or home carer service, mental health and health departments.

The ensuing Local Authority Social Services Act 1970 laid down in section 7(1) that the newly created departments were to 'act under the guidance of the Secretary of State' which meant that such guidance would become equivalent to a set of rules. This part of the Act is still in force and is regularly used by ministers to direct that local authorities act in a certain way by saying that the guidance is issued under section 7(1) of the Local Authority Social Services Act 1970. Such 'guidance' is therefore mandatory.

Serious case reviews are required by the Children Act 2004 when

a child dies or suffers serious neglect or abuse, in circumstances where safeguarding agencies knew or suspected abuse or neglect. The serious case reviews were designed to ensure that the families understand what happened, and the safeguarding services learn where they need to improve practice. The name and process of the reviews were amended by the **Children and Social Work Act 2017**. The reviews are now known as the Child Safeguarding Practice Reviews. They are either held by local safeguarding partners, or a national panel where incidents are considered to be particularly complex or of national importance. There is a repository held by the NSPCC of the outcomes of serious case reviews (NSPCC, 2021) and the Department for Education has a Child Safeguarding Practice Review Panel which is an independent panel commissioning reviews of serious child safeguarding cases (Department for Education, 2021).

Serious case reviews, adult See Safeguarding Adults Reviews.

Services for children and families are provided under Part III

of the **Children Act 1989**, which is designed to prevent the need for compulsory intervention by providing services to support children and their families. The engagement of families and children in service provision is voluntary.

Under section 17 of the Children Act 1989, local authorities have duties and powers to provide services to a broad range of children in need, including disabled children and young carers.

Local authorities can ask other agencies to support them in delivering and providing services under section 27 Children Act 1989. Day care services are also provided for in section 18.

Part one of Schedule 2 Children Act 1989 provides more details about local authority duties and powers, and the services that can be provided. The wording of many duties allows discretion about whether, and how, local authorities provide services. For example, local authorities shall take reasonable steps to:

- prevent children from suffering ill treatment or neglect through the provision of services under Part III;
- avoid children being in court proceedings;
- enable children to live with their family and promote contact if separated from them;
- provide family centres as appropriate for needs identified by the local authority;
- provide guidance counselling and activities;
- identify children in need and publish information about services available.

Some duties are worded more specifically than others. For example, local authorities shall maintain a register of disabled children and provide services to minimise the effects on the child of their disability. In section 17 ZA, inserted into the Children Act 1989 by the Children and Families Act 2014, a local authority must assess a young carer if they appear to need support and similarly, under section 17 ZD, for a parent carer.

There are specific duties to provide accommodation to children under section 20, and children who meet the criteria for secure accommodation orders under section 25. Specific duties to **looked-after children** are set out in in section 22.

Sexual abuse A child under 16 should never be regarded as being capable

of sufficiently comprehending or giving consent to a sexual act. Abuse may involve a range of actions including direct contact through inappropriate touching or making the child engage in touching and is not limited to penetration. It may involve indirect abuse where the child is made to share images of themselves or where the child is exposed to sexual images or acts. A child may be afraid to tell someone, and their behaviour may change. Allegations require a joint police and local authority investigation (Ministry of

Justice, 2011) and may form the category of abuse at a **child protection conference** (HM Government, 2018).

Sexual activity with a person under 18 is also deemed to be sexual abuse if the adult concerned is in a position of trust – a social worker, foster carer or teachers, for example (section 16 Sexual Offences Act 2003). Likewise, there are specific offences in relation to exploiting adults: for example, section 38 Sexual Offences Act 2003 makes it an offence to engage in sexual activity with a person with a 'mental disorder' which presumably includes a learning disability.

Sexual Harm Prevention Orders may be made by a criminal
court where someone is convicted of certain offences contrary to the Sexual Offences Act 2003. These are rape, sexual assault of a child, incest, murder, manslaughter, or kidnapping. They can also be made where the offender receives a caution, including a **youth caution**. Where the offender is under 18, courts should only consider Sexual Harm Prevention Orders in exceptional cases, and in practice they are only exceptionally used for young offenders.

Such orders can be quite wide-ranging since their aim is to protect the public from sexual harm, particularly children and vulnerable adults. They will mean that the offender's name is placed on the Sex Offenders' Register, and that a police record will be kept indefinitely. The orders last for a minimum of 5 years and have no maximum length (unless they include travel restrictions). Where they are made, they generally focus on restricting employment, travel or use of the internet.

Sexual Offences Prevention Orders were replaced in 2015
by **Sexual Harm Prevention Orders**, for which see separate entry.

Significant harm See Threshold criteria (care proceedings).

Social work education, alongside the methods by which people can
formally become social workers, has been regulated by legislation going back to the Care Standards Act 2000. Since the introduction of 'social worker' as a protected title, social work has been an all-graduate profession with a registration process for those higher education establishments wishing to offer social work degree courses. This has meant requiring approval for such courses as able to award the dual qualification of a degree combined with professional accreditation. The current legislation relating to this is section 43 **Children and Social Work Act 2017** with its associated Regulations. These nominate **Social Work England** as the body that accredits higher education providers that award social work degrees (different arrangements apply in Wales). Social Work England is not just the body to approve courses at basic qualifying level, it also has responsibility for approval of post-qualifying courses, such as for **Approved Mental Health Professionals** and **Approved Mental Capacity Professionals**.

Social Work England is the social work profession regulator. See **Social worker accountability and registration**.

Social worker accountability and registration is of
critical importance to people who use social work services. The principal safeguard is that 'social worker' is a protected title, which means that it is a criminal offence for someone to describe themselves as a social worker unless they are registered as such with the appropriate professional body. For England, that body is **Social Work England**; for Wales, it is Social Care Wales. Social Work England was created by Part 2 **Children and Social Work Act 2017** (Social Care Wales by the Regulation and Inspection of Social Care (Wales) Act 2016). Besides maintaining a national register of social workers, Social Work England enforces a code of conduct backed up by a disciplinary system, and also regulates professional training – basic qualifying courses, post-qualifying courses and advanced practice awards.

Until 2015, there was a College of Social Work responsible for assuring quality practice and high professional standards, which it did through promoting its **Professional Capabilities Framework** extending from basic qualifying to advanced practice levels. Responsibility for the Professional Capabilities Framework is now the responsibility of the **British Association of Social Workers**.

Social workers who are in employment therefore have two strands of accountability.

First, as employees they have a duty to their employer to carry out their allocated tasks and responsibilities in a competent manner. Any failure to do that may result in disciplinary action and ultimately dismissal from employment.

Second, as professionals they have an obligation to their professional body, with which they must be registered in order to work, to act in a way that is consistent with being ethical and trustworthy. To do this, they must comply with the Social Work England Professional Standards which Social Work England describe as 'the threshold standards necessary for safe and effective practice'. These standards set out what 'a social worker in England must know, understand and be able to do'. Breaches of the standards can be reported and are then investigated to determine the social worker's fitness to practise, since this could place members of the public at risk of harm or damage public confidence in social workers generally. Where there is evidence of potential unfitness to practise, there will be a hearing which ultimately could result in the social worker being disqualified from practice, which would also debar them from being employed as a social worker. The legal authority for these hearings, which can be challenged in some circumstances through the **judicial review** process, is section 44 and Schedule 3 Children and Social Work Act 2017.

Solicitors See **Courts and the court system**.

Special educational needs, sometimes referred to as special educational needs and disability, or SEND – a term used particularly in a school educational context – refers to acute difficulties socialising, intellectual disabilities related to reading, writing or understanding, and concentration difficulties, as well as the more obvious physical disabilities. The law concerning special educational needs, originally to be found in the Special Educational Needs and Disability Act 2001 (some of which is still in force), now derives primarily from the **Children and Families Act 2014** Part 3. Practitioners also need to be aware of the associated Regulations (especially the Special Educational Needs and Disability Regulations 2014 and Special Educational Needs (Personal Budgets) Regulations 2014) and Guidance (Department for Education and Department of Health, 2015; Special Educational Needs and Disability Regulations, 2014; Special Educational Needs (Personal Budgets) Regulations, 2014). The principal requirements in the Children and Families Act 2014 relate to:

- definition of special educational needs, including assessment processes;
- local authority and health service duties to provide support;
- Education, Health and Care Plans (see **Education, Health and Care Plans**);
- appeals and dispute resolution concerning assessment and service provision.

Section 77 Children and Families Act 2014 makes it mandatory to observe the relevant Code of Practice.

Special guardianship is an order made by the Family Court providing exclusive exercise of parental responsibility of a child to an adult over 18 who is not the child's parent. Introduced by section 115 Adoption and Children Act 2002 which added section 14(A) to the **Children Act 1989**, it enables a child to have permanency other than through an adoption order. For example, a child's relative may wish to care for the child without ending the child's legal relationship with their parents. Before making the order, a court must have a report from the relevant local authority that assesses the proposed arrangements. Local authority support may be available to special guardians, and there is statutory guidance (Department for Education, 2017b).

Specific Issue Orders are private law orders (section 8 **Children Act 1989**) that enforce requirements relating to a specific decision about an aspect of a child's upbringing, when those who hold **parental responsibility** cannot agree. For example, separated parents, who are unable to agree on a child's schooling or medical treatment. Specific Issue Orders can be applied for and made alongside other orders, such as a **Child Arrangement Order**, or on its own. The effect of the order generally ceases when the child reaches 16. This order does not apply to looked-after children.

Statute law is a primary source of legal rules that is contained in documents enacted by Parliament. What distinguishes statute law from common law is the fact that statute law is always written down and can be checked by consulting official sources. Statute law generally starts with passing a Bill through both Houses of Parliament, culminating in royal assent provided by the Crown and resulting in an Act of Parliament. Statute law both codifies government policy and implements it. The **Children Act 1989** and the **Mental Capacity Act 2005** are both examples of statute law. For more information see **Acts of Parliament**.

Statutory guidance directs practitioners' actions where an Act stipulates that practitioners must comply with that law's associated guidance. The guidance thus becomes 'statutory' in the sense that it effectively becomes a series of written down rules. The reason for delegating instructions to statutory guidance is that this enables the relevant government minister to vary the guidance from time to time without having to gain Parliamentary approval for what is in effect a change in the law. For example, in child safeguarding, *Working Together* (HM Government, 2018) is regularly revised and procedures can change significantly, as happened with the abolition of formal child protection registers.

Among the key examples of statutory guidance in social work law are:

- **Care Act 2014** Care and Support Statutory Guidance;
- Care of Unaccompanied Migrant Children and Child Victims of Modern Slavery: Statutory Guidance for Local Authorities;
- **Children Act 1989** Guidance and Regulations (5 volumes);
- Working Together to Safeguard Children: A Guide to Inter-Agency Working to Safeguard and Promote the Welfare of Children;
- Appropriate Adults: guide for youth justice professionals;
- Cautions Guidance for Police and Youth Offending Teams;
- Code of Practice for Youth Conditional Cautions;
- Referral Order Guidance;
- Standards for Children in the Youth Justice System.

Statutory instruments are the legal means by which law is put into practice. **Acts of Parliament** often grant government ministers the power to make more detailed orders, such as Regulations and Rules. They are often referred to as secondary, or subordinate, legislation. Their purpose varies, some being technical; for example, simply stating when particular sections of an Act come into force. Other statutory instruments are more wide ranging and can be used to implement the Act in certain ways, or to amend or update the primary Act. They can be quite detailed, thus avoiding the complications of making Acts of Parliament overly complex and enormously lengthy.

Statutory instruments must be laid before Parliament before they can be enacted but would not normally be debated, although the procedure does allow for the possibility of a challenge.

For a list of examples of statutory instruments relevant to social work see **Regulations and Rules**.

Substitute care See **Accommodation of children**.

Supervision orders are made under section 35 of the **Children Act 1989** obliging a local authority to advise, assist and befriend a child for up to one year. Schedule 3 Para 6 of the Children Act 1989 provides for an extension of the order for up to three years. An order may be accompanied by conditions that the child, for example, attends a particular place. The threshold for a supervision order is the same as that required for a care order but with a very different effect. It does not provide the local authority with parental responsibility, and the child remains living at home.

An education supervision order, for which the grounds are primarily non-attendance at school, can be made under section 36 Children Act 1989. This will also be for up to 12 months, extendable for up to three years.

Supreme Court See **Courts and the court system**.

T

Tariffs, youth offending For a general overview of the way the youth justice system sets out tariffs for young offenders, see **Youth justice**.

Threshold criteria (care proceedings) have to be met before

the state, acting through the local authority or court, may make an order for compulsory intervention in a child's life. Significant harm must be proved before any kind of order can be made in care proceedings. A reading of the relevant sections of the **Children Act 1989** will reveal different levels of threshold; for example, for an interim care order under section 38 there needs to be 'reasonable belief' that the threshold is crossed, whereas for a full care order or supervision order section 31(2) says the court must be 'satisfied' that the threshold has been crossed.

The threshold is that the child must be suffering, or is likely to suffer, significant harm, and that the harm or likelihood of harm must be attributable to either:

1   the care given to the child, or likely to be given to the child if the order was not made, not being what it would be reasonable to expect a parent to give;
2   or the child being beyond parental control.

Harm

Sections 31(9) and (10) Children Act 1989 includes ill-treatment of a child or harm to a child's development or health. Neglect, physical, emotional or sexual abuse would be included. The Adoption and Children Act 2002 (section 120) expanded the definition to include harm caused by seeing or hearing the ill-treatment of another; this would include domestic abuse. When considering the impairment to health or development, consideration is given to that expected of a similar child. For example, not feeding a child or keeping them from school so that their physical and educational development is behind what could be expected of a similar child, might amount to significant harm.

Significant

The link between harm and significant harm is not defined by the legislation. **Case law** reminds us that 'significant' should be given its ordinary meaning, for example, considerable, noteworthy or important. Significant is a question of fact not law. Many children suffer harm, and parents make mistakes, but for harm to be 'significant', it must be more than commonplace parental failure or inadequacy (*Re L (Care: Threshold Criteria)* [2007]).

Attributable to the care being provided by the parent

There must be a link between the significant harm and the care provided by the parents. The standard of care expected is an objective one; that is, parenting that could be reasonably expected of a hypothetical reasonable parent, not the particular parent in the case. Regrettably, there will be parents who are doing their best, but the child is still being harmed by their parenting.

Is suffering

While the word suggests the present tense, case law has interpreted 'is suffering' to be the time when the local authority took protective measures, for example, the circumstances that existed prior to and precipitated the application for a care order.

Is likely

A child, for example, a new-born baby, may not as yet have experienced any harm, but there is a real possibility that without a **care order**, it will. The history of a family does not in itself predict the future, so there would need to be an assessment of risk based on facts, not suspicion. Patterns of parenting, relationships and things done and not done by the parents will be relevant to establishing the likelihood of significant harm.

Beyond parental control

A child or young person may be beyond parental control and placing themselves at risk through no fault of the parents. This may include staying away from home or taking drugs. If the harm is significant, then notwithstanding the parents doing their best, the child may still be subject to **care proceedings** because this threshold will be crossed. Contextual safeguarding factors may be relevant here.

Transition to adulthood, moving on from adolescence to full adulthood, is a challenge for all young people, but particularly for young people who have been **looked after** by a local authority. It is also a challenge to young people with special educational needs.

Research suggests that young people who had been looked after by local authorities were especially vulnerable to homelessness and generally emerged from local authority accommodation with far fewer educational qualifications and employment prospects than the general population (Cocker and Allain, 2019, Chapter 10). Unbelievably, for many years it was standard practice to expect looked-after young people to leave foster care or residential care placements on their eighteenth birthdays totally unsupported, with no rights to request help or support. This changed with the implementation of the Children (Leaving Care) Act 2000 which gave local authorities additional duties and responsibilities. These were inserted into the **Children Act 1989** and can now be found in sections 23A–23E and 24A–24D of that Act.

These additional duties relate primarily to young people who, as 16- and 17-year-olds, were looked after by local authorities prior to those ages. In law these are designated 'eligible' children who, once they cease being looked after by the local authority, become 'relevant' children, and once they attain the age of 18, 'former relevant children'. The specific duties towards these young adults are to provide a personal adviser and to prepare a 'Pathway Plan' for them. Young people themselves must be involved in formulating this plan which must clearly identify their needs. Generally, Pathway Plans should cover level of support, health needs, further education, employment plans, accommodation and family relationships. The role of the personal adviser is to provide advice, participate in reviews, and liaise and co-ordinate services, providing a focal point for support to the young person.

Pathway Plans and the appointment of **personal advisers** were placed on a stronger legal footing by section 3 **Children and Social Work Act 2017** (see **Pathway plans**), while section 1 of that Act clarifies that in carrying out their responsibilities to a 'relevant' or 'former relevant child under the age of 25', the local authority must:

- act in the young person's best interests, and promoting physical and mental health and well-being;
- encourage care leavers to express their views, wishes and feelings, and take them into account;
- help those young people gain access to, and make the best use of, services provided by the local authority and its relevant partners;
- promote high aspirations in, and seek to secure the best outcomes for care leavers;
- ensure the safety of care leavers, and stability in their home lives, relationships and education or work;
- prepare them for adulthood and independent living.

Duties and responsibilities were extended to 'former relevant children' up to the age of 25 by section 2 Children and Social Work Act 2017 which mandates local authorities in England to publish a 'Local Offer for Care Leavers'. This Local Offer must contain information about services offered by the local authority for care leavers and should cover health and well-being, relationships, education and training, employment, accommodation and participation in society (section 2(2) Children and Social Work Act 2017). It is now accepted that this should include 'staying put' arrangements whereby young people remain with their foster carers following their eighteenth birthday. Section 98 **Children and Families Act 2014** added a requirement for local authorities to monitor and support such arrangements.

Where a young person between 16–21, or 16–25 if still in full-time education, was looked after by a local authority when they were 16 or 17 but for a total of less than 13 weeks (between ages 14–17) they are designated as a 'qualifying care leaver' and are entitled to advice and assistance from social workers including possible help with living expenses. However, they are not entitled to the same level of support as 'relevant' and 'former relevant' children.

In carrying out their duties towards 'relevant' children and 'former relevant' children, local authorities must 'have regard' to government guidance (section 1(4) Children and Social Work Act 2017).

Legislation addressing the needs of young people with special educational needs moving through to adulthood is to be found in section 37 Children and Families Act 2014. This created Education, Health and Care Plans which are birth-to-25 documents drawn up by local authority children's services to provide a co-ordinated approach to addressing needs of young people with special educational needs. Regulations give further guidance (Department for Education, 2015b, 2018a, 2018b, 2018c). This legislation is explored more fully under **Education, Health and Care Plans**.

Treatment, community orders See Community treatment orders.

Treatment, compulsory See Compulsory treatment.

Tribunals are less formal than courts being reserved for civil cases: tribunals do not convict people and do not pass sentences. There is legally very little difference between courts and tribunals, in the sense that tribunal decisions are as valid and binding as those made by courts. They are also specialist with panel members who decide cases appointed for their expertise. Being more accessible than courts means that tribunals expect most people to present their own cases, or be represented by someone who is not a lawyer; for example, a trade union official at an employment tribunal. There are dozens of different kinds of tribunals hearing a very wide range of cases, and they have their own processes and rules. Since the implementation of the Tribunals, Courts and Enforcement Act 2007, in some areas there has been a division between first-tier and upper-tier tribunals, the latter operating as an appeal mechanism. Beyond that level, tribunals connect to the court structure at the Appeal Court level, above which lies only the Supreme Court.

The tribunals of most relevance to social work practitioners are Mental Health Tribunals which regularly hear appeals against detention orders made under the Mental Health Act 1983, particularly longer-term orders where the consideration is whether someone can return to live in the community and, if so, under what arrangements. Here, the tribunal will rely on a report from a social worker, usually an **Approved Mental Health Professional**.

Social workers do not normally contribute to the functioning of any other tribunal, but do need to be aware of the role of the:

- Care Standards Tribunal, which hears appeals against the decisions by regulators to bar someone from a register to work with children or adults;
- Criminal Injuries Compensation Tribunal, which hears appeals against awards made or not made for **criminal injuries compensation**;
- Employment Tribunal, which deals mainly with allegations of unlawful or unfair treatment by employers;
- Immigration and Asylum Tribunal, which hears appeals against decisions by the Home Office concerning permission to stay in the UK;
- Rent Tribunal, which settles rent disputes, but only for certain categories of tenants;
- School Admissions Tribunal and School Exclusions Tribunal which hear appeals against decisions by local authorities and school governors;
- Special Educational Needs and Disability Tribunal, which hears appeals against local authority decisions on education, health and care assessments.

U

Ultra vires See **Local authorities, accountability**.

United Nations Convention on the Rights of Persons with Disabilities
was first agreed in 2006 and was ratified by the UK government in 2009, although it is not incorporated into law in the same way as the **European Convention on Human Rights** is through the Human Rights Act 1998. The Convention's purpose is 'to promote, protect and ensure the full and equal enjoyment of all human rights and fundamental freedoms by all persons with disabilities, and to promote respect for their inherent dignity' (United Nations, 2006). Its principles fully accord with social work ethics and include:

- respect for dignity, autonomy and the freedom to make choices;
- non-discrimination;
- full and effective participation and inclusion in society;
- respect for difference and acceptance;
- equality of opportunity;
- access rights;
- gender equality;
- respect for 'the evolving capacities of children with disabilities and respect for the right of children with disabilities to preserve their identities'.

Unaccompanied asylum-seeking children
are children who are claiming asylum in their own right, separated from both parents and not being cared for by an adult who has responsibility for them in law or custom.

The UK signed the Geneva Convention in 1951 that provides a right to adults and children to seek asylum in another country when there is well-founded fear of persecution. This relates to both children and adults. Under Article 22 **United Nations Convention on the Rights of the Child 1989**, states are expected to provide appropriate humanitarian protection. Social workers play an important role in assessment, treatment and support of unaccompanied asylum-seeking children.

Asylum process

The Home Office is required under section 55 Borders, Citizenship and Immigration Act 2009 to make arrangements to safeguard and promote the welfare of children while carrying out its immigration functions. The Department of Education and Home Office issued a joint safeguarding strategy for unaccompanied asylum-seeking children and refugee children in 2017 (Department for Education and Home Office, 2017).

Unaccompanied asylum-seeking children may present at ports such as Dover or Heathrow, or have entered through different routes and turned up at the Croydon asylum intake unit, or be identified as unaccompanied asylum-seeking children if they encounter the police. They will then need to make an application to claim asylum. In order to assess their claim and before making a decision, a Home Office assessment process must be completed, starting with an initial welfare interview, followed some weeks or months later by a more in-depth interview. The Home Office will conduct an initial interview with the child where they will take a statement, a photograph, and fingerprints from the child.

Unaccompanied asylum-seeking children must be provided with access to legal representation as soon as possible. Processes have been developed to ensure that unaccompanied asylum-seeking children receive access to support and information from the point the child seeks asylum – the Home Office must make a referral to the child advice project, which is part of the Refugee Council, who offer initial advice and support that is independent from The Home Office Border Agency or local authority. The duty social worker from the local authority where the child is will also be contacted.

Unaccompanied asylum-seeking children should not be detained save for exceptional reasons. While they await a Home Office decision, suitable care arrangements will need to be made. The Home Office will inform the local authority that covers the area in which the child was found or presented. That local authority will then become responsible for the child until the Home Office makes a decision about the claim for asylum.

In recognition of the large number of unaccompanied asylum-seeking children being held in ports by just a few local authorities, such as Kent, a National Transfer Scheme was established in 2016 to provide a mechanism whereby other local authorities with the capacity to help can, in certain circumstances, be asked to assume responsibility for unaccompanied asylum-seeking children. So, if a child is at the border in Dover, the local authority can use the National Transfer Scheme to see whether other local authorities are able to support and accommodate the child.

An unaccompanied asylum-seeking child will be a **child in need** under section 17 **Children Act 1989** and therefore may be provided with services under Schedule 2; these may include counselling, guidance and financial support. All those working with unaccompanied asylum-seeking children must be alert to the risks associated with trafficking and refer the child to a National Referral Mechanism which is a scheme for identifying potential victims of modern slavery to ensure they receive appropriate support.

The circumstances of unaccompanied asylum-seeking children come within the meaning of section 20 Children Act 1989 because the unaccompanied asylum-seeking child has no one who can accommodate them in the UK, or because they can be considered to be abandoned or lost. Therefore, the local authority could use this section to provide suitable accommodation depending on the child's age and circumstances. Once in accommodation, section 22 Children Act 1989 requires a local authority to safeguard and promote the welfare of children when it is planning for and delivering services to children. Services include education, health, emotional and behavioural development. The Care Planning And Placement Care Review (England) Regulations 2010 must be observed with unaccompanied asylum-seeking children in the same way as it is applied to other children looked after by a local authority.

Age assessments

Age will dictate the way the Home Office processes the asylum application and the type of support the local authority provides. It is not uncommon for there to be disputes about age. By the very nature of the circumstances that brought unaccompanied asylum-seeking children to the UK, they often arrive without documentary evidence of their age. The dispute may begin with the Home Office at the port of entry, and it is the local authority that is likely to conduct a full age assessment. **Case law** establishes that simply assessing age on physical appearance or demeanour is, in itself, insufficient because different cultures, backgrounds and experiences, shape how a child presents (*R (B) v Merton London Borough Council* [2003]). The Association of Directors of Children's Services has issued official Guidance (Association of and Directors of Children's Services, 2015). The guidance sets minimum standards to ensure a safe and fair process for children who are already likely to have experienced great difficulty. They should be ideally completed by two suitably experienced social workers who are alert to the difficult experiences and trauma unaccompanied asylum-seeking children may have experienced. The social workers will gather information to understand the history and events of the unaccompanied asylum-seeking children. An **Appropriate Adult** and interpreter should be made available through the process. The assessors must give clear reasons for their decision which may be subject to **judicial review**. If the unaccompanied asylum-seeking child is assessed to be over 18, they will be transferred to adult services. At the time of this book going to press, the government has proposed a National Age Assessment Board. Social work organisations are seeking assurances that the process will be a child-centric one.

Accompanied asylum-seeking children

Children who enter the UK in company of caregiving adults are not able to access section 17 child in need support unless the child has a disability. Section 122 Immigration and Asylum Act 1999 says local authorities may not provide family support even if they are destitute, as long as the family is receiving support under section 95 Immigration and Asylum Act 1999.

United Nations Convention on the Rights of the Child is an international Convention containing 54 articles of general rights relating to young people under 18, which the UK ratified in 1991 (United Nations, 1990). The rights range from freedom from abuse and neglect, having children's views heard and decisions made in their best interest, as well as having special protection when their own families are unable to look after them. The treaty is not part of English law, but courts interpret legislation in a way that reflects the Convention. The UK government has also introduced or amended legislation and policy to reflect the broad rights in the Convention. Examples include the **Children Act 2004** and the Adoption and Children Act 2002.

The Convention came into force in 1992, having been ratified by every member of the UN apart from the USA. Although the UK is a signatory, the Convention is not incorporated into law in the same way as the **European Convention on Human Rights**. For example, the Article 31 Convention right to leisure, play and recreation does not appear in UK law. Even so, it still acts as a benchmark and every Convention country is assessed at least once every five years on the extent to which they conform to the Convention.

The Articles cover a wide range of rights, some of which do connect directly to the law of England and Wales. For example, Article 3 of the Convention says the best interests of the child should be a primary consideration in formal decision-making and that is the starting point of the **Children Act 1989**. The Children Acts 1989 and 2004 both provide comprehensive ways of meeting the requirements of Article 19 to provide protection from abuse. The expectations of the Convention right to education (Article 28) are manifestly met by the UK education system. However, whether the UK system is entirely consistent with the Article 40 principle of an age-appropriate youth justice system is debatable. Some say that the minimum **age of criminal responsibility** in England and Wales, currently 10, is too low and should be raised to 12 as it is in Scotland (Commission on Justice in Wales, 2019).

Universal Declaration of Human Rights, agreed between all UN members in 1948, forms the bedrock of human rights. The Declaration itself consists of 30 Articles, asserting such basic rights as life, liberty, security, equality before the law, fair treatment, privacy, nationality, freedom of movement, marriage, ownership of property, freedom of thought, expression and association, peaceful demonstration, participation in elections, social security, work, leisure, education and basic standard of living. The UN Declaration asserts the inherent dignity and worth of every individual and underpins social work practice.

It is, however, a declaration, not law. For UK social workers, the **European Convention on Human Rights**, which is based on the UN Declaration, is of greater day-to-day significance, being integrated into all UK legislation.

Other basic instruments concerning human rights worth noting as they relate directly to social work principles are:

- International Convention on the Elimination of All Forms of Racial Discrimination (1965);
- Convention on the Elimination of All Forms of Discrimination Against Women (1979);
- Convention on the Rights of the Child (1989);
- International Convention on the Protection of the Rights of all Migrant Workers and Members of their Families (1990).

Unsound mind is included because it is the term used in the **European Convention on Human Rights** Article 5, and therefore underpins how the law authorising detention of vulnerable people is to be judged internationally. Article 5 of the Convention concerns the right to liberty and 'security of person'. Article 5(1)(e) has provisions for 'laws for detention of … persons of unsound mind' among others; in other words, it is permissible under the Convention for countries to have laws compelling people to enter hospital or a care home against their wishes. Exactly what those laws are, and how they operate, is for each country to decide, but the Convention offers an overriding framework. In England and Wales, the key Acts that need to conform to that framework are the **Mental Health Acts 1983 and 2007,** the **Mental Capacity Act 2005** and the Mental Capacity (Amendment) Act 2019.

The list of safeguards the **European Court of Human Rights** expects to exist in order to protect people's fundamental rights regarding compulsion was drawn up in a key legal case, *Winterwerp v The Netherlands* [1979]. In this case, the complainant was compelled to enter a psychiatric hospital by an agreement between a relative and a local mayor, neither of whom could claim any clinical competence in the diagnosis of mental disorder. There was also no avenue for appealing against their decision. So, the Court ruled these procedures inadequate and declared that in order for a health or well-being detention law to comply with the Convention:

- the determination that someone was of 'unsound mind' or 'mentally disordered' had to be made by a clinician with experience in diagnosis of mental disorders;
- the mental disorder had to be of a kind or degree that warranted compulsory confinement;
- reasons had to be stipulated as to why someone was to be detained; and
- there had to be rights to appeal against continued detention so that the validity of confinement was justified.

Hence Convention law does not declare what the phrase 'unsound mind' actually means, but rather sets out who decides, in what circumstances, and with what legal safeguards.

Mental health and mental capacity laws in England and Wales comply with this in that they require a declaration by a qualified medical practitioner that the person has a mental disorder, and also involve other professionals, usually social workers, in confirming the need for detention specifying the circumstances and reasons. They also comply by providing avenues of appeal or redress through **tribunals** or the **Court of Protection**.

V

Victims is a term still widely used in the legal system although it is not a term favoured in social work, implying a weakness that runs contrary to the core social work principle of empowerment, and interestingly the term is studiously avoided in the **Care Act 2014** sections 42–46 safeguarding provisions. However, there are a number of legal arrangements that affect 'victims' that social workers need to know about. These are:

- what happens where there is a prosecution and victims are involved in the legal process, including in some cases submitting to the court an overview of the impact it has had on them or challenging a decision not to prosecute;
- related to that, possible involvement in restorative justice;
- prevention of harassment and intimidation of witnesses;
- entitlement to compensation even if there has been no prosecution.

For further information on these, there are several guides issued by the Crown Prosecution Service and Ministry of Justice (Crown Prosecution Service, 2016; Ministry of Justice, 2015, 2020a, 2020c). The aspects of these that are most directly relevant to social work law are:

- the challenges posed to the judicial system where victims have limited ability to be effective witnesses in court, for example, children or vulnerable adults – see **Vulnerable witnesses**;
- procedures in place to protect and safeguard people who are the 'victims' of domestic violence – see **Domestic abuse**;
- safeguarding procedures generally – see **Adult safeguarding** and **Child safeguarding** entries.

Victoria Climbié case See **Laming Inquiry**.

Video links in court evidence See **Vulnerable witnesses**.

Vulnerable adults is a term that was widely used in legislation and guidance, and also features in some case law, but is now recognised as a disempowering, rather negative, term begging the question: vulnerable to what? It also implies that it is the 'vulnerable' adult who is the problem, not those who perpetuate abuse. The **Care Act 2014** eschews the term, referring instead to an adult who 'has needs for care and support, is experiencing, or is at risk of, abuse or neglect, and as a result of those needs is unable to protect himself or herself against the abuse or neglect or the risk of it' (section 42 Care Act 2014).

Defining vulnerability has, however, been of concern to the courts. The **Mental Capacity Act 2005** makes the Court of Protection responsible for safeguarding the health and well-being, including financial well-being, of those adults who have lost the capacity to protect themselves. However, courts may still have to use **inherent jurisdiction** in cases where an adult has capacity but nevertheless is vulnerable to abuse.

This was decided in *DL v A Local Authority and others* [2012] where the court intervened to protect a couple who had capacity from being coerced by their son through threats to give up their home in his favour (for summary see **Adult safeguarding**). The judges in the case declared that it was not easy to define vulnerability but that the courts did have the right to intervene in particular cases. However, judges did reiterate, in paragraph 76 of the judgment, people's right to be 'eccentric', 'unorthodox', 'obstinate' or 'irrational' yet 'there can be no power of public intervention simply because an adult proposes to make a decision, or to tolerate a state of affairs, which most would consider neither wise nor sensible'. Intervention needed to be justified as 'necessary' and 'proportionate'.

Vulnerable witnesses
refers to witnesses involved in police investigation and court proceedings who are deemed vulnerable due to being under 18, having communication difficulties, having mental health issues, a learning disability, or being the 'victims of sexual offences and the most serious crimes' or 'persistently targeted victims' (Crown Prosecution Service, 2020).

Special arrangements for police interviews of vulnerable witnesses are to be found in the Code of Practice linked to section 66 Police and Criminal Evidence Act 1984 as amended by the Serious Organised Crime and Police Act 2005 (Home Office, 2019). This directs that an 'Appropriate Adult' should be present while they are interviewed in order to assist and advocate, but not to give legal advice. See **Appropriate Adult** for more information.

There are a number of means through which vulnerable witnesses may be assisted through the court process. These include:

- giving evidence in court behind a screen or through a video link;
- having evidence recorded in advance and subsequently played in court;
- giving evidence in private;
- courts being less formal and more child friendly;
- using communication aids including voice synthesisers or symbol boards;
- using an intermediary who can help a witness understand questions and make their answers understood by the court.

There is further information on the Crown Prosecution Service website.

It is not envisaged that children should ever give evidence in care proceedings or other **Children Act 1989** related cases.

W

Wardship

Wardship is an aspect of inherent jurisdiction. When a child is made a ward of court, the custody of the child is vested in the court, but the day-to-day care of the child is given to an individual and no important steps can be taken in the child's life without the court's consent. Wardship may be used for a range of issues, including: preventing publicity about a child; preventing abduction; or, for example, complex matters relating to medical treatment. Wardship ends when a child turns 18 or the order is revoked, or a care order is made. Wardship should not be used where care proceedings are appropriate (Ministry of Justice, 2020b).

Welfare checklist

Welfare checklist is to be used when making decisions about a child's upbringing under the **Children Act 1989**. Courts must consider and weigh up certain matters that are deemed to be relevant in determining what is in a child's best interests. These are listed in section 1(3) (a) – (g) Children Act 1989:

- wishes and feelings;
- physical, educational and emotional needs;
- the effect on the child of changes in circumstances;
- their age, sex and background and other relevant characteristics;
- any harm suffered or at risk of suffering;
- parents' or relevant person's ability to meet the child's needs;
- the range of powers available to the court.

These are accepted to be critical aspects of a child's development and used as an aide memoir by professionals working with children.

Well-being

Well-being is a core concept in law relating to adults, indeed the Welsh equivalent of the **Care Act 2014** is actually entitled the Social Services and Well-being (Wales) Act 2014.

Section 1 Care Act 2014 begins by declaring that a local authority has a duty to promote an individual's well-being. Subsection 2 clarifies that well-being is to be interpreted as it relates to:

- personal dignity;
- physical and mental health;
- emotional well-being;
- protection from abuse and neglect;
- control by the individual over day-to-day life;

- participation in work, education, training or recreation;
- social and economic well-being;
- domestic, family and personal relationships;
- suitability of living accommodation;
- the individual's contribution to society.

Westlaw, together with Lawtel, provides a reference source for checking what the law currently says. See **Legal databases**.

Whistle-blowing See Confidentiality and privacy.

White papers are government proposals for future legislation. They most often take the form of a draft Bill which it is intended to introduce into Parliament. The purpose of publishing a white paper is so that people can see how it is proposed to convert government policy to legislation, thereby affording an opportunity for interested parties to comment and possibly influence the shape of the legislation that is about to be proposed. For example, in January 2021 the government published a white paper setting out its proposals to amend and update the Mental Health Acts 1983 and 2007 (Department of Health and Social Care, 2021).

Wishes and feelings of adults are referred to in several places in the **Care Act 2014**, its associated guidance (HM Government, 2020a) and in the **Mental Capacity Act 2005**.

Section 1(3) of the Care Act 2014 lists matters to which local authorities must 'have regard'. Many of these reflect core social work values, including:

- people should generally make their own decisions about what is best for them;
- an emphasis on prevention;
- anti-discrimination principles;
- maximising participation;
- attention to carers' needs;
- safeguarding duty;
- principles of autonomy.

Subsection 1(3)(b) Care Act 2014 refers specifically to 'the individual's views, wishes, feelings and beliefs'. The **Care and Support Statutory Guidance** (HM Government, 2020a) confirms that adults' wishes should be taken into account when undertaking a person-centred approach to assessment (paragraph 6.42), when creating and revising a care and support plan (section 10). Representing and articulating people's wishes and feelings is clearly relevant to the role of the advocate appointed under section 67 (see **Independent Care Act Advocates**).

The **Mental Capacity Act 2005** stipulates that in determining someone's '**best interests**' in accordance with section 4, the professional must consider that person's wishes, feelings, beliefs and values.

Wishes and feelings of children
Before judges in family proceedings make an order that affects the welfare of a child, for example in relation to an order under section 8 **Children Act 1989**, **Special Guardianship**, or an order in relation to part V of the Children Act 1989, the **welfare checklist** in section 1 (3) of the Children Act 1989 must be considered. Within that checklist is a requirement to consider the ascertainable wishes and feelings of the child (considered in the light of the child's age and understanding). There is not a definition in the legislation, so the words must be given their ordinary meaning.

With a slight variation in wording, Section 1(4)(a) **Adoption and Children Act 2002** also requires the court, and therefore a social worker preparing a report, to consider the child's ascertainable wishes and feelings regarding the decision about adoption, which will be subject to their age and understanding.

The child's wishes and feelings do not necessarily determine the decision, or which order will be made. The weight attached to a child's wishes and feelings will vary according to the particular child's level of maturity and their circumstances. The legislation does not specifically set an age at which a child's views have greater influence on the outcome of a decision made about them, but courts are likely to give greater weight to the views of a child who is older.

Case law recognises that sometimes, for a variety of reasons, there might be a difference between the child's expressed wishes and what the child feels. For example, a child, whose parents apply to the court for a Child Arrangement Order, may not wish to upset one of their parents by expressing a preference to spend more time with one parent over the other.

To understand what the child's wishes and feelings, it might be the court will ask for a report from a social worker or guardian. The report should detail how the child's wishes and feelings have been ascertained and considered in forming any recommendations made by the social worker in their report to the court.

Outside of court proceedings, when social workers are providing and planning for services for a **child in need** under section 17 Children Act 1989, they should also, if reasonably practicable and consistent with the child's welfare, ascertain the child's wishes and feelings regarding the provision of those services (section 53 Children Act 2004).

When plans are being made about services and accommodation for children who are looked after by the local authority, sections 20 and 22 of the Children Act 1989 require their wishes and feelings to be considered. The importance of this is underlined in section 1 of the **Children and Social Work Act 2017** which makes the consideration of children's wishes and feelings a corporate parenting principle.

Legislative provision to ensure children's wishes and feelings are considered reflects Article 12 of the **United Nations Convention on the Rights of the Child 1989** and learning from serious case reviews.

Withdrawal of services can only occur through due process. What

happens if a local authority assesses that an adult has needs which it agrees to meet or fund, and then subsequently reduces the extent to which it provides services to meet those needs? That is what happened in *R v Gloucestershire County Council, ex parte Barry* [1997] when someone appealed against a decision by a local authority to cut adult care services across the board without reference to his individual case. As his needs had not changed, how could the local authority reduce its services? The House of Lords, then the highest court of appeal, agreed, although this turned out to be a pyrrhic victory, for the courts also declared that it was feasible and legal for a local authority to reassess needs on the basis of its own new financial situation. So, it could, for example, assess Mr Barry according to new eligibility criteria and, as a result, amend its support for him. Nevertheless, the principle is clear: services cannot be withdrawn unless there is a reassessment of need, a principle that is restated in the **Care Act 2014** statutory guidance.

What if someone is in residential care and there is a plan to withdraw services by closing that home? Here the position is more complex as it depends on the status of the home, but some appeals alleging that closing a home breached Article 8 were allowed, since long-term care was effectively a substitute for family life. For a fuller discussion of this see **Closure of care homes**. If the home does close, the local authority has responsibilities to ensure that care is still provided under sections 48–56 Care Act 2014.

What rights of redress are there when services are withdrawn? Adults or their representatives could, of course, complain to the organisation concerned or, if the withdrawal has an impact on the ability to meet assessed needs, to the relevant local authority. Section 72 Care Act 2014 provides for appeals and complaints, obliging local authorities to comply with the Local Authority Social Services and NHS Complaints (England) Regulations 2009. In essence, these provide for a formal process of escalating complaints within the local authority. Specific complaints about reductions in quality of service provider care could also be made to the **Care Quality Commission**. Apart from **judicial review** as in the Barry case cited above, it is also possible to complain to the Local Government Ombudsman about the process, but not about the decision itself. So, for example, in September 2020, a complaint was upheld that Mr. F's care hours were reduced without taking into account a G.P. report on support after a hospital admission. As a consequence, the local authority apologised, paid compensation, and agreed to review the cases of all people with visual impairments to ensure that there is provision to meet eligible unmet needs (Local Government & Social Care Ombudsman, 10/09/2020).

Witnesses See **Evidence in court**.

Working Together to Safeguard Children provides vital

guidance on how key legislation, including the **Children Acts 1989 and 2004** and the **Children and Social Work Act 2017**, should be applied in practice to ensure that relevant individuals and organisations have clear processes for sharing information and integrating services to promote the welfare of children and safeguard them where necessary. It lays out certain processes to be followed when carrying out a range of assessments and statutory investigations. As the guidance is statutory, professionals and organisations must 'have regard' to it. Compliance is required because it is issued under section 7 Local Authority and Social Services Act 1970 which applies to local authorities, as well as sections 10 and 11 Children Act 2004 which apply to non-local authority organisations and people involved in the child safeguarding system. The latest version was published in 2018 (HM Government, 2018).

W

Y

Young person, definition of, matters in youth justice legislation which distinguishes between children and young persons: the law sometimes stipulates that certain orders can only be made in respect of young persons and not children. In youth justice, a child is aged 10–13, a young person 14–17 (section 107 Children and Young Persons Act 1933).

Elsewhere, the term young person is not generally used in legislation. So, for example, the **Children Act 1989** defines a child as 'a person under the age of eighteen' (section 105 Children Act 1989). In practice, this means that legally a 'child', so long as they were 16 or 17, could be married, or serving in the armed forces: in April 2020, there were 2,690 under-18s in the armed forces, comprising just over 1.8% of total personnel (HM Government, 2020b). The UK is the only country in Europe that allows under-18s to be recruited to the armed forces.

Youth cautions are applicable to under-18s. If a young person (under 18) admits to committing an offence, the police may decide to administer a caution of which there are two kinds: a youth caution and a youth conditional caution. The relevant law is the Legal Aid, Sentencing and Punishment of Offenders Act 2012.

A youth caution, previously known as a reprimand or warning, is simply a formal warning which is recorded. It is a way of avoiding court proceedings, but it is important to understand that it is entered on someone's record, so a caution should not be accepted without careful consideration of the repercussions. It is tempting for families to pressurise youngsters to agree on the grounds that it is an easy way out and stops the matter being taken any further, which it does but only up to a point. Cautions must be declared as criminal convictions. In 2019, the **Supreme Court** declared that insisting that adults have to declare to potential employers cautions or convictions received several years earlier, especially if that caution was received when under 18, was a breach Article 8 of the **European Convention on Human Rights** (R (on the application of P, G and W) (Respondents) v Secretary of State for the Home Department and another (Appellants) [2019]). The Supreme Court also pointed out that the entire point of a youth caution was that it was supposed to be a diversionary measure, allowing children to move on from their mistakes.

Under-17s must receive their youth caution in the presence of an **Appropriate Adult** (sections 136–8 Legal Aid, Sentencing and Punishment of Offenders Act 2012). There is no official limit to the number of youth cautions that can be given. A caution means automatic referral to the local **Youth Offending Team** who, in the case of a second youth caution, should normally offer a voluntary rehabilitation programme. Both the police and Youth Offending Teams are directed to observe the official guidance (Ministry of Justice, 2013a, 2013b).

Where a young person has previously been convicted of an offence, the police could administer a youth conditional caution. Its purpose is to stop criminal proceedings which would otherwise have taken place in order to test whether the young offender might respond to other interventions. It is intended to be more robust since it has implications for any hearing in court, for example, by being taken into consideration when courts may be considering conditional discharges (section 135 Legal Aid, Sentencing and Punishment of Offenders Act 2012).

Youth Courts are specialist Magistrates' Courts that hear criminal cases where the person accused is aged 10–17. Generally, the court comprises three magistrates who are lay people who have received specialist training, but in some areas, cases will be decided by a district judge who is a qualified experienced specialist lawyer.

If a young person is accused of committing an offence with someone aged 18 or over, the case will initially be held in the adult Magistrates' Court, to determine whether the alleged offenders are guilty or not, and then remitted to the Youth Court (section 24 Magistrates Court Act 1980). If a young person is accused of committing a serious offence, the hearing may take place in the Crown Court, but generally the majority of cases concerning under-18s are heard in the Youth Court.

Compared to courts hearing adult cases, there are some significant differences:

- The hearings are less formal, with magistrates seated at the same level as the accused, who will normally have parents seated next to them. The accused young person is addressed by their first name.
- The Youth Court expects pre-sentence reports on all offenders, not just in specific cases as happens in adult courts.
- There is an additional responsibility to take account of the welfare needs of the child (section 44 Children and Young Persons Act 1933). Youth Courts have to consider this as well as their broader sentencing purpose of punishment, reform and rehabilitation of offenders, protection of the public and offenders making reparation (section 9(1) Criminal Justice and Immigration Act 2008).
- The range of sentences available to the magistrates is quite different: see entries on **Youth justice** and **Criminal Justice And Immigration Act 2008**. For first offenders, the court must make a **Referral Order**.
- Members of the public are not allowed to observe. The press are allowed to attend, but press reports must not identify anyone involved without the court's permission. In addition, the law prohibits the publication of any report or picture which might help reveal the name, address or school of the young person concerned.

However, these restrictions may be lifted if the court considers it is in the public interest to do so. For example, they might do so where the court thinks publicity will help the young person desist from offending (section 49 Children and Young Persons Act 1933, as amended) or if the crime is particularly serious (*R v Aziz (Ayman)* [2019]). Furthermore, reporting restrictions are automatically lifted if the Youth Court is considering the breach of injunctions or **Criminal Behaviour Orders** (section 30 Anti-Social Behaviour, Crime and Policing Act 2014).

There are practice directions that set out the principles on which Youth Court cases are heard, together with guidance on sentencing principles in the Youth Court (Judicial College, 2017; Ministry of Justice, 2019; Sentencing Council for England and Wales, 2017). **Case law** has established that special consideration should be made even when the offender has become 18 by the time the case is heard (*R v CW* [2020]).

Youth detention accommodation is an umbrella term that applies to the following kinds of accommodation which are used both for remands and sentences passed by the Youth Court:

- a secure children's home;
- a secure training centre;
- a young offender institution.

Remands would normally be remands to care, for which see **Remands to care or custody**.

A court can only order a remand to youth detention accommodation where all the conditions in both sections 98 and 99 Legal Aid, Sentencing and Punishment of Offenders Act 2012 have been met. The section 98 conditions may be summarised as follows:

- the alleged offender is 12–17 years old;
- the offence of which they are accused is violent, sexual, terrorist or one that if committed by an adult is punishable with a term of imprisonment of 14 years or more;
- the court is of the opinion that, after considering all the options including remand in local authority (non-secure) accommodation, only remanding in youth detention accommodation would be adequate for the protection of the public from death or serious personal injury occasioned by further offences committed by the young person, or to prevent the commission of further imprisonable offences;
- legal representation requirements have been met.

The section 99 conditions in summary form are either:

- a recent history of absconding while subject to local authority accommodation or youth detention accommodation;

- the offence to which the remand proceedings relate is alleged to have been committed while the young person was remanded to local authority accommodation or youth detention accommodation; or
- the offence to which the remand proceedings relate, together with any other imprisonable offences of which they have been convicted, would amount to a recent history of committing offences while on bail or remanded to local authority accommodation or youth detention accommodation.

Where the young person is actually placed is a decision made by the Youth Custody Service Placement Team, a division of HM Prison and Probation Service, which also issues guidance for practitioners (HM Prison and Probation Service, 2017, 2020).

Youth justice is a term that, ironically, does not refer to justice *for* young people, but rather to the system for addressing illegal or anti-social behaviour carried out *by* young people. Youth justice legislation in effect refers to the criminal youth justice system – youth in this context meaning anyone under 18.

Since the nineteenth century, the law has acknowledged that young people should not be punished for illegal activity in the same way as adults. Hence the use of imprisonment for young people was gradually reduced, or rather refined as a separate system of detention, originating with the founding of the first borstal in Kent in 1902. Reformatories and industrial schools for less serious offenders or young people in need of care gave way to Approved Schools by virtue of the Children and Young Persons Act 1933. The Children and Young Persons Act 1969 in turn abolished these in favour of Community Homes run by local authorities, a system that fell into disuse in the 1980s and 1990s. The Criminal Justice Act 1982 replaced borstal training orders with youth custody orders, which sat alongside the shorter-term detention centre orders. The principal non-custodial sentence for most of the twentieth century was the probation order, although in the 1970s and 1980s local authority social services departments played a significant role in supervising and making other provision for young offenders. The current system derives principally from legislation passed in the late 1990s and 2000s (Goldson and Muncie, 2015).

Youth justice legislation currently covers the following areas:

Prevention of youth crime

Section 40 Crime and Disorder Act 1998 states that local authorities must work towards the reduction of crime and disorder, principally through its annual youth justice plan.

Who qualifies as a young person

The law is clear that on a person's eighteenth birthday they become an adult and may not be tried by **Youth Courts** or awarded any youth justice sentence. This applies even if the offence was committed before the person became 18. There is sometimes a distinction between a child, meaning aged 10–13, and a young person, aged 14–17 (**Children Act 1989** section 105, Children and Young Persons Act 1933 section 107).

No one under 10 can be prosecuted for an offence, although there are procedures for supervising a child under 10 who has committed an act that would have been deemed an offence had they been 10 or over: a **Child Safety Order** under section 11 Crime and Disorder Act 1998.

Anti-social behaviour other than specified criminal offences

This can be addressed through Acceptable Behaviour Contracts or, if more serious, anti-social behaviour injunctions or orders. For more detail see separate entries: **Acceptable Behaviour Contracts** and **Anti-social behaviour orders**.

Arrest for alleged criminal offence

When someone under 18 is arrested by the police, they should be interviewed in the presence of an **Appropriate Adult**. If the police are satisfied there is a case to answer, and the offence is admitted, they can be given a **youth caution** or a youth conditional caution. They may be reported for the offence, which means the case will be referred to the local **Youth Offending Team** and thence to the **Youth Court**, in the meantime either being given **bail** or being subject to a **remand to care or custody**.

First-time offenders

Offences may have resulted in a caution or some other action by the police or **Youth Offending Team**, but the next stage brings in a diversionary mechanism for keeping young offenders away from the **Youth Court** itself, even at this stage. This special provision for first-time offenders who would otherwise have gone to court takes the form of a **Referral Order**.

Youth Court

Subsequent offences will in almost all cases be referred to the **Youth Court**. Prior to the actual appearance in court, there will be a **pre-sentence report** prepared by the **Youth Offending Team**. Options open to the Youth Court range from:

- absolute discharge, rare, only used for very minor offences;
- a conditional discharge – no penalty unless the offence is committed again within a fixed period of time (up to three years) in which case the offender could be resentenced for the original offence as well as being punished for the new offence;
- a fine may be imposed on the parent or young person themselves;
- **compensation** for damage caused;
- a **reparation order** – doing something to pay back for the harm caused;
- a **Youth Rehabilitation Order**;

- electronic monitoring, if the legal criteria laid down in section 1 (4) Criminal Justice and Immigration Act 2008 are met;
- Intensive Supervision and Surveillance – a mix of education, training or employment, restorative justice, addressing offending behaviour, family support and interpersonal skills development;
- Intensive Fostering, requiring the offender to live with a local authority foster carer for up to 12 months.

The **Youth justice system** involves the police, **Appropriate Adults**, solicitors, the **Youth Offending Team**, the **Youth Court**, and the **Youth Justice Board**. The last is responsible for oversight of the operation of the youth justice system generally and is an important resource for information on the provisions of the youth justice system.

Special court procedures

By law, offenders under 18 must be dealt with separately from adults, the general principles of this separation deriving from the Children and Young Persons Act 1933. Section 44 of that Act stipulates that courts hearing cases concerning young people must pay attention to the welfare needs of the child. Section 49 restricts public reporting of court cases involving them. This reflects an ideological debate that underpins all youth justice legislation between the needs of justice (for the public who want to see offences punished) and the welfare of the young person who cannot be held accountable for their actions in quite the same way as applies to an adult. Swings in attitudes and policies have resulted in different approaches at different times. During the 1970s, courts were quite severely constrained as to what orders they could impose: binding over, supervision or local authority care. This resulted in offenders being 'sentenced' by reference to their welfare needs as determined by their family background, rather than by the severity of the offence committed. The current system reflects much more of the 'justice' approach with sentences being determined primarily by the nature of the offence (Case, 2018; Goldson and Muncie, 2015; Pickford and Dugmore, 2012; Staines, 2015).

Youth Justice Board is a public body responsible for overseeing the entire

youth justice system. Its members are appointed by the Ministry of Justice. It carries out its functions primarily through monitoring the operation of the system, more specifically it:

- advises the Ministry of Justice about how the system is operating with recommendations for improvements;
- offers guidance to practitioners;
- identifies and shares best practice;
- promotes the voice of young people involved in the youth justice processes;
- commissions relevant research;
- makes grants for certain projects and services;
- provides relevant information technology for youth justice services.

The overarching principle declared by the Youth Justice Board is to see a youth justice system that sees children as children first, and offenders second. The Youth Justice Board, which covers both England and Wales, has a well-resourced website which is part of the government's (gov.uk) online portal.

Youth Offender Panels are responsible for implementing **Referral Orders** by helping young first offenders who admit breaking the law to address their offending behaviour. The panel is drawn from the local community – two volunteers trained for their role who make the decisions, assisted by one **Youth Offending Team** member.

The panel is less formal than court. Its function is to discuss in depth with the offender and their family why they are in trouble and what steps can be taken to put right what they did wrong, with the aim of preventing further offences. In this process, social worker involvement is important in terms of assessment and putting into effect the panel's decision, but the professional role is strictly advisory. Any victim of the crime is expected to be involved, although obviously their participation is voluntary. Normally there are three panel meetings to institute the contract and then review it.

Youth Offending Teams are multi-disciplinary teams consisting of practitioners with qualifications that relate to criminal justice, education or social work. They are employed by local authorities and are independent of the police and courts. They are an integral part of the youth justice system, which is overseen by the **Youth Justice Board**.

Their main roles are to:

- investigate why young people have got into trouble;
- advise courts accordingly by submitting reports to them;
- assist young people who have been arrested;
- prevent crime, support young people and their families through the court process;
- implement community sentences made by the court;
- maintain contact with young people awarded custodial sentences.

Youth Offending Teams have a duty to co-operate with Children's Services in making arrangements to improve the well-being of children in the local authority's area (section 10(4) **Children Act 2004**). They are also legally obliged to have arrangements that reflect the importance of the need to safeguard and promote the welfare of children (section 11 Children Act 2004) and to that end must appoint a safeguarding lead person (HM Government, 2018: paragraph 49).

Youth Offending Teams often provide invaluable placements for students on professional qualifying social work courses.

Youth Rehabilitation Orders are the main non-custodial options for

courts when dealing with young offenders. They are sentences of the court and recorded as such, unlike **Referral Orders** and **youth cautions.** They last for a maximum of 3 years (extendable once for up to 6 months in certain circumstances) and can take many different forms. These are laid down in section 1 Criminal Justice and Immigration Act 2008, amplified in the Schedules attached to that Act. The list is as follows (all legal references under each requirement refer to Criminal Justice and Immigration Act 2008 Schedule 1 Part 2):

Activity Requirement

'Activity' is not defined or specified by law, although it is clear that it may include something residential. An activity requirement can be made for any number of days up to an aggregate of 90 (paragraph 6).

Supervision Requirement

This requirement compels the convicted offender to attend appointments with a responsible officer (usually a member of the **Youth Offending Team**) or their nominee (paragraph 9).

Unpaid Work Requirement

This can only apply to 16- to 17-year-olds and means exactly what it says – offenders are required to carry out specified work without payment. The minimum amount of work is 40 hours, the maximum 240, to be completed within a 12-month period (paragraph 10).

Programme Requirement

This is very similar to the Activity Requirement except that the programme is a designed set of activities. Again, what activities is not defined, except that the Regulations are clear that they may include residential activities (paragraph 11).

Attendance Centre Requirement

This means the offender must attend an **attendance centre** for the number of hours stipulated in the order, the maximum number depending on age: 12 hours for under-14s, between 12 and 24 for 14- to 15-year-olds, and 12–36 hours for those aged 16 or above (paragraph 12).

Prohibited Activity Requirement

The offender must refrain from participating in certain activities. Specifically included as a prohibited activity is carrying or possessing firearms (paragraph 13).

Curfew Requirement

A curfew can be imposed for up to 16 hours per day for up to 12 months (section 81 Legal Aid, Sentencing and Punishment of Offenders Act 2012). It can apply to different places and different times each day.

Exclusion Requirement

This requirement prohibits entry to a specified place, a prohibition that can last up to three months (paragraph 15).

Residence Requirement

For 16- to 17-year-olds only, this requirement can stipulate that the young person resides with a specific individual or at a specified place (paragraph 16).

Local Authority Residence Requirement

This requires the young person to reside in local authority accommodation and can prohibit residence with people specified in the order. It lasts for a maximum six months or until age 18, whichever is the sooner (paragraph 17).

Mental Health Treatment Requirement

This can only apply where recommended by medical practitioners. Can apply to in-patient or out-patient treatment, but would not be used if the young person qualified for compulsory admission and detention under the **Mental Health Act 1983** (paragraph 20).

Drug Treatment Requirement

Clearly this only applies where there is evidence of addiction, and again must be on the recommendation of medical practitioners and must also be with the offender's consent. Can include in-patient and out-patient treatment (paragraph 22).

Drug Testing Requirement

This is a requirement to submit to regular tests regarding drug use. The order must specify the numbers of tests and has to run alongside Drug Treatment Requirement (paragraph 23).

Intoxicating Substance Treatment Requirement

This may be applied where there is clear evidence of addiction or misuse of intoxicating substances, and also requires the offender's consent. Can include in-patient and out-patient treatment (paragraph 24).

Education Requirement

This requires the offender to comply with local authority approved arrangements for education. It terminates automatically on attainment of school leaving age (paragraph 25).

Electronic Monitoring

This applies where certain additional criteria laid down in section 1(4) Criminal Justice and Immigration Act 2008 apply. The requirement means that the offender, while under supervision, may also be required to submit to electronic monitoring which has to be under the supervision of a responsible officer (paragraph 26).

Intensive Supervision and Surveillance

Again, applies where certain additional criteria laid down in section 1(4) Criminal Justice and Immigration Act 2008 apply. This requirement is a mix of punishment and opportunities, incorporating education, training or employment, restorative justice, addressing offending behaviour, family support and interpersonal skills development (paragraph 3).

Intensive Fostering

This requirement cannot run alongside Intensive Supervision and Surveillance. It requires the young offender to reside with a local authority foster carer and lasts for a maximum of 12 months (paragraph 18).

Guidance

Clearly only some combinations of requirements make sense, and certain combinations are not allowed. Furthermore, if there is more than one offence, there are rules in place to ensure that overall maxima are not exceeded. There is further guidance on this issued by the **Youth Justice Board** (Youth Justice Board, 2019a).

References

A, B and C (Adoption: Notification of Fathers And Relatives) [2020] EWCA Civ 41.

Airedale NHS Trust v Bland [1993] AC 789.

Associated Picture Houses Ltd v Wednesbury Corporation [1948] 1 KB 223.

Association of and Directors of Children's Services (2015) *Age Assessment Guidance*. Association of Directors of Children's Services. Available at: https://adcs.org.uk/assets/documentation/Age_Assessment_Guidance_2015_Final.pdf.

Barber, P., Brown, R. and Martin, D. (2019) *Mental Health Law in England & Wales: A Guide for Mental Health Professionals* (4th edition). London: Sage.

Barnett, D. (2019) *The Straightforward Guide to Safeguarding Adults*. London: Jessica Kingsley.

BASW (England) (2021) *Domestic Abuse Practice Guidance for Children and Family Social Workers*. Birmingham: BASW. Available at: https://www.basw.co.uk/system/files/resources/181181_basw_england_domestic_abuse_guidance_v5.pdf.

BF (Eritrea) v Secretary of State for the Home Department [2021] UKSC 2019/0147.

Brammer, A. (2020) *Social Work Law*. London: Pearson.

Brammer, A. and Pritchard-Jones, L. (2019) *Safeguarding Adults*. Basingstoke: Red Globe Press.

Braye, S. and Preston-Shoot, M. (2019) *The Care Act 2014: Well-Being in Practice*. London: Sage.

Brown, R (2019) *The Approved Mental Health Professional's Guide to Mental Health Law* (5th edition). London: Sage.

Brown, R., Barber, P. and Martin, D. (2015) *The Mental Capacity Act 2005: A Guide for Practice* (3rd edition). Post-qualifying Social Work Practice series. London: Sage.

Butler-Sloss, E. (1988) *Report of the Inquiry into Child Abuse in Cleveland 1987*. London: The Stationery Office.

Bywaters, P., Bunting, L., Mason, M., et al. (2016) *The Relationship Between Poverty, Child Abuse and Neglect: An Evidence Review*. York: Joseph Rowntree Foundation.

Cardiff County Council v Ross and Davies [2011] COP 12063905.

Carr, H. and Goosey, D. (2021) *Law for Social Workers* (16th edition). Oxford: Oxford University Press.

Case, S. (2018) *Youth Justice: A Critical Introduction*. Abingdon: Routledge.

Catt v United Kingdom [2019] 43514/15.

Caxton, M. (2021) *Social Worker's Guide to Liberty Protection Safeguards* (ed. P. Feldon). St. Albans: Critical Publishing.

CC v KK and STCC [2012] EWHC 2136, (COP).

Cheshire West and Chester v P [2014] UKSC 19.

Chisnell, C. (2019) *Safeguarding in Social Work Practice: A Lifespan Approach*. Second edition. London: Sage.

Cocker, C. and Allain, L. (2019) *Social Work with Looked after Children* (3rd edition). Transforming Social Work Practice series. London: Sage/Learning Matters.

Commission on Justice in Wales (2019) *Justice in Wales for the People of Wales*. Cardiff: Commission on Justice in Wales.

Cooper, A. and White, E. (eds) (2017) *Safeguarding Adults under the Care Act 2014: Understanding Good Practice*. Knowledge for Practice series. London: Jessica Kingsley Publishers.

Cooper, P. (2014) *Court and Legal Skills*. Basingstoke: Palgrave Macmillan.

Courts & Tribunals Judiciary (2021) *Recommendations to achieve best practice in the child protection and family justice systems*. London: HM Government. Available at: https://www.judiciary.uk/wp-content/uploads/2021/03/March-2021-report-final_clickable.pdf

Coventry City Council v C [2012] EWHC 2190 (Fam).

Crown Prosecution Service (2016) *Victims' Right to Review Guidance*. Director of Public Prosecutions. Available at: www.cps.gov.uk/sites/default/files/documents/publications/vrr_guidance_2016.pdf.

Crown Prosecution Service (2020) *Vulnerable Witnesses*. HM Government. Available at: https://www.cps.gov.uk/publication/vulnerable-witnesses.

D (A Child) [2019] UKSC 42.

Davis, L. (2014) *The Social Worker's Guide to Children and Families Law*. Second edition. London: Jessica Kingsley Publishers.

Department for Constitutional Affairs (ed.) (2007) *Mental Capacity Act 2005: Code of Practice*. London: The Stationery Office.

Department for Education (2011) *Looked-after Children: Educational outcomes*. London: HM Government.

Department for Education (2013) Statutory Guidance on Adoption. London: Department for Education.

Department for Education (2014a) *Adoption: National Minimum Standards*. London: Department for Education.

Department for Education (2014b) *Schools Admissions Code*. London: Department for Education.

Department for Education (2014c) *Children Act 1989 Guidance and Regulations Volume 1: Court Orders*. London: Department for Education.

Department for Education (2015a) *Children Act 1989 Guidance and Regulations Volume 2: Care Planning, Placement and Case Review*. London: Department for Education.

Department for Education (2015b) *Children Act 1989 Guidance and Regulations Volume 3: Transition to Adulthood for Care Leavers*. London: Department for Education.

Department for Education (2015c) *Children Act 1989 Guidance and Regulations Volume 4: Fostering Services*. London: Department for Education.

Department for Education (2015d) *Children Act 1989 Guidance and Regulations Volume 5: Children's Homes Regulations, Including Quality Standards*. London: Department for Education.

Department for Education (2017a) Exclusion from Maintained Schools, Academies and Pupil Referral Units in England. London: Department for Education.

Department for Education (2017b) *Special Guardianship Guidance.* London: Department for Education. Available at: https://assets.publishing.service.gov.uk/government/uploads/system/uploads/attachment_data/file/656593/Special_guardianship_statutory_guidance.pdf.

Department for Education (2018a) *Applying Corporate Parenting Principles to Looked-after Children and Care Leavers: Statutory Guidance for Local Authorities.* London: Department for Education. Available at: https://assets.publishing.service.gov.uk/government/uploads/system/uploads/attachment_data/file/683698/Applying_corporate_parenting_principles_to_looked-after_children_and_care_leavers.pdf.

Department for Education (2018b) *Extending Personal Adviser Support to All Care Leavers to Age 25: Statutory Guidance for Local Authorities.* London: Department for Education. Available at: https://assets.publishing.service.gov.uk/government/uploads/system/uploads/attachment_data/file/683701/Extending_Personal_Adviser_support_to_all_care_leavers_to_age_25.pdf.

Department for Education (2018c) *Local Offer Guidance: Guidance for Local Authorities on the Local Offer for Care Leavers.* London: Department for Education. Available at: https://assets.publishing.service.gov.uk/government/uploads/system/uploads/attachment_data/file/683703/Local_offer_guidance_final.pdf.

Department for Education (2021) *Child Safeguarding Practice Review Panel.* London: Department for Education. Available at: www.gov.uk/government/organisations/child-safeguarding-practice-review-panel.

Department for Education and Department of Health (2015) *Special Educational Needs and Disability Code of Practice: 0 to 25 Years.* London: Department for Education and Department of Health.

Department for Education and Home Office (2017) *Safeguarding Strategy for Unaccompanied Asylum-Seeking and Refugee Children.* London: Department for Education and Home Office.

Department of Health (1991) *Child Abuse: A Study of Inquiry Reports 1981–1989.* London: HMSO.

Department of Health (2000) *Framework for the Assessment of Children in Need and Their Families.* Norwich: Her Majesty's Stationery Office.

Department of Health (2015) *Mental Health Act 1983 Code of Practice.* Norwich: Her Majesty's Stationery Office.

Department of Health and Social Care (2018) *National Framework for NHS Continuing Healthcare and NHS-Funded Nursing Care.* London: Department of Health and Social Care. Available at: www.gov.uk/government/publications/national-framework-for-nhs-continuing-healthcare-and-nhs-funded-nursing-care

Department of Health and Social Care (2021) *Reforming the Mental Health Act.* London: Department of Health and Social Care. Available at: https://assets.publishing.service.gov.uk/government/uploads/system/uploads/attachment_data/file/951741/mental-health-act-reform-print.pdf.

Dhinsa v Serco and Another [2011] ET/1315002/09

DL v A Local Authority and others [2012] EWCA Civ 253.

Equality and Human Rights Commission (2019) *Torture in the UK: Update Report Submission to the UN Committee Against Torture in Response to the UK List of Issues.* London: Equality and Human Rights Commission.

Evans, R. (2012) 'Parenting Orders: The parents attend yet the kids still offend', *Youth Justice*, 12(2): 118–133. DOI: 10.1177/1473225412447163.

Feldon, P. (2021) *The Social Worker's Guide to the Care Act 2014* (2nd edition). St. Albans: Critical Publishing.

G (A Child) [2013] EWCA Civ 965.

Gaskin v United Kingdom [1989] 10454/83.

Gillick v West Norfolk and Wisbech Area Health Authority [1986] AC 112.

Goldson, B. and Muncie, J. (eds) (2015) *Youth Crime & Justice* (2nd edition). London: Sage.

Golightley, M. and Goemans, R. (2017) *Social Work and Mental Health* (6th edition). London: Sage.

Heart of England Foundation Trust v JB [2014] EWHC 342 (COP).

Henry, D. (2020) *Young Refugees and Asylum Seekers: The Truth about Britain.* St Albans: Critical Publishing.

Herczegfalvy v Austria [1992] 15 EHRR 437.

HL v United Kingdom [2004] 40 EHRR 761.

HM Government (2018) *Working Together to Safeguard Children: A Guide to Inter-Agency Working to Safeguard and Promote the Welfare of Children.* London: HM Government. Available at: https://assets.publishing.service.gov.uk/government/uploads/system/uploads/attachment_data/file/779401/Working_Together_to_Safeguard-Children.pdf.

HM Government (2020a) *Care and Support Statutory Guidance.* London: HM Government. Available at: www.gov.uk/government/publications/care-act-statutory-guidance/care-and-support-statutory-guidance.

HM Government (2020b) *UK Armed Forces Biannual Diversity Statistics: 2020.* London: HM Government. Available at: www.gov.uk/government/statistics/uk-armed-forces-biannual-diversity-statistics-2020.

HM Prison and Probation Service (2017) The Youth Custody Service Placement Team. London: HM Government. Available at: https://assets.publishing.service.gov.uk/government/uploads/system/uploads/attachment_data/file/647093/Placement_Guidance_Sept_2017_YCS.pdf.

HM Prison and Probation Service (2020) *Guidance on Youth Custody Service Placement Team.* London: HM Government. Available at: www.gov.uk/guidance/placing-young-people-in-custody-guide-for-youth-justice-practitioners.

Holt, K. (2019) *Child Protection.* 2nd ed. Basingstoke: Palgrave Macmillan.

Home Office (2013) *Information for Local Areas on the Change to the Definition of Domestic Violence and Abuse.* London: HM Government. Available at: https://assets.publishing.service.gov.uk/government/uploads/system/uploads/attachment_data/file/142701/guide-on-definition-of-dv.pdf.

Home Office (2019) *Police and Criminal Evidence Act 1984: Code C: Revised Code of Practice for the Detention, Treatment and Questioning of Persons by Police Officers.* Norwich: The Stationery Office.

Hubbard, R. and Stone, K. (2018) *The Best Interests Assessor Practice Handbook.* Bristol: Policy Press. Available at: www.vlebooks.com/vleweb/product/openreader?id=none&isbn=9781447335580 (accessed 27 February 2021).

Humberside County Council v B [1993] 1 FLR 257.

Johns R. (2014) *Capacity and Autonomy.* Basingstoke: Palgrave.

Johns, R. (2020) *Using the Law in Social Work* (8th edition). London: Sage.

Jones, R.M. (2020) *Mental Health Act Manual.* London: Sweet & Maxwell.

Judicial College (2017) *Youth Court Bench Book.* HM Government. Available at: https://www.judiciary.uk/publications/youth-court-bench-book-and-pronouncement-cards/ (accessed 13 November 2019).

K v A Local Authority [2012] EWCA Civ 79.

Kannan v Newham LBC [2019] EWCA Civ 57.

Lammy, D. (2017) *The Lammy Review – An independent review into the treatment of, and outcomes for, Black, Asian and Minority Ethnic individuals in the Criminal Justice System.* London: HM Government. Available at: https://assets.publishing.service.gov.uk/government/uploads/system/uploads/attachment_data/file/643001/lammy-review-final-report.pdf.

Lancashire County Council v M (COVID-19 Adjournment Application) [2020] EWFC 43.

Local Government & Social Care Ombudsman (10/09/2020) 'Investigation into a complaint against Westminster City Council (reference number: 19 007 605)'. Local Government & Social Care Ombudsman. Available at: 'www.lgo.org.uk/decisions/adult-care-services/assessment-and-care-plan/19-007-605.

Local Government Association (2018) *Ordinary Residence Guide: Determining Local Authority Responsibilities under the Care Act and the Mental Health Act.* London: Local Government Association. Available at: www.local.gov.uk/sites/default/files/documents/CHIP%20Ordinary%20Resident_FINAL%20COPY.pdf

Local Government Association (2020) *Making Safeguarding Personal. Local Government Association.* Available at: www.local.gov.uk/our-support/our-improvement-offer/care-and-health-improvement/making-safeguarding-personal.

Mandelstam, M. (2019) *Safeguarding Adults: An A-Z of Law and Practice* (3rd edition). London: Jessica Kingsley.

Medway Council v M & T [2015] EWFC B164.

Ministry of Housing, Communities & Local Government and Department for Education (2018) Prevention of Homelessness and Provision of Accommodation for 16 and 17 Year Old Young People Who May Be Homeless and/or Require Accommodation. London: HM Government. Available at: https://assets.publishing.service.gov.uk/government/uploads/system/uploads/attachment_data/file/712467/Provision_of_accommodation_for_16_and_17_year_olds_who_may_be_homeless.pdf.

Ministry of Justice (2008) *Deprivation of Liberty Safeguards: Code of Practice to Supplement the Main Mental Capacity Act 2005 Code of Practice.* London: The Stationery Office.

Ministry of Justice (2011) *Achieving Best Evidence in Criminal Proceedings: Guidance on Interviewing Victims and Witnesses, and Guidance on Using Special Measures.* London: Ministry of Justice.

Ministry of Justice (2013a) *Code of Practice for Youth Conditional Cautions.* London: Ministry of Justice.

Ministry of Justice (2013b) *Youth Cautions Guidance for Police and Youth Offending Teams.* London: Ministry of Justice.

Ministry of Justice (2015) *Code of Practice for Victims of Crime.* London: Ministry of Justice.

Ministry of Justice (2019) *Rules and Practice Directions.* London: Ministry of Justice. Available at: www.justice.gov.uk/courts/procedure-rules/criminal

Ministry of Justice (2020a) *Information for Victims of Crime.* London: Ministry of Justice. Available at: https://assets.publishing.service.gov.uk/government/uploads/system/uploads/attachment_data/file/746330/victims-of-crime-leaflet-2018.pdf.

Ministry of Justice (2020b) *The Victims' Code: Young Victims of Crime: Understanding the support you should get.* London: Ministry of Justice. Available at: www.cps.gov.uk/sites/default/files/documents/victims_witnesses/childs_victims_code_leaflet.pdf.

Ministry of Justice (2021) *Youth Justice Statistics 2019-2020 England and Wales.* London: Ministry of Justice. Available at: https://assets.publishing.service.gov.uk/government/uploads/system/uploads/attachment_data/file/956621/youth-justice-statistics-2019-2020.pdf.

Ministry of Justice and Youth Justice Board (2018) *Referral Order Guidance.* London: Ministry of Justice.

Mockute v Lithuania [2018] ECHR 66490/09.

National Appropriate Adult Network (2018) *National Standards for the Development and Provision of Appropriate Adult Schemes in England and Wales.* Ashford, Kent: National Appropriate Adult Network.

NSPCC (2021) *Repository of Serious Case Reviews.* NSPCC. Available at: https://learning.nspcc.org.uk/case-reviews/process-in-each-uk-nation.

Office for National Statistics (2020) *Domestic Abuse in England and Wales Overview: November 2020.* HM Government. Available at: www.ons.gov.uk/peoplepopulationandcommunity/crimeandjustice/bulletins/domesticabuseinenglandandwalesoverview/november2020.

Peters, E. (2012a) 'I blame the mother: educating parents and the gendered nature of parenting orders', *Gender and Education,* 24(1): 119–130. DOI: 10.1080/09540253.2011.602332.

Peters, E. (2012b) 'The weight of my words: the role of confession and surveillance in parenting programmes', *Journal of Social Welfare and Family Law,* 34(4): 411–424. DOI: 10.1080/09649069.2012.753736.

Pickford, J. and Dugmore, P. (2012) *Youth Justice and Social Work.* London: Sage/Learning Matters.

Poole Borough Council v GN and another [2019] UKSC 25.

Portsmouth NHS Trust v Charlotte Wyatt [2005] EWHC 117 (Fam).

R (A) v London Borough of Lambeth [2010] EWHC 1652.

R (B) v Merton London Borough Council [2003] 4 All ER 280.

R (Cornwall) v Secretary of State for Health [2015] UKSC 46.

R (G) v Nottingham County Council [2008] EWHC 152 Administration.

R (on the application of Heather and others) v Leonard Cheshire Foundation [2001] EWCA Civ 366.

R (on the application of P, G and W) (Respondents) v Secretary of State for the Home Department and another (Appellants) [2019] UKSC 3.

R v Aziz (Ayman) [2019] EWCA Crim 1568.

R v CW [2020] EWCA Crim 970.

R v Gloucestershire County Council, ex parte Barry [1997] UKHL 58.

R v North East Devon Health Authority ex parte Coughlan [1999] EWCA Civ 1871.

Re A (A Child) [2015] EWFC 11.

Re B (A Child) [2013] UKSC 33.

Re B-S (Children) [2013] EWCA Civ 1146.

Re L (Care: Threshold Criteria) [2007] Fam Law 297.

Re SA (Vulnerable Adult with Capacity: Marriage) [2005] EWHC 2942 (Fam).

Rogers, J., Bright, L. and Davies, H. (2015) *Social Work with Adults*. London: Sage.

Sentencing Council for England and Wales (2017) *Young People and Sentencing*. London: Ministry of Justice. Available at: www.sentencingcouncil.org.uk/about-sentencing/young-people-and-sentencing/

Sexton, M. (2020) *Social Worker's Guide to Liberty Protection Safeguards*. St. Albans: Critical Publishing.

Social Care Institute for Excellence (2020) *Safeguarding Adults*. Social Care Institute for Excellence. Available at: www.scie.org.uk/safeguarding/adults/

Special Educational Needs and Disability Regulations (2014).

Special Educational Needs (Personal Budgets) Regulations (2014).

Staines, J. (2015) *Youth Justice*. Basingstoke: Red Globe Press.

Starns, B. (2019) *Safeguarding Adults Together under the Care Act 2014: A Multi-Agency Practice Guide*. St. Albans: Critical Publishing.

Traveller Movement and Others v J. D. Wetherspoon plc [2015] 2CL01225.

United Nations (1990) *UN Convention on the Rights of the Child*. United Nations. Available at: www.ohchr.org/en/professionalinterest/pages/crc.aspx.

United Nations (2006) *UN Convention on the Rights of Persons with Disabilities*. United Nations. Available at: www.un.org/development/desa/disabilities/convention-on-the-rights-of-persons-with-disabilities.html.

W v Edgell [1989] 1 All ER 1089 175.

Walker v Northumberland County Council [1995] IRLR 35 177.

Watts v UK [2010] ECHR 53586/09.

Wesseley, S. (2018) *Modernising the Mental Health Act: Increasing choice, reducing compulsion – Final report of the Independent Review of the Mental Health Act 1983*. London: HM Government. Available at: www.gov.uk/government/publications/modernising-the-mental-health-act-final-report-from-the-independent-review

Williams and another v London Borough of Hackney [2018] UKSC37.

Winterwerp v The Netherlands [1979] ECHR 6301/73.

X Council v B (Emergency Protection Orders) [2004] EWHC 2015 Fam.

YL v Birmingham City Council [2007] UKHL 27.

Youth Justice Board (2014) *Appropriate Adults: Guide for Youth Justice Professionals*. London: HM Government. Available at: www.gov.uk/guidance/appropriate-adults-guide-for-youth-justice-professionals.

Youth Justice Board (2019a) *How to Use Community Interventions: Section 6 Case Management Guidance*. London: HM Government. Available at: www.gov.uk/government/publications/how-to-use-community-interventions/how-to-use-community-interventions-section-6-case-management-guidance#guidance-for-workers-in-yots.

Youth Justice Board (2019b) *How to Use Reports: Section 5 Case Management Guidance*. London: HM Government. Available at: www.gov.uk/government/publications/how-to-use-reports/how-to-use-reports-section-5-case-management-guidance.

Youth Justice Board (2019c) Youth Justice Plan Guidance. London: HM Government. Available at: www.gov.uk/government/publications/youth-justice-plans-practice-note-for-youth-offending-partnerships

Yule v South Lanarkshire Council [1999] 1 CCLR 546.

Z and others v United Kingdom [2001] 34 EHRR 97.

Index